Woman's Day CHRISTMAS CRAFTS & FOODS

CHRISTMAS
Woman's Day
CRAFTS & FOODS

Sedgewood™ Press

For CBS Inc.

    Editorial Director: *Dina von Zweck*

    Project Coodinator: *Ruth Josimovich*

For Sedgewood™ Press:

    Editorial Director, Sedgewood™ Press: *Jane Ross*

    Project Director: *Virginia Colton*

    Managing Editor: *Gale Kremer*

    Designer: *Bentwood Studio/Jos.Trautwein*

    Production Manager: *Bill Rose*

Distributed in the Trade by Van Nostrand Reinhold.
ISBN 0-442-28101-3
Library of Congress Catalog Number 82-51037
Manufactured in the United States of America.

CONTENTS

THOUGHTS ON CREATING YOUR OWN CHRISTMAS

Long before the stores start their countdown of shopping days 'til Christmas, people who believe in making their *own* holiday are well into a bustle of Yuletide activities. Months ahead, while there is time for the thought and care that the season deserves, they are making plans, laying in supplies and moving merrily forward on all sorts of projects: do-it-yourself decorations, food specialties for presents and parties, gifts and cards that express seasonal sentiments in a uniquely personal way.

What is most miraculous about this annual effort: No matter how many times the ritual is repeated, the spirit is always willing. Christmas never fails to generate the necessary excitement and enthusiasm. What most of us *could* use, however, and what this book strives to provide, are *ideas,* the kind that point out new creative directions and inspire us to action.

Fanciers of handcrafts will love our ***Trimmings for Your Tree***, splendid complements to any family's treasured store of ornaments. Especially intriguing are the adaptations of tree-trimming customs from all over the world. For the sentimental, there are new versions of old-time favorites; for youngsters, captivating little creatures certain to be right at home on a tree.

Next we pay *Fresh Tributes to Cherished Traditions*, suggesting innovative approaches to the stockings, wreaths and gift wrappings that play such a big part in any Christmas celebration. *Dressing Up the Holiday House* offers help with home decoration, indoors and out. Don't be concerned if you're short on skill, space or money — our ideas are designed to work within practical limitations.

Christmas wouldn't be complete without something special for the little ones. For that, we have *Sights to Delight the Children*: first some eye-opening creations of cookies and candy, then their old friend Santa in many endearing forms.

We haven't exactly saved the best for last, but *Foods at Their Most Festive* does serve up some mighty good eating. And every single selection is meant for sharing, from the delicacies that make great gifts to the foods that guarantee great parties.

All of this should satisfy just about every creative urge, but these rewards are only the beginning. The real beneficiaries will be the lucky ones on the receiving end — the family and friends who get to enjoy the results. Since their joy and your pleasure are one and the same, you're doubly repaid for your creative efforts!

THE EDITORS

TRIMMINGS
FOR YOUR TREE

*We know the joy of bringing out those old familiar ornaments—it's like seeing old friends who've been away too long. But even the friendliest group gets a lift from some congenial additions, and it's in that spirit that this collection is offered. It is designed not merely to fit in beautifully with your family treasures but to complement and enhance them, and to make tree-trimming a newly exciting event. Our decorations have, as you will see, distinctive personalities, and just the warmth you want for this most convivial of occasions. In **Ornaments with a Folk-art Flavor,** you sample a world of intriguing tree-decorating traditions. **Trims Sparkling and Shiny** catch every twinkle of light to make a truly luminous contribution. Then come **Sentimental Favorites,** a nostalgic glance at Christmas as it used to be. The trimmings close with **Cunning Little Creatures,** a mini menagerie meant mostly (but not entirely) to enchant the children.*

Ornaments with a Folk-art Flavor

Add drama to your tree, and enrich your own traditions, by dipping into the folk heritages of other countries. It's a world of fascinating techniques and textures . . . of intense contrasts . . . of intriguing materials from time-honored yarn, felt and wood to present-day paper, plastic, cord, even drinking straws used in ingenious adaptations.

Crocheted Pockets

CIRCLE

SIZE: Circle measures 3¾″ in diameter.

MATERIALS: Knitting-worsted-weight yarn, small amounts of hot pink, lavender and orange; aluminum crochet hook size H (Canadian hook No. 8), **or the size that will give you the correct gauge.**

Starting at the center with hot pink, ch 4. Join with sl st to form ring. **1st rnd:** Ch 1, working in the back loop sl st to ch-1. **2nd rnd:** Ch 1, 2 sc in each sc around. Join (16 sc). **3rd rnd:** Ch1, * 2 sc in next sc, sc in next sc. Repeat from * around. Join (24 sc). Break off. **4th rnd:** Attach lavender to sl st of last round. Ch 1, working in back loop only, sc in each sc around. Join (24 sc). **5th rnd:** Repeat 3rd rnd (36 sc). Break off. **6th rnd:** Attach orange to sl st. Ch 1, working in back loop only, * work 2 sc in next sc, sc in each of next 2 sc. Repeat from * around. Join (48 sc). Break off.

Make another circle in same manner.

Finishing: With wrong sides of circles together, join them by working sc through both layers of next 36 sc, working through back loop of each sc. Ch 24 for handle and join to opposite side of opening. **Tassel:** Wind orange yarn 24 times around a 3″ piece of cardboard. Remove cardboard and tie yarn strands together ½″ below one folded edge. Cut through fold at other end. Sew tassel in place.

STAR

SIZE: Width of star is 5″.

MATERIALS: Knitting-worsted-weight yarn, small amounts of purple, lime and turquoise; aluminum crochet hook size H (Canadian hook No. 8), **or the size that will give the correct gauge.**

Starting at the center with purple, ch 4. Join with sl st to form ring. **1st rnd:** Ch 1, work 6 sc in ring. Join with sl st to ch-1. **2nd rnd:** * Ch 5, skip 2 ch, sc in each of next 3 ch, sc in next sc (1 spoke made). Repeat from * 5 times more (6 spokes made). Break off. **3rd rnd:** Attach lime to top of one spoke. Ch 3, sc in same place, * work sc in base of next 2 sc, skip next sc, hdc in sc at base of spoke, skip next sc, sc in each of next 2 sc, work sc, ch 2 and sc in top of spoke. Repeat from * around, ending last repeat with sl st in base of ch-3 at beg of rnd. Break off. **4th rnd:** Attach turquoise in ch-3 space at end of lime point. Ch 3, sc in same place, * sc in each of next 3 sc, skip hdc, sc in each of next 3 sc, work sc, ch 2 and sc in point. Repeat from * around, ending repeat with a sl st in sc at beg of rnd. Break off.

Make another star in same manner.

Finishing: Starting at one point, overcast stars together along 8 edges, leaving 4 edges (1 point) open. Attach turquoise at one free point, ch 15 for handle; join to adjoining free point. Break off.

Felt-circle Balls

MATERIALS: 2½″-diameter plastic-foam balls; dressmaker's pins with colored heads; bright-colored felt scraps; ¾″, ½″, ¼″, ⅛″ paper punches.

Using all four sizes of paper punches, punch out approximately 300 felt circles in different colors for each ball. Stack circles in three different colors and sizes, insert a pin through them and push pin into plastic-foam ball. Continue making and pinning stacks, covering surface of ball with slightly overlapping circles. Fill in between small spaces with a single ⅛" circle pinned in place. Make a loop from yarn or thread, knot ends and pin to ball for hanger.

Woven-yarn Balls

MATERIALS: 3"-diameter plastic-foam balls; yarn scraps in several colors; dressmaker's pins with colored heads (approximately 200 per ball); tapestry needle; masking tape; marking pen; small glass (about 2¾" diameter); comb.

General directions: To divide foam ball into 8 parts, place ball in the glass. Following rim, mark circumference guideline with pen. Turn ball so rim is perpendicular to first guideline; mark second circumference line. Draw two more circumferences to make 8 segments. Use first circumference to plan designs. Push pins two-thirds of the way in along guidelines, using 7 or 8 per inch, and following photograph for design.

Yarn covering on balls consists, first, of strands worked in basket weave in several colors and pinned in place. Next come areas where strands in solid color are wound around pins, concealing ends of basket weave. For basket weave, group together and tape down ends of 10 or 11 short yarn strands (about 2" lengths) of one color on a flat surface. Thread a longer strand of another color in needle and weave it in at right angles to taped strands. Tighten your weave as you go, pushing with teeth of comb. Remove tape; trim patch to approximate size. Tape to ball, pulling up bordering pins and repinning in place. Complete all woven areas as above.

For solid areas, select a long yarn strand, knot end and attach to corner of an open area on ball. Wind yarn back and forth around pinheads, keeping rows straight. Complete each open area separately, push an extra pin in corner to secure loose end and trim yarn length. Push all pins in as

Crocheted Pockets, Felt-circle Balls, Woven-yarn Balls

far as they will go at end of winding.

Make a small yarn loop, knot ends and pin to the top to use as a hanger.

Magenta ball: For each 1" x 1¼" basket-weave patch, weave various blue and green strands. Tape and pin to ball, making 4 vertical bands. To fill in between, wind magenta yarn around pins.

Gold ball: Using first circumference as guide, mark off four 1⅞" diagonal squares for basket-weave areas. Mark lines from upper and lower corners to center top and bottom; insert pins. Using pink and orange yarns, make basket-weave patches; tape and pin squares. To fill eight diamonds, wind gold yarn around pins.

Tyrolean-look Felt-and-sequin Garland

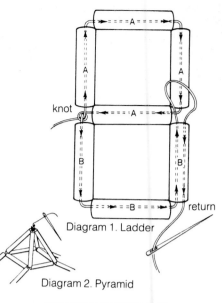

Diagram 1. Ladder

Diagram 2. Pyramid

STRAW STAR DIAGRAMS

Tyrolean-look Felt-and-sequin Garland

SIZE: 2″ wide.

MATERIALS: Scraps red, white and green felt; desired length of ⅜″-wide red grosgrain ribbon; assorted color sequins; white glue.

Trace the patterns below, both inner and outer lines. Following photograph, cut out, layer and glue hearts and flowers. Glue on sequins. Glue hearts and flowers to ribbon as shown.

HEART AND FLOWER PATTERNS

Lithuanian Straw Ornaments

SIZES: Star measures 8½″ across, flat snowflake 8¼″ and dimensional snowflake about 6″.

MATERIALS: Paper drinking straws; single-edged razor blade or sharp scissors; long (over 3″), large-eyed needle; kite string or heavy thread; white glue; shellac or clear plastic spray (optional finish).

General directions: Ornaments are made from paper drinking straws, cut into sections. The star sections are sewed together with needle and string or thread; the snowflakes are assembled with white glue. Finished ornaments can be sprayed with plastic or shellac.

STAR

Note: So that ornament will be firm, pull thread tightly after adding each straw section and after joinings. To add thread, remove needle, knot new strand to old strand and rethread needle. Knot will be hidden in straw.

Center wheel: Cut 30 straw sections 1″ long. Thread needle with a yard of thread and use single. Following Diagram 1, string 4 A sections on thread and tie in knot to form square. String 3 B sections, loop thread around thread at right corner of square (joining made); then bring thread back through a B section as shown (this is called a return). String 3 sections, join at left corner, return. Continue in this manner, using 28 sections and forming a ladder with 10 rungs. String 1 more section, form ladder into wheel and join to end of beginning rung; return through same rung, thread remaining section, join to end of last rung and return through rung (wheel

completed). Build small pyramids on outside of wheel as follows:

Small pyramids: Cut 40 sections 1½″ long. Continuing with thread, string 2 sections from last rung, join at next rung on same side of wheel, return through last pyramid section. String 3rd section, join at opposite end of rung, return through 3rd section. String 4th section, join at opposite end of first rung to form pyramid, return; join all threads firmly at top of pyramid as in Diagram 2; return through 3rd section. Build a pyramid over each square space around wheel. Return through 1 section to a rung of wheel. Build spokes as follows:

Wheel spokes: Cut 20 sections 1¾″ long. Continuing with thread, string 2 sections from rung, join at next rung, complete pyramid as before with top of pyramid at center of wheel. Do not return to base of pyramid. *String 5th section, join to end of next rung, return. String 6th section, join to other end of same rung, return. Repeat from * around, overlapping and joining sections at center of wheel when necessary to keep it firm. After joining last section, fasten center tightly and return to base (side of wheel). To form points of star, build large pyramids over small pyramids as follows:

Large pyramids: Cut 20 sections 3″ long. String 2 sections, skip 2 small pyramids and join at base of 2nd pyramid at end of rung (see photograph), return. String 3rd section, join at opposite end of same rung, return. String 4th section, join at opposite end of first rung, return; join all threads firmly at top, completing first large pyramid; return through 3rd section. Make 4 more pyramids, ending at top of last pyramid. Join threads at top firmly; make loop for hanging.

FLAT SNOWFLAKE

For rays, cut straws into three 8¼" and three 3⅝" sections. Crisscross sections as in photograph; tack at center with two or three kite-string stitches. Dab white glue between rays. Cut 2 straws into 8" sections; bend each into a 6-sided frame, cutting out triangular bits for easier bending. Trim off excess. Glue a frame to each side of center.

Using graph paper with 5 squares to 1", copy design A for center, B for long rays and C for short rays. Covering graph paper with heavy transparent plastic to protect it, cut straws to fit each design. Then glue pieces together over plastic (not *to* plastic), using designs as guides. Let dry. Glue A and B over center and long rays; glue C to ends of short rays.

DIMENSIONAL SNOWFLAKE

Use graph paper with 5 squares to 1" and copy design for one side and snowflake center. Cover graph paper with heavy transparent plastic to protect it and count squares for size of straw sections. For center and one side, cut 10 sections 1 square long, 45 sections 3 squares long, 18 sections 5 squares long. Put aside sections for center until ready to do assembly. Follow design to glue together straws for one side, leaving top and bottom end units separate at this time; let dry. Make three more sides.

To assemble, glue main portions of two opposite sides flat to center straws; add top and bottom units; let dry. Glue the 3rd side vertically to center; prop it at left and right with medium-weight books until dry. Place snowflake on edge of a table with 3rd side hanging down; glue 4th side to center and prop with one book until dry. Make a small extra ornament like an end unit. Punch hole in center top of snowflake; insert kite-string hanger and tie on extra ornament.

Lithuanian Straw Ornaments

STRAW SNOWFLAKES DIAGRAMS

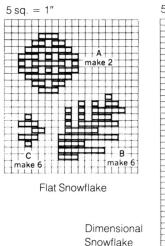

5 sq. = 1"

A
make 2

C
make 6

B
make 6

Flat Snowflake

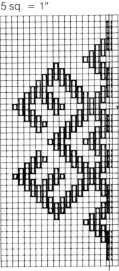

5 sq. = 1"

Dimensional Snowflake

center

Polish-inspired Pleated-paper Stars

Polish-inspired Pleated-paper Stars

MATERIALS: Tissue paper and 8½" x 11" plastic report covers in several bright colors; clear cement; ruler; stapler.

To make stars, mark and cut five 1" x 9" plastic strips for each. To pleat tissue, cut out 3¾" x 8½" rectangle. Fold crosswise to 3¾" x 4¼". With fold at bottom, mark point at top 1¼" to left of right corner. Round right edge from fold to mark; unfold. Accordion-pleat to ¼" width; pinching pleats together at bottom, enclose pleated fan in a plastic-strip "wall" to make a tear-shaped star point. Keeping paper and plastic ends together, staple. To hold pleated fan in centered position inside strip, dab cement on a toothpick along the outer pleats and press against the strip.

Repeat for other star points. Arrange points with rounded tops toward star center. To join, staple strips at inside to each other.

Cord Circles and Stars

MATERIALS: Several colors of gift-wrap tinsel cord (see photograph for colors and textures); cardboard; masking tape; white glue; sharp scissors; straight pins; compass; long-nosed pliers.

CIRCLE

First draw, then cut out 4"- to 6"-diameter circles from cardboard. On a flat working surface, position a cardboard circle and cut lengths of masking tape, sticky side up, to cover circle surface; tape ends of tape lengths down. For two-tone circle, work with two pieces of tinsel cord at the same time. Referring to photograph and beginning on outside edge of circle, leaving an 8" length of cord free to be tied into loop later, wrap cords snail-fashion on sticky circle surface, pressing cords firmly in place. Continue to center of circle; clip cords. Brush surface with white glue. When coating is dry, carefully pull cord circle away from taped cardboard and coat opposite side. Tie loose end into loop for hanging.

STAR

To produce a star shape, follow procedure above for circle but begin circle without leaving loose end for loop. When coated circle has dried thoroughly, use sharp scissors to cut it into six or eight equal wedges.

Following photograph, reassemble and glue into star shape. To hang star, push a straight pin into one point, cut off pin head and twist pin into loop with long-nosed pliers.

Use an ornament hanger or thread loop to hang either ornament on the tree.

Matchstick X's

MATERIALS: Box of long kitchen matches; several colors of vegetable dyes or acrylic paints; white glue; masking tape; straight pins; long-nosed pliers.

With sticky side up, cut several lengths of masking tape to cover a 6"- to 8"-square area. Tape ends down to work surface with masking tape. Cut off all match heads, leaving 2" matchsticks. For tricolored ornaments, use vegetable dye or acrylic paints, thinned with water, to stain several matchsticks before assembling X. Following pattern, press two unstained matchsticks end to end for center of X. At each side of joining, press down a matchstick at right angle to center to form a cross. Continue to put down matchstick lengths as shown. Apply white glue with finger, making certain to push glue between sticks to hold them together; let dry. Pull up holding tape and carefully remove tape from back of X. Rub glue on opposite side. To hang as a cross, push a straight pin into one center point; to hang as an X, push pin into V between two points. Cut off pin head and twist into loop with long-nosed pliers. Use ornament hanger or thread loop to hang on tree.

Cord Circles and Stars, Matchstick X's

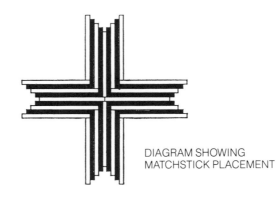

DIAGRAM SHOWING
MATCHSTICK PLACEMENT

A SCANDINAVIAN CHRISTMAS gets its great charm from woodcraft. **On and under the table-top tree:** Gingerbread-house Base made of plywood; Gingerbread Men, also of plywood; Stenciled Pine Blocks; and Garland of Wooden Beads. **In the foreground:** Layered-wood Partridges and Wooden-star Candleholders. Instructions begin at right.

A SCANDINAVIAN CHRISTMAS

Gingerbread-house Tree Base

MATERIALS: ¼ sheet of ⅛" plywood (2' x 4'); ½"-diameter and 1"-diameter dowels; red, green, white and brown artist's acrylic paints; white caulk in narrow-tip tube or gun; wood glue or hot-glue gun.

Cut out, following diagram and general directions below for working with wood. Cut dowels as shown. Paint all parts as indicated in diagram. Assemble with glue. Add caulking decoration as shown.

Gingerbread Men

MATERIALS: 1 square foot of ¼" plywood (enough for about 12 men); brown artist's acrylic paint; white caulking in narrow-tip tube or gun.

Enlarge pattern, following general instructions, page 189, and special directions below for wood. Cut out, again referring to general directions below; before cutting, drill hanging hole in top of head.

Paint brown; let dry. Using caulk, decorate as shown (2 designs given).

Layered-wood Partridge

MATERIALS: 3 square feet of ⅛" plywood (enough for 2 partridges); ³⁄₁₆"-diameter and ¼"-diameter dowel; wood glue.

Enlarge pattern, following general instructions, page 189, and specifics below for wood. Cut out, again referring to general wood directions below, being sure to drill holes before cutting. Assemble. Cut dowels as shown and glue in place.

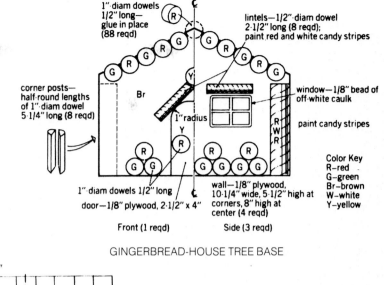

1"-diam dowels 1/2" long—glue in place (88 reqd)

lintels—1/2"-diam dowel 2·1/2" long (8 reqd); paint red and white candy stripes

corner posts—half-round lengths of 1"-diam dowel 5·1/4" long (8 reqd)

1" radius

Br

window—1/8" bead of off-white caulk

paint candy stripes

1"-diam dowels 1/2" long; door—1/8" plywood, 2·1/2" x 4"

wall—1/8" plywood, 10·1/4" wide, 5·1/2" high at corners, 8" high at center (4 reqd)

Color Key
R—red
G—green
Br—brown
W—white
Y—yellow

Front (1 reqd)   Side (3 reqd)

GINGERBREAD-HOUSE TREE BASE

Each sq. = 1"

center center

GINGERBREAD MEN

Each sq. = 1"

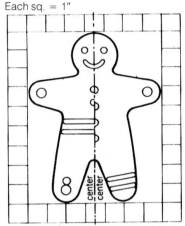

1: plume—drill for 3/16" diam holes, plug with 3/16" diam dowels 1/2" long, round ends (4 reqd)

4: drill 3/8" diam hole for eye; plug with 1/4" diam dowel 1/4" long; round end (4 reqd)

All layers are 1/8" birch veneer plywood

LAYERED-WOOD PARTRIDGE

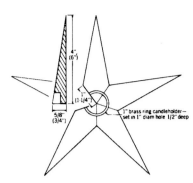

WOODEN-STAR CANDLEHOLDER

Wooden-star Candleholder

MATERIALS: 5' of 1 x 2 pine; 1"-diameter brass ring candleholder; wood glue; block plane; red stain (optional).

For each star, cut 5 pieces to either 4" or 6". Cut each to shape shown in diagram; after cutting, plane to form angle shown. Assemble with glue. When dry, drill 1"-diameter ½"-deep hole, as shown, for brass ring. Insert ring.

Stenciled Pine Blocks

MATERIALS: 6' of 2 x 2 pine (enough for 48 blocks); small screw eyes; letter stencils; red and green acrylic paints; stencil brush.

Cut 1½" pieces of pine. Tape stencil in place for each letter; paint, holding brush perpendicular to surface. If desired, some sides of blocks can be painted solid red or green. Let dry. Center screw eye in top for hanging.

Garland of Wooden Beads

MATERIALS: Bag of ⅝"-diameter wooden beads (enough for 5' garland); heavy string. Beads may be all natural wood or interspersed with color, depending on the effect you prefer.

Thread beads on string; knot ends together.

Layered Felt Brilliants, "Lacquerware" Baubles

General directions for working with wood: To cut, enlarge patterns if this is required, (enlarging instructions, page 189) preferably onto oaktag or manila file-folder paper. Lay out pattern part (or parts) and mark with pencil on wood or plywood. If making a number of the same item, mark one piece and stack on several others to cut at one time. Use a band or jig saw if possible. With a band saw you can cut up to a 3" thickness at one time; with a craft-type jig saw, about 1" at a time. If using a coping saw, cut no more than about 1" at a time, with pieces clamped to the work surface and section being cut extending beyond. Do any interior cuts shown. (**Note:** If any holes are required, mark and drill them *before* you cut out pieces.)

Separate and sand all pieces smooth.

To glue layers together, you can use hot-glue gun or dabs of wood glue placed where they won't ooze. Glue and press in pairs, let dry and glue pairs together. Let dry completely.

To stain, apply stain after sanding but before gluing (many pieces are not stained).

Layered Felt Brilliants

MATERIALS: Felt scraps in various colors; rickrack; knitting-worsted-weight yarn; cotton or fiberfill stuffing.

Note: Ornaments can be trimmed on one or both sides.

Enlarge patterns for star, bird and butterfly (enlarging instructions, page 189). Draw a triangle with 4¾" base and 5¼" height for appliqué tree, 3¾"-diameter circles for other trims, shaping ends of some into points.

Cut two felt pieces for each ornament from either matching or contrasting colors. Then, following photograph for colors and shapes, cut felt for appliqué and rickrack. Machine-stitch trimming to one or both pieces. With wrong sides facing, topstitch pieces together with ¼" seam, leaving opening at top for stuffing. Stuff; pin a 4½" yarn braid inside opening for hanging and sew closed. Trim ⅛" from edge of top piece so contrasting underpiece forms a border.

"Lacquerware" Baubles

SIZES: From 2″ disk to 9″ double cone.

MATERIALS: Cardboard for flat ornaments 2″, 2½″ and 3″ in diameter; 2″ and 3″ plastic-foam balls; cone-shaped paper cups; bright-colored tissue paper; white glue; lacquer and lacquer thinner.

Follow photograph to cut cardboard flat ornaments; glue cups to balls for dimensional shapes.

To decorate, apply thinned glue to shape and let dry until tacky. Cover completely with a layer of tissue paper, first crushing paper. Apply glue and more layers of paper, keeping glue from outer surface. Let dry when several layers have been applied; coat with thinned lacquer.

For scrolls, cut paper strips into different widths. Roll and twist strips between fingers, keeping tissue taut as you work. Apply a thin line of glue to the shape, then press twisted paper along line; hold and let dry. Also shape tissue into balls; cover tightly with paper and twist to underside. Glue in place. Bend border scrolls into a loop for hanging or add a screw eye. Finish with 2 or 3 coats of thinned lacquer and let drip dry.

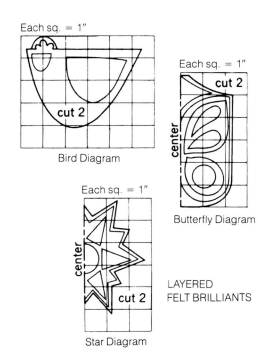

Each sq. = 1″

cut 2

Bird Diagram

Each sq. = 1″

cut 2

center

Butterfly Diagram

Each sq. = 1″

center

cut 2

Star Diagram

LAYERED FELT BRILLIANTS

"Cloisonné Eggs"

"Cloisonné" Eggs

SIZE: 3″ x 4″.

MATERIALS: Egg-shaped pantyhose container; gold cord; vinyl plastic varnish; model glue; white glue; acrylic paints; paintbrush; toothpicks.

Cut a small hole at end of larger half of egg. Make 1″ loop from gold cord. Knot ends, insert loop through hole from inside and secure knot with white glue. Glue egg halves together with model glue. Following photograph, make 3″ pattern of flower and leaves on tracing paper and cut out 4. Tape to egg and trace with pencil; remove patterns. Mark detail lines.

To decorate egg, for first coat mix a drop of white paint into each color. When dry, add second coat without adding white, then third coat if necessary.

Do one area at a time. Use toothpick to spread white glue around outline of flowers, leaves and center circle and along veins of leaves, pressing cord into glue. Set egg in a glass and varnish upper half. Let dry. Turn over and varnish other half.

Trims Sparkling and Shiny

*Deck the boughs with dazzle, magically made from every-day, easy-to-find materials—pipe cleaners, pasta shapes, ribbon scraps. The trims get their glow from gold spray and sequins, pocket mirrors, foil gift wrap and glitter. **You get a tree that is a festival of lights!***

Pleated-foil Stars, Foam-tray Snowflakes

Pleated-foil Stars

MATERIALS: Blue, silver and green foil gift-wrap paper; sharp scissors.

Cut one 5″ square from each paper color. Fold each diagonally in ⅜″-wide accordion pleats. Wrap together at center (see photograph) with ⅜″ width of foil paper; glue to hold. Glue on hanging loop.

Foam-tray Snowflakes

MATERIALS: Foam trays; sharp knife; nylon line.

Enlarge pattern (enlarging instructions, page 189). Cut out two pieces of foam in pattern shape. Fit together at notches. Thread nylon line through top center of snowflake; knot ends.

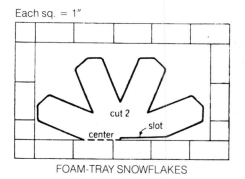

Each sq. = 1″

cut 2

slot

center

FOAM-TRAY SNOWFLAKES

Pasta Wreaths

MATERIALS: 2"-long bow-tie macaroni; wire; clear cement; aluminum foil; ⅛"-wide ribbon; gold spray paint.

Bend a length of wire into 3"-diameter circle. Twist ends together. Place wire on foil working surface. Cement bow ties to wire, overlapping each to center of preceding bow tie. Let dry. Spray-paint gold. Let dry. Glue on bow; attach hanging wire.

Honeycomb Fans

MATERIALS: Metallic honeycomb ribbon; metallic pipe cleaners; small Christmas bells.

For each fan, cut 20" length of 3¼"-wide metallic honeycomb ribbon. Fold in 1" accordion pleats. Wrap pipe cleaner around base. Decorate with wired bells or pieces of pipe cleaner.

Glittering Stars and Sphere

MATERIALS: Metallic pipe cleaners in several colors; wire.

STARS

Twist two different-color 12"-long metallic pipe cleaners together to form double strand. Repeat with two more. Wire double strands together, end to end. Bend at 2½" intervals to form 6" five-pointed star. For multiple star, make two double-strand and two single-strand stars. Wire all four stars together. Make wire hanging loop in either case.

SPHERE

Bend eight pipe cleaners into 3¼"-diameter circles. Wire ends of each circle and wire circles together at top and bottom, making hanging loop from top wire. Spread to form sphere shape shown.

Pasta Wreaths and Honeycomb Fans

Glittering Stars and Sphere

Satiny Ribbon Ornaments

Satiny Ribbon Ornaments

SIZES: Vary from as small as 2″ to 3″ wide and high to as large as 7″ (Comet from star to tail).

MATERIALS: Posterboard; cardboard; satin-finish ribbon in bright colors; invisible transparent tape; double-stick tape; sequins or small mirrors; glue; toothpicks; scissors; pencil.

General directions: Trace the patterns here and on pages 24 and 25 (they are full-size). Cut out pattern shapes; make duplicate shapes when necessary. Side strips are joined along the edges of front and back shapes with transparent tape. Make loops for hanging ornaments by gluing a 4″ strip of ribbon in half lengthwise, folding it in half widthwise and taping ends to posterboard forms before applying decorative ribbon.

Ornaments are covered with double-stick tape on all sides, then decorative ribbon is pressed onto tape. Side strips are covered with a strip of ribbon. Front and back pieces of the tree, moon, star, comet and heart are decorated with thin overlapping strips of ribbon. These strips are 1″ long, cut in half lengthwise; a V-shaped notch forks the strip at one end. When applying these strips, overlap them in rows with the forked ends all pointing in the same direction.

HEART

Cut two heart shapes from posterboard and a long 1″ strip from cardboard, and join. Make a loop, following General Directions above. Cover side strip and back of heart with red ribbon. Cover front of heart with overlapping rows of forked red ribbon strips (see General Directions). Cut six 1½″ strips of ⅜″-wide green ribbon and fork one end of each. At top center of heart front, use these to make three overlapping V shapes, attaching the ribbon to the heart with double-stick tape. Dot back of small mirror with glue and press it over the point of the V.

STAR

Cut two star shapes from posterboard and one long 1″ strip from cardboard. Following General Directions above, join strip to star shapes, make loop, and cover strip with red ribbon. Glue circles of blue ribbon ¾″ in diameter all along strip. Cover the back of the star with double-stick tape and strips of red ribbon; cut off excess. On star front, glue concentric circles of silver, green and blue ribbon, ¾″ in diameter, from dead center to beginning of star points. Cover star points with forked strips of red ribbon (see General Directions); start from edges of concentric circles and work outward toward points. All forked ends point toward center; cut off any excess ribbon at star points.

CRESCENT MOON

Cut two crescent shapes from posterboard. Cut one long 1″ strip from cardboard. Join strip to shapes and make a loop for hanging ornament following General Directions above. Dot backs of mirrors or sequins with glue and decorate ribbon-covered side strip (see photograph). Overlap rows of forked strips of silver ribbon (see General Directions) along the front and back moon shapes, keeping forked ends all pointing down.

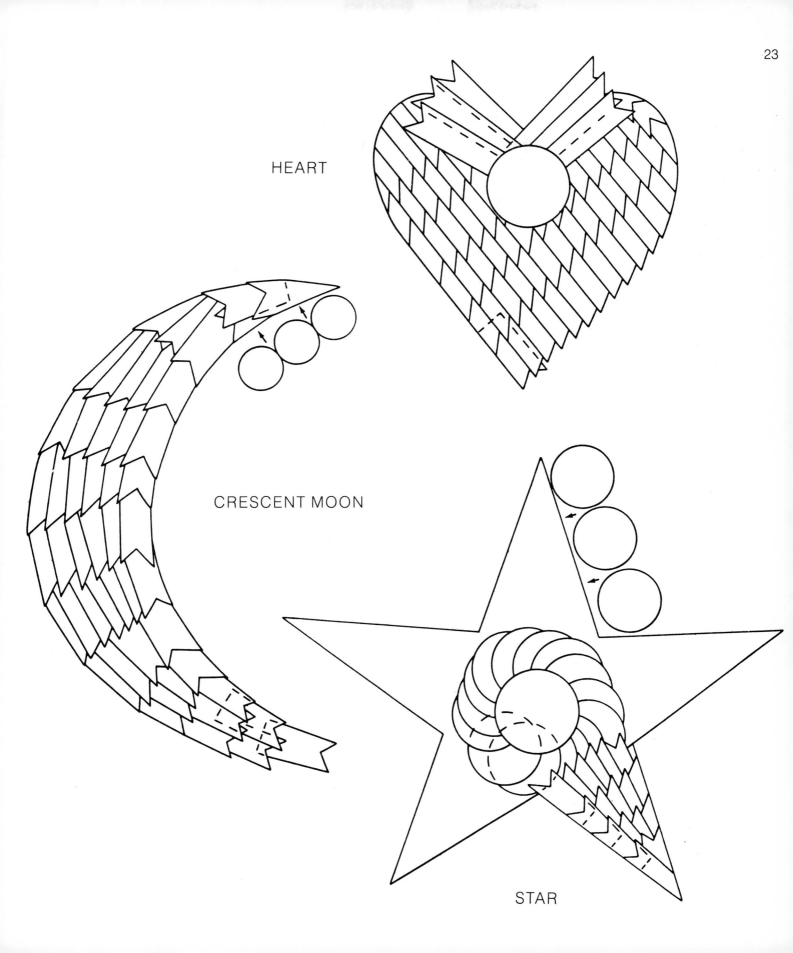

HEART

CRESCENT MOON

STAR

BIRD

Cut two bird shapes from poster-board and a cardboard strip ½" wide, and join. Add loop, following General Directions above. Apply double-stick tape and strips of silver ribbon to bird, front and back. Cut off excess ribbon, dot dull side of ribbon ends with glue and press down. Cut ¾" pieces of red and green ribbon in half lengthwise; fork the ends. Dot with glue and overlap on neck of bird. Cut 3" strips of green ribbon, cut a curve into one edge that will conform to the curve of bird's underbelly. Zigzag other edge, and glue to bottom of bird front. Cut a 4½" strip of green ribbon in half, zigzag one edge of each half lengthwise and glue to top and bottom strip of bird.

Cut a tear-shaped piece of poster-board for the wing. Cover both sides with double-stick tape and green ribbon. Bend slightly so wing will stand away from bird's body. Glue round end of wing to front of bird.

Cut 1½" strips of ribbon in half lengthwise and fork one end. Dot straight edge with glue and press to head and tail area of bird. Make a beak by cutting a strip of ribbon 2" long. Fold in half and cut a V shape in it. Using a toothpick, dot shiny side center with glue and press across strip of bird's head. Glue on mirror or sequin eye. Add mirrors or sequins around curve of bird's body.

TREE

Cut four triangles from posterboard. Join at their long sides with transparent tape. Stand the joined triangles on posterboard, trace around, and cut out a square base. Attach with tape. Apply strips of double-stick tape to base of tree, cover with green ribbon, and cut off any excess. Attach loop for hanging ornament to top of tree. Cover entire tree with double-stick tape and ½" strips of forked green ribbon—see General Directions above. Begin at bottom of tree and work toward the top, forked ends pointing down. Cut twenty ½"-diameter circles from red ribbon. Apply glue to back of each. Place four around top of tree, others at random on tree. First putting a dab of glue on the back, center a mirror or sequin on each red circle.

BIRD

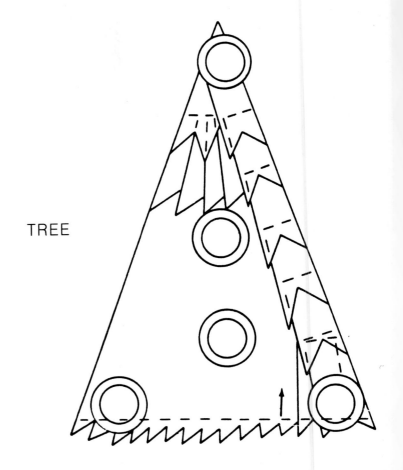

TREE

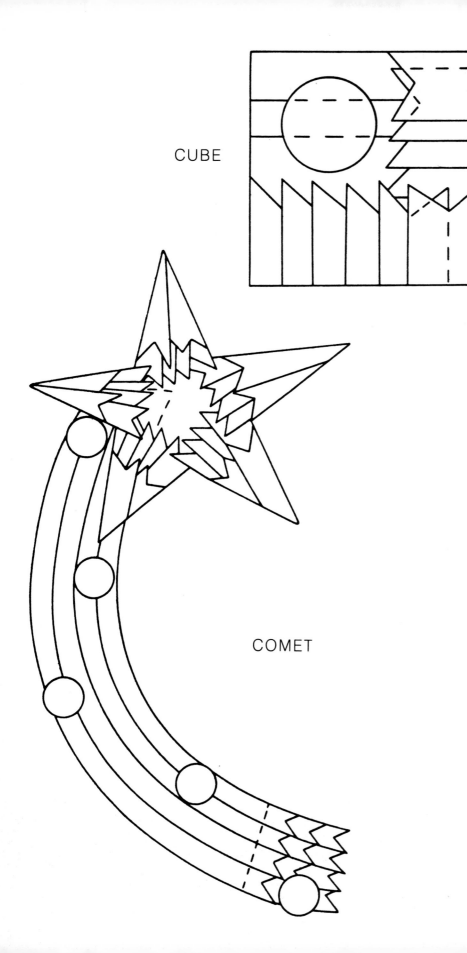

CUBE

COMET

Cut six 2" x 2" squares of posterboard and place four of them side by side. Join these together with transparent tape so they will fold at tape joints. Form a box shape and tape 4th side together. Tape remaining two squares on ends to form a closed cube. Glue a 4" strip of blue ribbon in half lengthwise, fold in half widthwise and tape to any corner of cube to form loop for hanging the ornament.

Apply double-stick tape to two opposite sides of cube and cover with red ribbon. Apply a ½" strip of blue ribbon ½" from edge of one side and glue a small mirror over it. Cut 2" strips of blue and yellow ribbon, fork both short ends (see General Directions). Apply double-stick tape to remainder of cube and overlap rows of these strips to cover tape.

COMET

Cut out two star shapes and one comet tail shape from posterboard, plus a ½" strip of cardboard. Join strip along edges of two star shapes with transparent tape, cover strip with silver ribbon, folding strip at each angle of star. Following General Directions above, attach a loop and cut forked strips of red, light green, dark green and blue ribbon. Overlap blue pieces in a row along top of curve of comet tail. Make sure all forked ends point toward end of tail. Directly under this row, form another horizontal row of dark green pieces, then a row of light green and a row of red at the bottom. Glue five small mirrors or sequins along tail of comet, as shown in photograph. Glue beginning of comet tail securely to back of star. Glue mirror or sequins to center of star, front and back. Cut forked pieces from silver ribbon, just as you did for the comet tail. Cover star points with double-stick tape and apply silver pieces so they overlap all forked ends pointing toward the center.

Snowflake Sparklers

MATERIALS: Sheets of acetate (available at art supply stores); silver or white glitter; thread or nylon line; compass; scissors; pencil; large needle; double-stick transparent tape.

Make paper patterns for circles 4″, 4½″ and 5″ in diameter. Cut acetate according to patterns. Mark pattern circles into six equal parts, like spokes. Place under acetate and apply strips of double-stick tape to top of acetate over lines. Add extra strips of tape crosswise or midway between first strips to give basic shape of a snowflake. Cut away all untaped portions of acetate. Make additional cuts—notches, pointed ends, shaped ends (refer to photograph for ideas). Place acetate, tape side up, on large smooth sheet of paper. Sprinkle glitter heavily on tape. Pat glitter firmly in place. Pick up snowflake and shake excess glitter onto paper. Lightly brush off any remaining loose glitter. Use paper to funnel excess glitter back into container. Punch hole in snowflake with needle and insert thread. Knot thread ends to make loop for hanging on tree.

Snowflake Sparklers

Flashing-lights Mirror Ornaments

MATERIALS: Assorted small round, oval, diamond- and pear-shaped mirrors; strung pearls in various colors and sizes; plastic jewels; clear cement; aluminum foil; thin gold thread.

Work on a foil-covered surface so that if the glue runs, the ornament can be peeled away without damaging the decoration. Cut a 6″ or 8″ length of gold thread; fold in half. Cement two mirrors of the same shape back to back, inserting loose ends of folded gold thread between mirrors for hanger loop. Following photograph for color and design, cement string of pearls around outside edge of mirror. Arrange jewel design on mirror surface and cement in place. Let dry. Turn ornament over and cement same design on other side.

Flashing-lights
Mirror Ornaments

Sentimental Favorites

These ornaments take a fond look back to Christmas as it was long ago: to quaint fabrics and cards saved from other seasons...early handwork techniques...satin ornaments reminiscent of the Victorian era...truly personal expressions of holiday wishes. To anyone yearning for simpler, more sentimental times, these "handmades with heart" are warmly recommended!

Memento Ornaments

Memento Ornaments

MATERIALS: Old ornaments of various sizes and shapes; steel wool; spray paint in several colors; pencils or hors d'oeuvre skewers; rectangle of plastic foam; self-stick tape in several widths (¹⁄₁₆″ to ½″) and colors; for personalizing and decoration, self-stick or glue-back letters and numerals, signal dots, plastic tape for flowers and other motifs; acrylic spray; varnish (optional).

Use steel wool to buff away any cracked or peeling lacquer from old glass ornaments such as the balls and tapered ornaments shown. Wipe clean with a damp cloth and remove hangers. Slip ornaments on pencils or hors d'oeuvre skewers; spray or brush on 2 coats of paint. Push holders into the plastic foam and allow the ornaments to dry.

Divide ornaments into areas and decorate with bands of colored self-stick tape in varying widths and shades. Apply letters and numerals for names and dates; use signal dots and bits of tape for flowers and other motifs. Finish with acrylic spray; varnish if desired. Replace hangers.

Nostalgia Cornucopias

MATERIALS: Old Christmas or other greeting cards or construction paper; assorted braid or tinsel trims; gold and silver seals and doilies; colored tissue papers; gold thread; glitter, sequins; ribbon; white glue; spring-type clothespin; masking tape.

Cut and shape a 5½" long cone from Christmas card or construction paper; overlap and glue edges together at back. Use a spring-type clothespin to clip top edges together until glue is dry and use masking tape down seam to hold glued edges. Trim top edge even. Following photograph, decorate cornucopia with cut-out motifs from other cards, seals and touches of glitter or sequins glued in place.

The top of each cornucopia is closed with tissue paper. Cut 3"-wide strips of tissue paper to go around top edge. Plan to use at least four layers of tissue for each top; this can be one continuous strip, unless you would like a two-tone effect. Glue tissue paper along top edge of cornucopia; let dry. Pinch tissue together as in photograph and tie with ribbon or tinsel. Make a loop from gold thread and attach to cornucopia ribbon for hanging. Glue braid or tinsel trim around top border to conceal edge of tissue. Shape tissue paper into floral topknot.

Nostalgia Cornucopias

Old-fashioned Pomanders

Old-fashioned Pomanders

For each:
- 1 small thin-skinned orange or medium lemon
- 1 box or jar (about 1⅛ ounces) whole cloves
- 2 or 3 teaspoons mixed spices (mace, cinnamon, nutmeg, allspice, ground cloves)

With skewer or tip of small knife, starting ¼" from top, pierce entire surface of fruit at ⅛" intervals to ¼" from bottom. Insert cloves in punctures. Sprinkle with spice mixture to cover completely so no peel shows. Store uncovered in cool, dry place 2 to 3 weeks. (Don't be concerned if mold and slight odor develop; both disappear with drying.) Tie ribbon around fruit, leaving excess on top for hanging. Makes 1.

Scrap-bag Christmas Shapes

MATERIALS: Fabric scraps (preferably gingham, calico or other old-fashioned cottons); cardboard; scissors; fabric glue; bits of trimmings for ornamentation (used here: rickrack, lace, eyelet, upholstery fringe, yarn and gold braid); string or cord.

Following photograph for contours, cut cardboard to the desired shapes and sizes. Cut fabric to cover cardboard shapes, adding ½" at all edges. Glue fabric to cardboard, applying glue in a thin, even layer so it won't soak through. Glue ½" allowance at edges of fabric to back of cardboard.

Decorate ornaments with trim, following photograph or devising your own decorations. Glue trim to ornament. Some trims should extend beyond the edges and be glued to the back (see photograph).

Glue string loop to backs of ornaments as hangers.

Cut matching fabric to the shape of the cardboard. Glue to back to cover the lapped materials and to secure the string used for hanging.

Scrap-bag Christmas Shapes

30

Painted Satin Bell and Clothespin Candle

MATERIALS: Marking pens for fabric in colors shown; ¾ yard polyester fleece (makes 5 bells) and ¼ yard polyester fleece (makes 4 candles); ⅛ yard 60"-wide metallic knit fabric (enough for 5 bells and 4 candles); ½ yard (45"- wide) white acetate satin (enough for 5 bells and 4 candles); 15" piece of #5 width red satin ribbon for each ornament; gold thread or cord for bell hangers; 1" or 2" yellow bump chenille (1 bump per candle); metallic chenille stems in gold for candles (1 stem is enough for 3 ornaments); small wooden clip clothespins (1 per candle); gold paint for clothespins; yellow and white sewing thread; needle; scissors; ruler; white paper; fine-tip black marking pen; pencil; Sobo glue; blotter.

Note: Designs on ornaments can also be worked in stitchery, following decoration diagrams and description of elements (flowers and leaves) that are not shown.

SATIN BELL

Enlarge patterns for bell, clapper and clapper cover (enlarging instructions, page 189). For each ornament, cut 6 of bell shape and 5 of clapper from fleece. Place bell shapes in two stacks of 3 each. Whipstitch around edges of stacks to hold them together. Pull stitches to make sharp edge. Make single stack of clapper pieces and sew in same way. Cut satin covering for each bell stack. (Cut satin 1" larger on curved sides and 2" wider at bottom edge than fleece.)

Make pattern of design (flowers and leaves are not shown). Go over lines with black marking pen. Let dry thoroughly. Place under satin piece for bell, keeping centered with 2" excess at bottom. Lightly trace design on satin with pencil. Repeat for second satin piece. Place one of the satin

Painted Satin Bell and Clothespin Candle, Satin Balls with Glue Flowers, Knotted-cord Mini Candy Cane, Finger-knit Mini Wreath, Instructions, pages 30-33

pieces on a blotter and go over lines with fabric pens in colors shown in photograph. Add flowers after basic lines are finished. Rosebuds are an oval of red with a stroke of green at each side and two or three little leaves at tip of oval. Other flowers are one yellow dot surrounded with petal-color dots and dashes. Leaves are fat dashes. Repeat decorative steps for second piece. Let dry.

Place fleece shape on wrong side of painted satin with design centered over fleece. Turn excess satin to fleece. Catchstitch satin to fleece to fasten. Turn up bottom edge last. Place the two matching covered forms together with right sides out and stitch together invisibly along all but bottom edge. Using enlarged pattern, cut two pieces of metallic knit fabric for clapper cover. Sew with right sides together, leaving opening for turning. Turn to right side and insert fleece clapper. Pull covering up tight and stitch with about half of clapper visible. Make bow of ribbon and sew or glue to top of bell. Make hanger loop of gold cord and glue to top of bell.

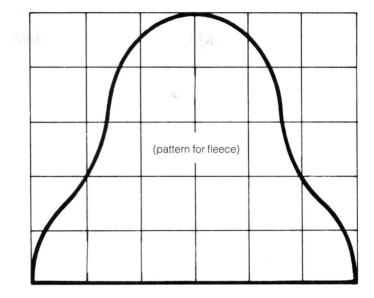

(pattern for fleece)

SATIN BELL

In all diagrams, each sq. = 1″

(other project diagrams, page 32)

decoration for upper bell

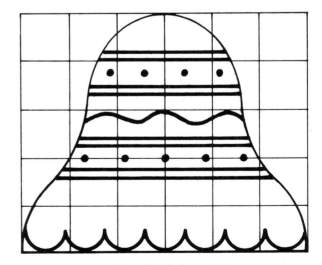

decoration for lower bell

CLOTHESPIN CANDLE

Paint clip clothespin gold. Let dry. Enlarge candle and holder diagrams (enlarging instructions, page 189) and cut fleece candle shapes (5 for candle, 6 for holder). Assemble like bell—single stack for candle, two stacks of 3 for holder. Cut satin for candle 6" x 4½". Make up pattern in same way as for bell and center satin on it. Trace and paint in same way as for bell, following photograph. Cover candle shape by wrapping painted satin around it and stitching it in place. Turn in at top and back to hide raw edges. Use candleholder pattern to cut four pieces of metallic knit fabric 1" larger on all sides than candle-holder shape. Cover each piece of holder in same way as for bell. Hold pair of holder pieces together, knit side out, and stitch invisibly together along all but top edge. Glue base of candle into holder. Let dry. Glue holder to painted clothespin so that the clothespin can grip branch to hold candle upright. Let dry.

Cut one chenille bump and shape metallic stem piece around it to outline the bump. Wrap at bottom to hold together. Cut off excess metallic chenille. Glue to candle top as flame; insert cut ends into seam at top of candle. (Punch hole with awl or icepick if necessary.) Tie ribbon into bow and glue to front bottom of holder.

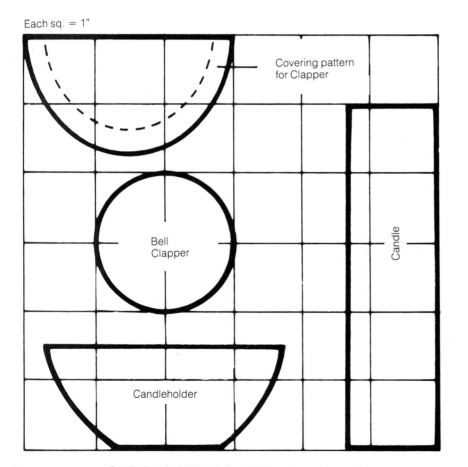

Each sq. = 1"

Covering pattern for Clapper

Bell Clapper

Candle

Candleholder

CANDLE, HOLDER AND CLAPPER (patterns for fleece)

Satin Balls with Glue Flowers
(shown on tree in photograph on page 30)

MATERIALS: 2-ounce bottles Sobo glue (one for each color used); liquid food colors; quick-drying glue; gold paper lace doilies; small pearl beads; white satin balls (about 3" in diameter); plastic wrap; skewer; clear acrylic spray paint; gold soutache braid; scissors.

Note: Not all clear plastic wraps will release the glue when dry. Test with a dab of glue before doing entire project.

Remove top from one bottle of Sobo glue. Add 7 or 8 drops of one of the food colors to bottle; stir well with skewer. Clean skewer. Replace bottle top. Repeat for each color desired

Spread plastic wrap on a flat, level surface that can be left undisturbed for 24 to 48 hours. Place drops of colored glue (¼"-diameter for small petals, ⅜"-diameter for larger petals). Make ⅜" to ½" dashes of green for leaves. Make an ample supply of each color so any that are imperfect can be discarded. As the glue dries, it becomes transparent. When the drops can be easily removed from the plastic wrap, turn them over to hasten drying. When almost dry, but still tacky, make flowers. For larger flowers, overlap 5 dots (petals). When the last two are overlapped, a cupped flower will form. For smaller flowers, use 4 of the smaller dots and arrange them in cross shape. Leave some dots plain to use as buds or trim. Let dry thoroughly. Spray all flowers, leaves and buds on both sides with clear acrylic.

Cut doilies apart to form medallions and swags. Glue these, using the quick-drying glue, to satin balls in any desired arrangement. (Use very small amounts of this glue; a small brush may be helpful.) Glue flowers, leaves and buds to gold trim. Let dry. Glue on pearls as flower centers. Glue on pieces of gold soutache braid.

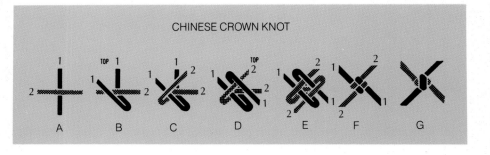

CHINESE CROWN KNOT

A   B   C   D   E   F   G

Knotted-cord Mini Candy Cane

(shown on tree in photograph on page 30)

MATERIALS: 2½ yards each red and white Maxi-cord Twisted Polypropylene (**Note:** Any shiny, textured macramé or gift cord, in appropriate colors, can be substituted); 16" floral wire (16 gauge); fabric glue; scissors.

Candy cane is made with a continuous series of Chinese Crown Knots working around the floral wire. To complete your first Chinese Crown Knot, follow Illustrations A to G along with the sequence of written instructions that follows.

1. Lay the red and white cords (shown as Cords 1 and 2 in illustrations) across each other at centers to form a cross (Illustration A). Tie each end into an Overhand Knot (see drawing) to prevent fraying.

2. Fold Cord 1 up over Cord 2 (B).

3. Fold Cord 2 up over both Cord-1 strands (C).

4. Fold Cord 1 down over both Cord-2 strands (D). Loosen Cord 1 to make a loop.

5. Fold Cord 2 down over Cord 1, putting it through loop formed by first Cord-1 strand (E).

6. Gently pull each of the cords to tighten the square (F).

7. Turn the square over (Illustration G) and set aside.

Make a small bend in the wire and slip the hook of it under the top cord of the overturned square (again, see Illustration G). Squeeze the hook closed.

Resting the wire on your shoulder, repeat steps 2 through 6 (starting 1-over-2 as in Illustration B) until knotted length measures 8½". Squirt glue into the last knot to secure, and pull ends tight. Allow glue to dry, then trim ends very close. Trim excess wire with scissors. Bend finished length into candy-cane shape.

Finger-knit Mini Wreath

(shown on tree in photograph on page 30)

MATERIALS: 3 yards Maxi-cord Twisted Polypropylene Christmas color combination (see Note about substitutions under Mini Candy Cane, above).

Christmas wreath is knitted with fingers from one 3-yard cord. No needles are necessary.

To prepare for finger knitting: Tie a small knot at each end of the 3-yard cord.

1. Beginning at one end, wrap the cord around the fingers of your left hand as shown in the first illustration. You have created two loops, loop A on one finger and loop B on the other.

2. Pass the cord across the front of both fingers as shown in the second illustration. **First step of stitch:** With your right hand, lift loop A up over this crossing cord and your fingertip. The crossing cord becomes the new loop A. **Second step of stitch:** Lift loop B up over the crossing cord and your fingertip. The crossing cord becomes the new loop B.

Repeat instructions under 2 three times. After the third repeat, release cord C from your grasp and pull it to the back of your left hand. After every stitch, pull on the forming wreath to keep the tension even. Continue working in this manner until wreath part measures 7".

To finish: Pull the working end of the cord through both loops to secure. Tie cord ends together into a knot so wreath ends come together in a circle. Tie remaining cord into a bow.

OVERHAND KNOT

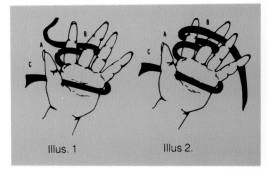

FINGER KNITTING

Illus. 1   Illus 2.

Cunning Little Creatures

Plush bears, pompon elves and reindeer, clothespin clown and pony, a whole felt menagerie! As if that weren't enough, there are also small trims of birds and butterflies, mice, kittens and pups—and, to represent "people," Mr. and Mrs. Santa and a sweet eyelet angel. These go fast, so plan on making a few extras to tuck into presents.

Pompon Dolls Plush Bears

Plush Bears

MATERIALS: Two 3¼" x 4" rectangles velour in appropriate color for each bear; scraps brown, red, white and green velour; black embroidery floss; cotton or fiberfill stuffing; gold thread.

For either bear: Enlarge bear pattern (enlarging instructions, page 189). Cut out 2 body pieces, adding ⅛" seam allowance to all edges. With right sides together, stitch outer edges, leaving opening. Clip curves, turn right side out, stuff firmly and sew closed. Make tiny stitches through front side only at dotted lines.

Cut out muzzle (see photograph for color). Work running stitch ⅛" from edge, pull up and stuff. Turn under edges and sew. Embroider eyes, nose, mouth. Cut neck bow from ¼"-wide velour. Notch ends. Attach 6½" gold thread to head for hanger; knot ends.

For tan bear: Cut four ⅜" x ⅝" ovals of brown velour for paws. Turn under raw edges and sew in place.

For brown bear: Cut white stomach. Turn under and sew raw edges.

Each sq. = 1"

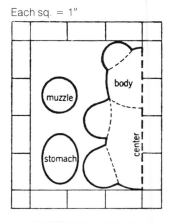

PLUSH BEAR PATTERN

Pompon Dolls

MATERIALS: Knitting-worsted-weight yarn (see colors under individual directions, 1 ounce or less needed of each). For all, felt scraps (see photograph for colors); gold hanging cord; 6" length of thin wire.

Note: For general pompon instructions, see page 189.

ELF

Make following yarn pompons: 2½" green body, 2" white beard, 1½" pink face, 1" red feet and ¾" red hands. Glue together. Cut and glue felt cheeks, nose, eyes and mouth.

For hat, cut 1¼" x 3½" strip green felt. Fold and glue into ring. Glue to head. Cut red felt feather; glue. Glue ends of hanging loop in hat.

For glasses, make two ⅜" loops on wire, ⅛" apart. Bend ends and poke into pompon with loops over eyes.

RUDOLPH

Make following white yarn pompons: two 1¾" for body, a 1½" head and a 1" muzzle (see photograph).

For legs, cut two 2¾" x 5¾" pieces yellow felt. Glue together. When dry, cut out 2"-wide x 2¾"-deep sections from ends of piece, leaving 4 legs. Fold legs down; glue center to body.

Cut 1¼" x 2" yellow felt neck; roll tight and glue, then glue upright to end of body. Cut 1½"-diameter red-felt collar. Cut points around edge. Cut hole in center to fit over neck. Glue head to top of neck and muzzle to head. From felt, cut ears, nose, mouth, eyes and two ⅝" x 1¾" yellow antlers; glue on. Attach cord to head.

SNOWMAN

Make following white yarn pompons: 3½" body, 2¼" head and 1" hands. Glue on features. For hat, from green felt, cut 1½" x 3½" crown and 2¼"-diameter circle for brim. Fold crown and glue into ring. Cut hole in center of brim to fit crown; glue together. Add red felt hat band. Glue hat to head. Cut ½" x 7" red felt strip for tie. Knot center, tie in bow and notch ends; glue to throat. Poke hole in back of brim, insert ends of hanging loop, knot and glue.

SANTA

Make following pompons: 3½" red body, 1" red hands, 3" white beard, 1" white for hat, two 1½" black for feet, 1½" pink face, tiny pink nose.

For hat, from red felt, cut, form and glue 3"-deep cone. Bend slightly to side and sew. Cut tiny hole in back, insert ends of hanging loop, knot and glue. Glue hat to head and pompon to tip.

Glue on felt cheeks and mouth. For mustache, knot two 1½" strands white yarn together; glue in place.

Fabric-scrap Mouse Ornament

Fabric-scrap Mouse Ornament

SIZE: About 3" high.

MATERIALS: Scraps striped and polka-dot fabric, ⅜"-wide lace and ⅛"-wide ribbon; Indian seed beads; embroidery floss; large-eyed crewel needle; cotton or fiberfill stuffing.

Trace the full-size body and ear patterns given below. Cut out 2 body and 4 ear pieces, adding ¼" seam allowance to all edges. With right sides facing, stitch curved edge of pairs of ears together, sandwiching lace between. Turn right side out. Stitch body pieces together, leaving opening for turning at top. Turn right side out, stuff, insert ribbon loop for hanging and sew opening closed. Turn under raw edges on ears, pleat and sew in place. Sew bead to nose. Embroider satin-stitch eyes. For feet, thread ribbon on needle. Insert ribbon at position of front foot and pull it out at position for back foot. Knot ends close to fabric and cut, leaving ½" end at each position. Sew on ribbon tail.

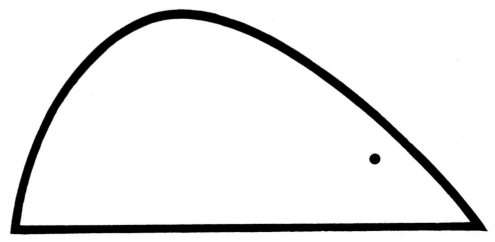

Candy Cane and Mouse Ornament

to outer ears, glue in small pleat at base, then glue to large pompon head. Glue on next smaller pompon cheeks with bead nose between; add eyes and thread whiskers.

For hat, cut red felt pie wedge shape with 2" radius and 4" measurement along curved edge. Fold and glue into cap shape. Add white felt band and ¼" pompon. Bend and glue hat to shape, then glue to head.

Twist pipe cleaners to form candy cane. Trace holly leaf pattern and cut out 2 felt leaves. Make small red bow. Sew mouse, leaves and bow to candy cane.

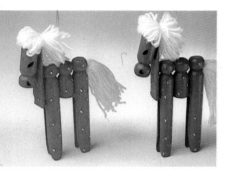

Clothespin Pony Ornament

Candy Cane and Mouse Ornament

SIZE: About 7" high.

MATERIALS: One 1"-diameter, two ½"-diameter and one ¼"-diameter white pompons per mouse head (instructions, page 189); scraps white, pink, green and red felt; red ribbon; ¼" moveable animal eyes; small red beads (nose); heavy black thread; red and white pipe cleaners; white glue.

For ears, cut out two white felt 1"-diameter circles and 2 pink felt circles slightly smaller. Glue pink inner ears

Clothespin Pony Ornament

SIZE: About 3" x 5".

MATERIALS (for 1): 4 wooden clothespins; scraps white yarn; acrylic paint; white glue; hand saw; gold cord.

For head, cut 1⅜"-long piece from top of clothespin. For neck, use one side of remainder. For body, cut 1⅜"-long piece from top of 2nd clothespin. Following photograph, glue clothespins together to form horse. Paint; add contrasting color dots.

For mane, cut twenty-four 4" strands yarn. Holding strands together, fold in half; tie with another strand about ¾" from fold. Glue to top of head and neck as shown. For tail, cut fourteen 4½" strands yarn; wrap a longer strand around neck of last clothespin on horse and tie around center of strands; trim ends even.

Thread 9" piece of gold cord between clothespins and tie ends together for hanging.

Clothespin Clown Ornament

SIZE: About 4½" high.

MATERIALS (for 1): Wooden clothespin; ½ ounce yarn; 2" x 8" piece fabric; acrylic paints; white glue; thread.

Following photograph, paint background, polka dots and face on clothespin. Make 1¼" pompon (for instructions, see page 189) and glue on clothespin top for hair. For ruff, press longer raw edges of fabric under ¼"; press in half lengthwise, right side out. Sewing through both thicknesses, run gathering stitches ⅛" from folded raw edges. Pull up to fit around neck, overlapped at back. Add thread loop for hanging.

Clothespin Clown Ornament

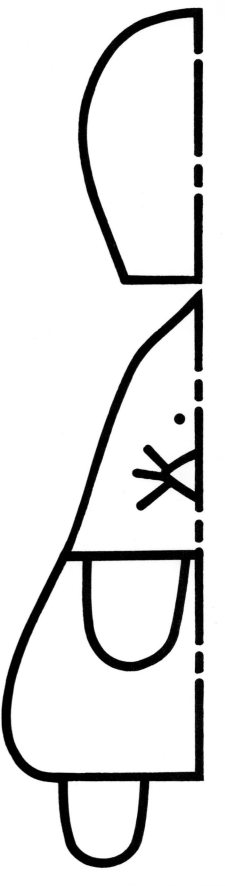

Big-eared Stuffed Mouse Ornament

Big-eared Stuffed Mouse Ornament

SIZE: About 6″ high.

MATERIALS: Scraps solid-color, polka-dot and striped fabrics; embroidery floss; cotton or fiberfill stuffing; small brass curtain ring.

Trace full-size patterns at right. Cut out 2 face pieces, 2 body pieces, 4 ears, 4 hands and 4 feet, adding ¼″ seam allowance to all edges.

With right sides facing, sew pairs of ear, hand and foot pieces together, leaving straight edges open. Turn right side out. Sew head to body, sandwiching hands between with raw edges matching.

With right sides facing, stitch front to back with feet sandwiched between, leaving 2″ opening at top of head. Turn right side out. Stuff.

Stuff ears lightly, pleat at center of raw edges, insert in opening and sew in place. Embroider features. Attach ring at top of head between ears.

Felt Animals, Tassel Doll

Felt Animals

SIZES: About 1½" to 3½" high.

MATERIALS: Felt scraps in assorted colors; cotton or fiberfill stuffing; ball fringe; embroidery floss, novelty braid, metallic cord, sequins and beads for trim; white glue.

General directions: Enlarge patterns (enlarging instructions, page 189); cut out paper enlargements and trace on felt. Cut two of each body shape, adding ¼" seam allowance. Cut ¼" x 1½" felt strips to hang three of the animals.

Seam pieces for rabbit, camel and elephant, leaving openings at underside. Trim seams; turn and stuff. Sew openings. Cut out and glue pink felt ears to rabbit; cut and sew felt ears in body colors to camel and elephant, matching A to A.

Topstitch together butterfly, cat and dog shapes, putting stuffing and felt hanging strips between layers. Trim seam allowances.

Follow photograph for decorations. On rabbit, tack white ball from fringe for tail and sew on sequin and bead trim. On butterfly, work embroidery with gray, red and orange floss. On cat, work features and orange chain stitch shown, then fill in with straight lines in blue and purple.

On camel and elephant, use cord for bridle, red and lavender braids for saddles, sequins and beads elsewhere. On dog, outline spirals with orange; embroider features and French knots with red. Add cord for hanging to these three.

Each sq. = 1"

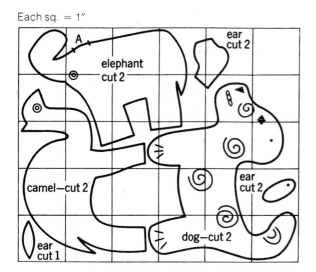

PATTERNS FOR CAMEL, ELEPHANT, DOG

Each sq. = 1"

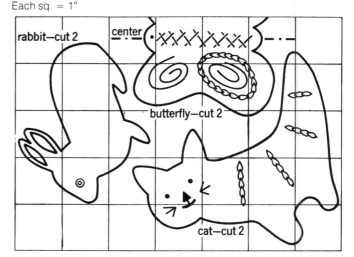

PATTERNS FOR RABBIT, BUTTERFLY, CAT

Tassel Doll
(shown at left)

SIZE: About 5″ from cap to toe.

MATERIALS: Yarn scraps, heavy-weight magenta (about 10 yards) and medium-weight purple; 4″ x 4″ scrap of purple felt; cardboard.

For body of doll, wind heavy yarn about 30 times around 4″-wide cardboard strip; for arms, wind yarn a dozen times around 2¾″ cardboard. Tie each set of loops once with matching yarn; slip off cardboard. Hiding knot inside body, run arm loops through. Wind 1″ at top of body for head. Wind waist, ankles and wrists with purple yarn; sew stitches on chest and features on face.

For cap, cut a felt triangle 3″ high and 3¼″ wide at base, or wide enough to fit, with seam, around doll's head. Turn up ¼″ cuff; fold triangle and sew back seam. Trim seam allowance.

Fanciful Art-foam Birds

MATERIALS: 18″ x 38″ sheets of ⅛″ colored art foam (enough for 4 to 6 birds); pinking shears; household cement; cotton or fiberfill stuffing; felt-tipped markers in various colors; ornament hangers or wire.

Enlarge six patterns on paper (enlarging instructions, page 189). Tape pattern temporarily to foam. Cut 2 layers together for each bird with pinking shears. Run a thin line of cement along head, back and tail of one piece; press second piece to it and let dry 15 minutes. Stuff very lightly; cement open edges together. Following photograph, decorate bird with markers. Attach to tree with ornament hangers or wire.

Fanciful Art-foam Birds

Each sq. = 1″

cut 2 of each

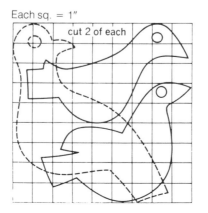

Each sq. = 1″

cut 2 of each

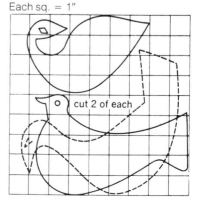

ART-FOAM BIRDS PATTERNS

Mr. and Mrs. Santa Ornaments

Eyelet Angel Ornament

Mr. and Mrs. Santa Ornaments

SIZE: About 4" x 6".

MATERIALS: Scraps red and white fabric, white jumbo rickrack, red and black embroidery floss; 1½" white pompons; cotton or fiberfill stuffing.

Trace pattern at immediate right. For each ornament, cut out one red full piece (hat and face) for back of head, adding ¼" seam allowance. Cut out one red hat piece and one white face piece, adding ¼" seam allowance.

Stitch hat to face. Topstitch rickrack to hat ½" above seam line. With right sides facing, stitch front to back, leaving opening for turning at lower edge. Turn right side out; press flat. Topstitch across broken line. Stuff face and hat below topstitching; sew opening closed. Embroider features following photograph. Make pompon (instructions, page 189) and sew it to the hat.

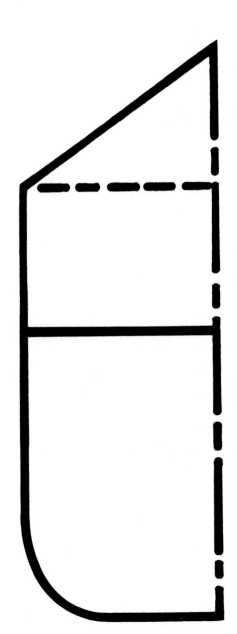

Eyelet Angel Ornament

SIZE: About 6" high.

MATERIALS: 8" piece 4"-wide eyelet lace per angel; scraps felt, nylon stocking, crochet thread and ribbon; pink acrylic paint; cotton or fiberfill stuffing; white glue.

For head, cut 4" circle from stocking. Work running stitches ¼" from outer edge, place 1½" ball of stuffing at center and pull up to form ball; fasten off. For dress, stitch ends of lace together to form tube. Hem raw edge; gather; pull up gathers to fit around neck. Sew to head. For hair, wrap strand of crochet thread around index finger about 30 times. Slip off finger, tie loops together and sew to head. Repeat until head is covered with "curls." Enlarge wing pattern (directions, page 189); cut out felt wings; glue to back. Straight-stitch eyes and mouth; paint cheeks. Add pink bow.

Each sq. = 1"

WING PATTERN

Doggy-in-a-basket Ornament

SIZE: About 1½" x 2¾" x 3".

MATERIALS (for 1): 1½" x 2¾" x 3" basket; one 1½"-diameter, one 1"-diameter and three ½"-diameter pompons; two ¼"-diameter, moveable animal eyes; scraps brown, red and green felt; ½ yard ¼"-wide red ribbon; white glue; dried flowers; pinking shears.

Make pompons (see page 189) with yarn scraps, or use purchased ones.

To make dog, glue 1½" pompon for body to 1" pompon for head; add ½" pompon for nose, and moveable eyes. Cut out and glue on felt ears, snout and mouth as shown. Glue body into basket. Glue red ribbon around basket and add ½" pompons for paws. With pinking shears, cut 1"-long leaves and glue in place. Insert dried flowers. Glue 2" ribbon bow to handle. Ornament hanger can catch center knot or a ribbon loop can be added.

Kitty-in-a-stocking Ornament

Kitty-in-a-stocking Ornament

SIZE: About 5½" high.

MATERIALS: Scraps red, white and green felt; red and white pipe cleaners; ¼"-wide moveable animal eyes; ⅜"-diameter white pompons; heavy black thread; white glue.

Trace patterns below right for stocking, cat head and holly leaf. For each ornament, cut out 2 red felt stockings; stitch together with ⅛" seam. Cut out 2 cat heads and 2 leaves. Glue heads together, then glue head and leaves to stocking. Make pompons (instructions, page 189) and glue on for paws. Twist pipe cleaners together to form candy cane. Insert in stocking.

Doggy-in-a-basket Ornament

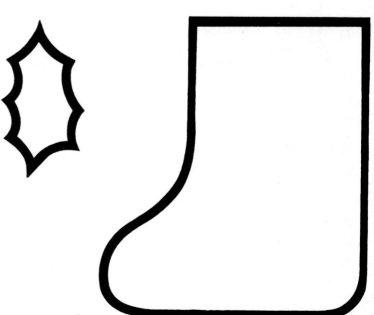

FRESH TRIBUTES TO CHERISHED TRADITIONS

*This section salutes a trio of customs second in esteem only to the traditional tree: **Christmas stockings,** hung with eager anticipation by generations of children; **wreaths**, sign of repose within, and welcome to, the family circle; **gifts and cards**, bearers of fond messages to loved ones near and dear, and to those farther away. **Stockings for Every Needlework Skill** bows to those who are handy with a needle— including the one on a sewing machine! Crafters of every variety will find projects to please in **A Roundup of Wreaths**: the customary kind in classic red-and-green, plus quite a few surprises. **Original, Ingenious Gift Wraps and Cards** recognizes the streak of individuality in all of us, with designs that say "Season's Greetings" in distinctive, personal style.*

Stockings for Every Needlework Skill

As far back as Christmas celebrations are remembered, children have been hanging stockings ''by the chimney with care.'' It's amazing, after all those years, that they still hold so many surprises (no pun intended!): color variety, design innovation and, most gratifying to needleworkers, techniques from needlepoint, knitting and crochet to simple machine sewing.

Quick-point Threesome

SIZE: About 11" by 16½".

MATERIALS: For each stocking: 14" x 20" piece of 5-to-the-inch Penelope needlepoint canvas, red woven fabric and heavyweight red felt; 1¼"-diameter plastic ring; large-eyed tapestry needle; bulky acrylic yarn, one 2-ounce skein each of any of the colors required for the stocking you are making (see color key with each chart): scarlet; maroon; white; yellow-orange; deep orange; turquoise; mint green; pink; black; tangerine; aqua; emerald.

CHARTS: Each square on charts equals 1 stitch. Follow charts for color and design only, not for number of stitches per inch. Where colors appear in small areas, symbols are given; large areas are marked with letters and symbols omitted (see color keys for symbols and letters).

NEEDLEPOINT: Holding canvas vertically, count 13 spaces over from lower left corner, then count 5 spaces up. Mark next mesh. Tape canvas edges to prevent raveling. Work first stitch over marked mesh (see first stitch marked on chart).

Following chart, work design in half cross-stitch (see diagram at top left on page 46).

FINISHING: Block stocking. Trim excess canvas to ½" seam allowance. Using canvas for pattern, cut out one piece red woven fabric for lining. With right sides together, stitch canvas to lining around outer edges, leaving top edge open. Trim seams; turn right side out. Turn under raw edges at top and slipstitch. Using this piece for pattern, cut out one stocking shape from felt. With wrong sides facing, whipstitch outer edges together, leaving upper edge open.

Wind red or maroon yarn around ring until it is covered; knot to secure. Sew to upper corner of stocking

CHRISTMAS STOCKINGS in quick-point are, from left to right: Noel, Boy with Wreath and Girl with Candle. Charts and color keys for each of them, as well as a diagram of the half cross-stitch, appear on pages 46 and 47.

Half cross-stitch

NOEL

Color Key

	▲	emerald
	—	mint green
S and	|	yellow-orange
R and	×	scarlet
	●	maroon
	○	tangerine
W and	□	white
	T	turquoise

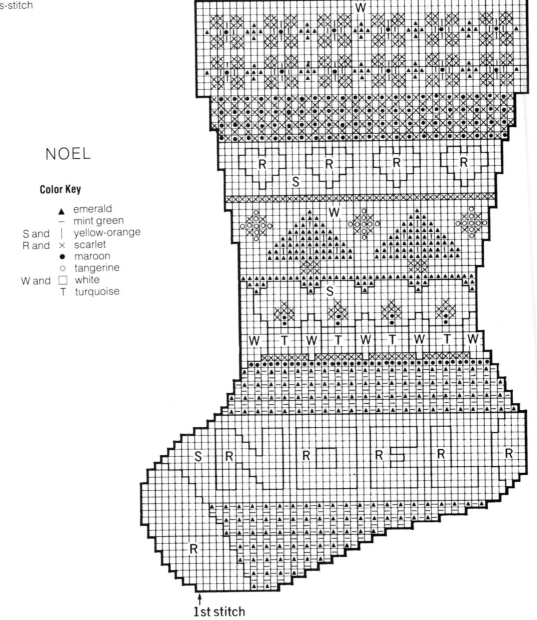

1st stitch

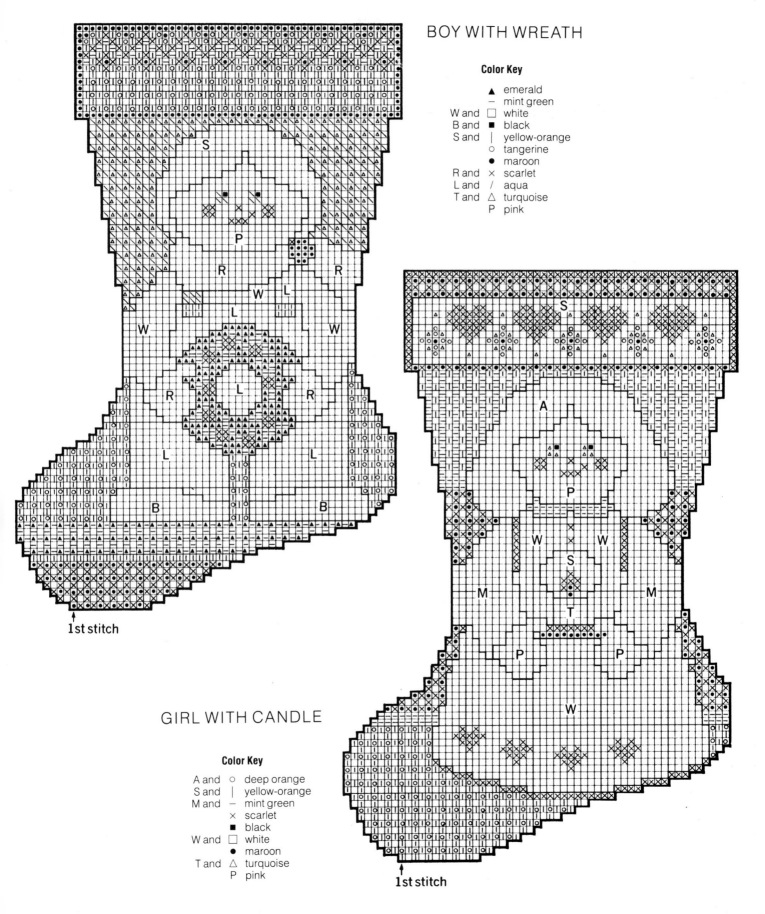

BOY WITH WREATH

Color Key

	▲	emerald
	–	mint green
W and	□	white
B and	■	black
S and	│	yellow-orange
	○	tangerine
	●	maroon
R and	✕	scarlet
L and	╱	aqua
T and	△	turquoise
P		pink

S

P

R   R

W   L

L

W   W

R   R

L

L   L

B   B

1st stitch

A

P

W   W

S

M   M

T

P   P

W

1st stitch

GIRL WITH CANDLE

Color Key

A and	○	deep orange
S and	│	yellow-orange
M and	–	mint green
	✕	scarlet
	■	black
W and	□	white
	●	maroon
T and	△	turquoise
	P	pink

Christmas Quartet

Christmas Quartet to Knit and Crochet

SIZE: Both knitted and crocheted versions are about 9" x 10½".

KNITTED STOCKINGS

MATERIALS (for 1 of each): Ombré stocking: Knitting-worsted-weight yarn, 2 ounces red-white-green ombré and 1 ounce white. **Striped stocking:** Knitting-worsted-weight yarn, 2 ounces green, 1 ounce each red and white. 1 pair size 8 (or English size 5) knitting needles, **or the size that will give you the correct gauge.**

GAUGE: 4 sts = 1".

BASIC STOCKING: (Note: Stocking is made in two pieces.) **Front:** Starting at lower edge, cast on 14 sts. Working in pattern given for individual stocking (see either Ombré Stocking or Striped Stocking, below), work 1 row, cast on 4 sts (heel edge), work 1 row, cast on 2 sts (toe edge), work 1 row, cast on 12 sts (heel edge), work 1 row, cast on 2 sts (toe edge), work 1 row (34 sts). Work even for 1½". At toe edge, bind off 2 sts every other row 3 times, then 6 sts once (22 sts). Work even for 5".

Cuff: Work even in garter st for 4".

Back: Work as for front, reversing shaping.

Finishing: Sew front to back along side and lower edges with cuff seam on outside; fold half of cuff down.

OMBRÉ STOCKING: Work basic stocking in ombré, cuff in white garter st.

STRIPED STOCKING: Work basic stocking in stripe pattern of 10 rows green stockinette st, 4 rows white garter st, 10 rows red stockinette st and 4 rows white garter st; work cuff in green garter st.

CROCHETED STOCKINGS

MATERIALS (for 1 of each): Ombré stocking: Knitting-worsted-weight yarn, 2 ounces red-white-green-metallic ombré and 1 ounce red. **Striped stocking:** Knitting-worsted-weight yarn, 2 ounces red, 1 ounce white and small amount red-white-green ombré. Aluminum crochet hook size G (or international hook size 4.50 mm), **or the size that will give you the correct gauge.**

GAUGE: 7 dc = 2".

BASIC STOCKING: (Note: Stocking is crocheted in one piece, then folded at center back. See Ombré Stocking or Striped Stocking, below, for colors). Starting at lower edge, ch 56. **1st row:** Work 2 dc in 4th ch from hook, dc in next 9 ch, sc in next 32 ch, dc in next 10 ch, 2 dc in last ch; ch 3, turn. **2nd row:** Work 2 dc in first dc, dc in next 13 sts, sc in next 28 sts, dc in next 13 sts, 3 dc in top of ch-3; ch 3, turn. **3rd row:** Dc in 1st 18 sts, sc in next 24 sts, dc in next 17 sts, 2 dc in top of ch-3; ch 3, turn. **4th row:** Sk first dc, dc in next 20 sts, sc in next 20 sts, dc in next 20 sts, dc in top of ch-3; ch 3, turn. **5th row:** Sk first dc, dc in each st across, dc in top of ch-3; turn. **6th row:** Sl st across first 3 dc, dc in each dc to last 3 dc; turn. **7th through 9th row:** Repeat 6th row (38 dc); ch 3, turn. **10th through 17th row:** Sk first dc, dc in each dc across, dc in top of ch-3; ch 3, turn.

Cuff: Repeat 10th row for 8 rows. Fasten off.

Finishing: Fold stocking in half; sew front and lower edges together; fold half of cuff down.

OMBRÉ STOCKING: Work 1st through 17th row with ombré, cuff with red.

STRIPED STOCKING: Work 1st through 7th row with red, 8th and 9th with white, 10th with ombré, 11th and 12th with white, 13th through 17th with red and cuff with white.

Easy Terrycloth Stockings

Easy Terrycloth Stockings

MATERIALS: Hand towels or terrycloth scraps; washable trim (see photograph, or trim as you wish); coordinating thread.

Cut two boot shapes from toweling; from same material, cut two rectangles (these will be extensions for cuffs) the length of the boot top and the depth of the desired cuff plus seam allowance. With **cuff right side** facing **boot wrong side** and raw edges matching, stitch a cuff extension to the top edge of each boot piece.

Extend cuff pieces up and, with right sides of **boot** pieces facing, stitch the two shapes together. Turn right side out and turn cuff down along seam (right sides of both will be showing). Add trim as in photograph or in any style you desire (trim will finish second raw cuff edge).

Multistriped Knitted Stockings

MATERIALS: Knitting-worsted-weight yarn, 4 ounces in variety of colors plus red or green; one pair dp needles No. 4; tapestry needle.

With red or green, cast on 60 sts loosely and divide on 3 needles. Join, being careful not to twist sts. Work in k 1, p 1 ribbing for 8 rnds. Break off.

9th–24th rnd: With red or green, k each rnd. Break off.

25th–32nd rnd: With new color, k each rnd. Break off.

33rd–36th rnd: With new color, k each rnd. Break off.

37th–44th rnd: With new color, k each rnd. Break off.

45th–48th rnd: With new color, k each rnd. Break off.

49th–56th rnd: With new color, k each rnd. Break off. Continue in this manner working Rnds 57 through 60, 61 through 68, 69 through 72, 73 through 80, 81 through 84 each in different colors as desired.

HEEL: Sl sts from 3rd needle to 1st needle and work on these 30 sts only.

1st row: With red or green, *sl 1, k 1, repeat from * across.

2nd row: P across. Repeat 1st and 2nd rows 10 times more, ending with a p row. **Turn heel.**

1st row: P 19, k 2 tog, k 1, turn.

2nd row: Sl 1, k 10, k 2 tog, k 1, turn.

3rd row: (P row): Sl 1, p 11, p 2 tog, p 1, turn.

4th row: (K row): Sl 1, k 12, k 2 tog, k 1, turn.

5th row: (P row): Sl 1, p 13, p 2 tog, p 1, turn. Continue working in this manner until 20 sts remain.

INSET GUSSET: K 10 sts on 1st needle and pick up 11 sts along side of heel tab. On 2nd needle k 30 sts from holder. On 3rd needle pick up 12 sts along side of heel tab and knit remaining 10 sts of heel from bottom of heel.

1st rnd: Knit around.

2nd rnd: K to last 3 sts on 1st needle, k 2 tog, k 1, k across sts on 2nd needle, k 1, sl 1, k 1, psso, k across sts on 3rd needle.

Multistriped Knitted Stockings

3rd rnd: K around. Changing colors as before, dec every other row until 56 sts remain — 13 sts on 1st needle, 30 sts on 2nd needle and 13 sts on 3rd needle; then sl 1 st each end of 2nd needle so that 14 sts remain on 1st needle, 28 on 2nd needle and 14 on 3rd needle. Continue to k around until 4 rows of 7th color are completed.

SHAPE TOE: 1st rnd: On 1st needle k 11 sts, k 2 tog, k 1. On 2nd needle sl 1, k 1, psso, k to within 3 sts of end, k 2 tog, k 1. On 3rd needle sl 1, k 1, psso, k to end.

2nd rnd: K around. Repeat 1st and 2nd rnds until you have 4 sts on 1st needle, 8 sts on 2nd needle and 4 sts on 3rd needle. K 4 sts from 1st needle and sl on 3rd needle. Cut off yarn 12" long. Weave 8 sts from 3rd needle to 8 sts on 2nd needle. Fasten off.

Each sq. = ½"

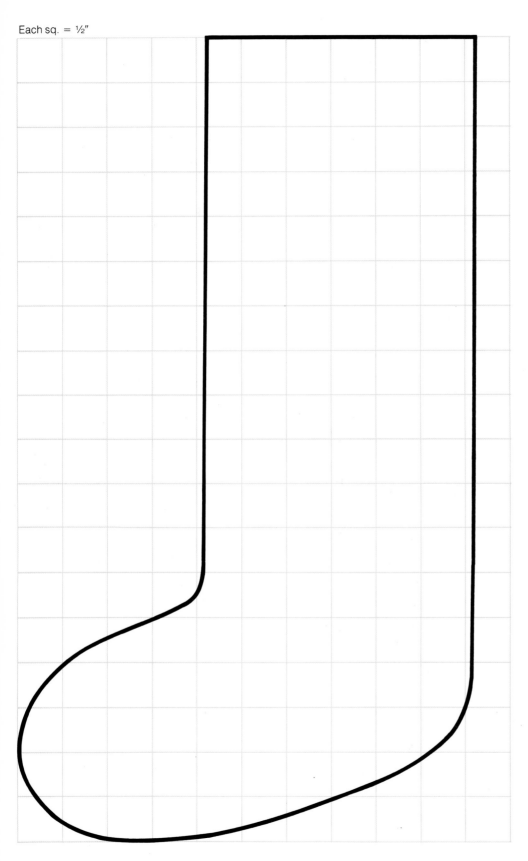

Quilted Trio

Quilted Trio

SIZE: About 10" x 15".

MATERIALS: ½ yard 45"-wide reversible prequilted print fabric (makes 2); scraps 1"-wide single-fold bias tape and 1"-wide eyelet lace.

FOR ALL STOCKINGS: Enlarge pattern, following instructions on page 189. Cut 2 pieces for each stocking, flopping pattern on 2nd piece so right sides of front and back will face out.

Mark off upper 3" for cuff. Cut a 7" piece of tape, fold in half lengthwise and topstitch prefolded edges together, then fold to form loop. With wrong sides of front and back stocking pieces facing, sandwich ends of loop where they will be caught in back seam 3¼" from upper edge. With raw edges matching and loop facing inward, stitch ⅛" seam along both sides of cuff.

STRIPED STOCKING: With wrong sides facing, encase raw edges of stocking below cuff with tape; topstitch. Encase upper edge. Turn cuff down.

POLKA-DOT STOCKING: With right sides of front and back facing, stitch ⅛" seam around stocking below cuff. Stitch lace to upper edge. Turn right side out. Turn cuff down.

TREE PATTERN STOCKING: With right sides of front and back facing, stitch ⅛" seam around stocking below cuff. Encase upper edge with tape; topstitch. Turn right side out. Turn cuff down. For bow, cut 15" piece of tape. Fold in half lengthwise; topstitch long edges. Tie in bow; tack to cuff.

A Roundup of Wreaths

Wreaths, with their serene circular shape, have come to symbolize unity and peace, the coming together of people of good will. We offer many ways to send your message of fellowship: designs for indoors and out; a mixture of the classic and the unusual (look especially for wreaths made of materials from your kitchen); a broad spectrum of crafting and handwork techniques.

Wreath with Chili Peppers

Crocheted Wreath with Satin Chili Peppers

CROCHETED WREATH

SIZE: About 15" in diameter.

MATERIALS: 14 ounces knitting-worsted-weight yarn; aluminum crochet hook size G (or international hook size 4:50 mm); wire coat hanger; 3 yards (plus 2 yards for long streamers) 3"-wide satin ribbon; double-stick tape.

Bend coat hanger to form circle. (Hook on hanger is used for hanging finished wreath.) Measure circumference of circle (about 15"). With yarn, make a chain this length. Join to form ring.

1st rnd: * Ch 7, sc in next sc, ch 7, sc in same sc. Repeat from * around; join. Break off. **2nd rnd:** * Sc in next ch-7 sp, ch 7, (sc in same sp, ch 7) 3 times. Repeat from * around; join. Break off. **3rd rnd:** * Sc in next ch-7 sp, ch 3, (sc in same sp, ch 3) 3 times. Repeat from * around; join.

Break off. Sew starting chain to coat hanger. Tie satin peppers to hanger between loops of crochet.

To make bow: Cut ribbon into 44" and 64" lengths. Notch ends. Tie center of shorter piece around wreath. Fold longer piece in thirds, pinch center together and tie shorter piece around it to make "bow." (Folds in streamers are held in place with double-stick tape.)

SATIN CHILI PEPPERS

MATERIALS: ½ yard each red and green satin (enough for about 15 per color); tubular elastic; dried tops of real chilies or green pipe cleaners; fabric glue; red or green rattail or narrow satin ribbon; matching sewing threads.

Enlarge pattern (enlarging instructions, page 189) and cut chilies. Cut elastic to fit inside and tack in place where shown. Fold in half lengthwise with right sides facing; sew along side dotted line in pattern. Turn right side out. Fold in ¼" and gather top closed with running stitches (top dotted line); glue real chili tops over stitches, using fabric cement. (Or fold pipe cleaner in half, and then make hook at each end. Insert about halfway into chili, pulling up gathers so chili fits tight around pipe cleaner.) To hang, use red or green rattail or satin ribbon tied to top.

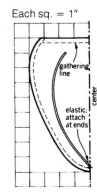

Each sq. = 1"

SATIN CHILI PEPPER

Classic Pine Cone Wreath

MATERIALS: Double wire wreath frame (from florist); assorted pine cones; stemmed artificial red berries; 2 yards red velvet ribbon; medium- to heavy-weight florist's wire.

Wire all cones by twisting wire among cone scales near base; leave 6″ ends for attaching to frame. First attach a row of large cones around outer edge, winding wire over both edges of frame. Attach smaller cones to inner edge. Fill in with cones and berries, wiring them invisibly to frame; attach bow.

Classic Pine Cone Wreath

Spiral-crochet Wreath

Spiral-crochet Wreath

SIZE: About 14″ in diameter.

MATERIALS (for 1): Knitting-worsted-weight yarn, 12 ounces green, 3 ounces red-white-green-metallic ombré; aluminum crochet hooks size G and I (or international hooks size 4.50 and 5.50 mm), **or the sizes that will give you the correct gauges;** heavy metal coat hanger; 3½″ x 50″ strip red felt; wire cutters; sewing thread.

GAUGES: With size G hook, 7 dc = 2″.

With size G hook and green, ch 300. **1st row:** Work 5 dc in 4th ch from hook and in each ch across; ch 3, turn. **2nd row:** Dc in each dc across; ch 3, turn. **3rd row:** With size I hook, repeat 2nd row; join ombré, fasten off green; ch 1, turn. **4th row:** Sc in first 3 dc, * ch 4, sc in next 3 dc; repeat from * across. Fasten off.

Cut hook off coat hanger; bend remainder into circle. Twist crocheted piece around wire; tack ends.

From felt strip, cut 6″ piece for center of bow, 25″ piece for bow and 19″ piece for ties. Fold bow piece into bow shape, pleating center; wrap center piece around it; tack. Pleat and fold tie piece at center to form diagonal ties; tack. Notch ends of ties.

Crocheted Loop-stitch Wreath

SIZE: 16″ in diameter.

MATERIALS: Bulky acrylic yarn, 8 (35-yard) skeins emerald; acrylic knitting-worsted-weight yarn, 1 (4-ounce) ball scarlet; aluminum crochet hook size K (or international hook size 7.00 mm); ¼ yard red felt; cardboard; red sewing thread.

POMPON (make 15): Cut 2 cardboard circles 1½″ in diameter. Cut ½″-diameter hole in center of each to make ring. Hold rings together and make cut from outer edge to hole. Wind scarlet yarn around and around rings, bringing it through cut with each wind. When cardboard is covered and hole filled, break off yarn. Snip wound yarn around outside edge of ring; separate cardboard rings slightly and tie yarn together tightly in center between rings. Remove cardboard and pompon will fluff out. Trim slightly if necessary to even.

WREATH FRAME: From cardboard, cut circle 14″ in diameter. Cut 9″-diameter hole in center to form ring. (**Note:** If cardboard is thin, cut 2 rings and tape or glue together.)

CROCHET: With crochet hook and emerald yarn, crochet chain to fit around outside of ring plus 1″. **1sr row:** Sc in 2nd ch from hook and in each ch across; ch 1, turn. **2nd row (wrong side):** Work lp sc in next sc as follows: * Make 2″-long lp over index finger of left hand; insert hook in next sc and draw a bit of both strands of lp through st; remove finger from lp, yo and draw through all lps on hook (lp sc made). Repeat from * across (lps appear on right side of work). **Break off. Do not turn. Always work with wrong side facing you. **3rd row:** Make lp on hook; work lp sc in each lp sc across. Repeat from ** until piece is large enough to cover both sides of ring. Break off.

FINISHING: With lps outward, fold crocheted piece over cardboard frame and sew edges together. (You will have to pull in the crochet around inner edge to fit cardboard frame.) From

Crocheted Loop-stitch Wreath

felt, cut 3″ x 20″ piece for bow and 2″ x 30″ piece for ties. Fold wider piece to form bow shape, lapping ends at center back. Fold narrower piece in half crosswise, wrap fold around bow and tack at back. Cut ends on a diagonal. Following photograph, tack pompons and bow to wreath.

Tissue Wreath

SIZE: About 18" in diameter.

MATERIALS: Heavy wire; colored tissue paper, 3 (20" x 30") sheets each red and light green, 2 each dark green and turquoise; paper towels; white glue; 26 cafe-curtain clip rings; pinking shears.

Cut 60" wire. Leaving 10" free at each end, wind with paper towels to pad to diameter of curtain rings. Glue ends. Cover with strips of tissue paper, wrapping on diagonal.

To form paper puffs, remove sheet of tissue paper from package. Refold as it was and, using pinking shears, cut crosswise at 6" intervals. Unfold. Gather each strip lengthwise and clip at center with curtain ring. Thread rings onto paper-wrapped wire about 2" apart. Join wire ends.

Tissue Wreath

Knotted-yarn Wreath

Knotted-yarn Wreath

SIZE: About 18" in diameter.

MATERIALS: About 7 ounces total of green and blue yarns in assorted shades, weights and types (yarns here are 7 shades of sport- and knitting-worsted-weight yarn, mohair, and nubby yarn); 2½" x 45" strip red felt or ribbon for bow; 21 red wooden beads for berries; 3 yards fine wire; two 12"-diameter hoops of sturdy wire or 2 coat hangers that can be bent to shape for wreath frame; pliers.

WREATH FRAME: Bind wire hoops together with a few strands of fine wire or cord, or make two hoops from coat hangers and bind together, as round and kink-free as possible.

KNOTTED FRINGE: Cut yarn in 10" lengths. Take 3 lengths (all same color or a mixture) and knot around frame, making 2 tight knots, 1 over the other. Con-

tinue around, knotting 3-strand lengths in this manner, pushing the knotted strands close together, until frame is covered.

BERRIES AND BOW: Cut 12" piece of thin wire, string a bead on it and wind wire around frame, squeezing it between knotted strands. String another bead, wind wire again, string third bead and bind ends of wire firmly together and around frame. Space bead (berry) clusters evenly around wreath (see photograph).

Tie felt or ribbon in bow, notch ends and sew to wreath.

Braided-fabric Wreath

MATERIALS: Cotton or cotton-blend fabrics in contrasting prints or solid colors (designer sheeting used here); stiff wire; wide ribbon.

To make tubes for braiding, cut three strips of fabric long enough to span the circumference of the desired wreath when they are stuffed and braided. (**Note:** To estimate the necessary length, test-braid some un-stuffed tubes about 1½ times the circumference and lay them out flat in a circle. From this, you will be able to tell whether you need to increase or decrease the length. Bear in mind that stuffing both "fattens" and shortens the circle.) Fold strips in half lengthwise with right sides facing; sew along the cut sides and across one end, taking a ⅝" seam. Turn tubes right side out.

Gather tube with your hands as you would when putting on socks, and begin to stuff. A ruler is handy for tamping down the stuffing as you get farther down the tube. When the tube is full, tuck in the ends and sew opening closed. Repeat for each tube. Braid the three tubes and attach to a stiff-wire circle the size of the wreath. Make a lavish bow with a wide ribbon, topped with a "ribbon" made from a scrap of the wreath fabric. Pin bow onto wreath where the ends of the tubes join, to cover any break in the overall pattern.

Ribbon Cylinder Wreath

Braided-fabric Wreath

Ribbon Cylinder Wreath

SIZE: 24" in diameter.

MATERIALS: Red readymade wreath bow; three 2-yard rolls each gift-wrap ribbon in three seasonal colors; 24" square corrugated cardboard; glue; green paper-backed foil 26" x 26" (**Note:** Glue does not adhere to metal foil); transparent tape; stapler.

Cut a 24"-diameter circle out of cardboard. Make this into a wreath by cutting out an inner circle with a 12"-diameter. Cover the cardboard wreath with the paper foil and tape to back.

The 34 telescoping cylinders are made in three sizes and three colors. Cut and staple all 34 cylinders before assembling. Small cylinders take 3½" of ribbon, medium 4½" and large 5½". Join by overlapping the ends of ribbon ½" and stapling.

Nestle the three sizes of cylinders so that they telescope as shown, with smallest cylinders at inner edge and both inner and outer edges even with wreath base. Glue in place. There will be a space for the large bow.

To mount the bow, cut an empty ribbon spool down to 1" in height. Glue in empty space with label side up. Make a green bow to center on the wreath bow. Tie the two together using the third color of ribbon. Glue the bow to the label side of the spool.

Each sq. = ½"

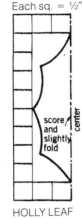

HOLLY LEAF

Each sq. = ½"

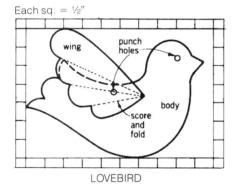

LOVEBIRD

Holly Wreath with Lovebirds and Garlands

Paper Holly-leaf Wreath with Lovebirds and Garlands

HOLLY-LEAF WREATH

SIZE: 15" in diameter.

MATERIALS: Heavy glazed paper (from art-supply store): 1 sheet each red and bright pink, 2 sheets green; 4 sheets green heavy construction paper; 15"-diameter plastic-foam wreath form; cotton swabs; red paint or liquid dye; short carpet tacks; white glue.

Enlarge leaf pattern, following instructions on page 189. Cut 100 full leaves from green construction paper; cut 100 half leaves from green glazed paper and glue to construction-paper leaves. Score lightly on center line after glue dries. Cut and make two lovebirds, following directions below, from pink and red paper. Dip 88 cotton swabs in red paint or dye; let dry; cut off tips and discard sticks.

Cut strips of green construction paper to fit around inside and outside edges of wreath form; glue in place. With carpet tacks, attach leaves to form, following photograph. Slip ends of groups of swabs under leaves and glue in place. Glue birds at top.

CUT-PAPER LOVEBIRD

MATERIALS: 1 or more sheets of at least 2 colors of heavy glazed paper (from art-supply store); rubber cement; hole punch; strings for hanging.

Enlarge lovebird pattern, following directions on page 189. For each lovebird, cut two bodies from one color, reversing pattern so that they can be glued together. Cut 4 wings, reversing 2. Glue body to body and wing to wing with rubber cement. Score and fold wings as shown; punch holes in body and glue wings in place. Tie short length of string to body hole, knotting ends for hanging.

TEDDY-BEAR AND GINGERBREAD-BOY GARLANDS

MATERIALS: Sheets heavy glazed paper; rubber cement.

Enlarge boy and bear patterns, following instructions on page 189 and using ¼" squares for 3"-high figures and ½" squares for 6"-high figures. Cut strips of paper 3" or 6" wide. Rubber-cement same-size strips together so that they are two-layered. Fold into accordion pleats 2½" or 5" wide. Place full-size pattern on top and cut as for paper dolls. For garlands, be sure to leave arms linked; for single figures, cut apart.

Each sq. = ½" for large garland, ¼" for small garland

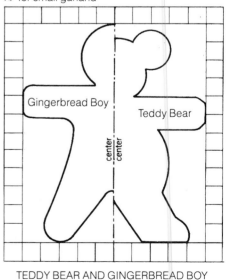

TEDDY BEAR AND GINGERBREAD BOY

Braided-yarn Wreath

SIZE: 10" in diameter.

MATERIALS: Knitting-worsted-weight yarn, 4 ounces green and 1 ounce red; wire coat hanger or No. 6-gauge aluminum armature wire; large-eyed needle; stemmed artificial red berries (optional).

Cut green yarn into 48" lengths; divide into 3 equal bundles. Tie bundles together at one end and braid. Tie braid at end and cut both tassel ends to an even 3". Cut 22" length of wire. Shape wire into 7"-diameter circle. Before joining ends of wire, work one end into braided length, then join wire ends.

To decorate wreath, embroider French knots in clusters of 3 as in photograph, or attach red berries, wiring stems to wreath frame at back. For bow, cut thirty 48" lengths of red yarn and divide into 3 equal bundles. Tie bundles together at one end, braid and tie, leaving 1½" tassels. Trim ends even and unravel plies for fuller tassels. Shape braid into flat bow with 12" streamers. Tack bow in place where wreath ends meet as shown.

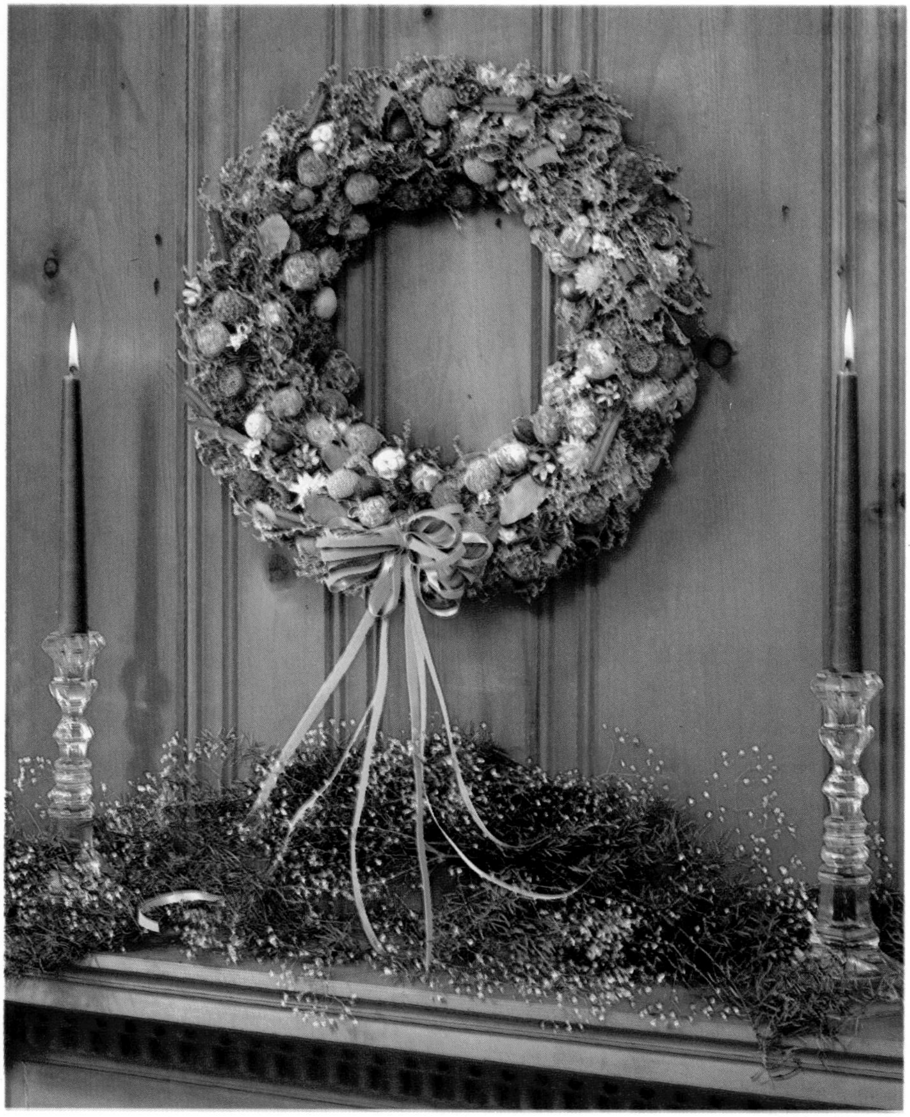

Spice Wreath

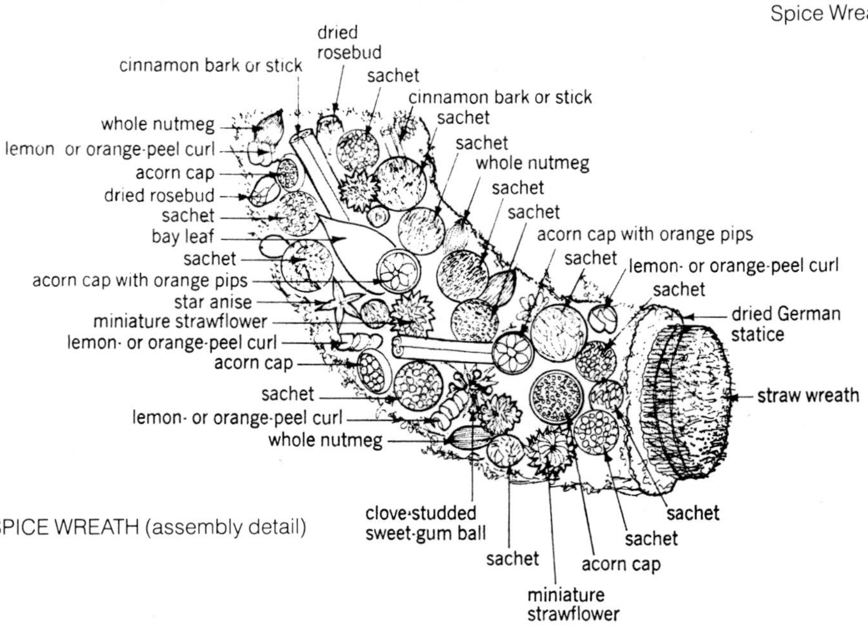
dried rosebud
cinnamon bark or stick
sachet
cinnamon bark or stick
sachet
whole nutmeg
lemon or orange-peel curl
acorn cap
dried rosebud
sachet
bay leaf
sachet
acorn cap with orange pips
star anise
miniature strawflower
lemon- or orange-peel curl
acorn cap
sachet
lemon- or orange-peel curl
whole nutmeg
sachet
whole nutmeg
sachet
sachet
acorn cap with orange pips
sachet
lemon- or orange-peel curl
sachet
dried German statice
straw wreath
clove-studded sweet-gum ball
sachet
miniature strawflower
acorn cap
sachet
sachet

SPICE WREATH (assembly detail)

WREATHS FROM YOUR PANTRY SHELF

Spice Wreath

SIZE: About 17″ in diameter.

MATERIALS: 14″-diameter purchased straw wreath; dried flowers: 4 to 6 bunches of German statice, 12 miniature strawflowers on 2″ wire stems and a few rosebuds or sprays of ammobium; 6 sweet-gum balls; 12 acorn caps; ¼ yard 72″-wide ivory nylon net; small rubber bands; floral picks; thin flexible wire; 2 yards ½″-wide pale-green velvet ribbon; glue gun and cartridge; white glue; various spices, herbs and dried flower petals.

Note: Though wreath is not difficult to assemble, it takes patience and care. Listed below are a few of the spices, herbs and dried flower petals used. You can substitute whatever is available in your area.

Use seed and spices such as star anise, caraway, cardamom, coriander, cumin, fennel, rosemary, mustard, poppy, sesame, whole or coarsely ground allspice, cloves, cinnamon bark or stick, nutmeg, ginger root and whole bay leaves. From pharmacies you can obtain orris root, frankincense and myrrh; also dried flower petals such as lavender, potpourri, sassafras bark, oakmoss, herbal and mint teas, lemon verbena, tansy and yarrow.

Sachets: Cut nylon net into 5″ squares. Prepare various potpourris of dried petals and herbs. Add a pinch of orris root to each mixture to preserve the fragrance. Place 2 teaspoons potpourri mixture in center of each net square. Pull up edges to form about a 1″-diameter ball. Bind sachet tightly with rubber band; cut away excess net. Also make sachets with combinations of sesame seed, rosemary, whole cardamom and caraway.

Acorn caps: Pour a few drops of glue in acorn cap and rub inside of cap to coat thoroughly. Sprinkle cap with seed spices such as mustard, whole allspice and whole cardamom. Also arrange orange pips in flower or star shape. Shake out excess seed and set caps aside to dry.

Sweet-gum balls: Dip tips of whole cloves in glue and insert one in each hole in sweet-gum ball until ball is half filled.

Lemon- and orange-peel curls: Remove peel from fruit in 4 lengthwise sections; scrape any pulp and soft white membrane away. Cut in thin strips. Allow strips to dry 1 to 2 hours, then twist pliable strips into spirals and secure with a toothpick. Allow to dry.

Wreath assembly: Using flexible wire, make a strong double hanger loop around straw wreath; bind wire firmly. Push loop to back of wreath and tuck any sharp ends into straw.

Cut statice into sprays of 3" to 5" including stems. Wire a pick to each spray. Cover front and all edges of wreath with statice, making sure that sprays all go in the same direction. Overlap sprays so that front and sides of wreath are completely covered. Do not cover back.

Following manufacturer's directions for using glue gun, touch the underside of prepared sachets, acorn caps, sweet-gum balls, peel curls and all the individual dried flowers, bay leaves, cinnamon bark, star anise, etc., with gun and arrange on wreath as in photograph and assembly detail.

To finish, make a loopy bow with streamers from velvet ribbon as in photograph; wire bow to wreath.

Note: To store, place wreath in large plastic bag.

Coffee-dough Wreath

Coffee-dough Wreath

Note: Follow recipe below to make dough for wreath, which is inedible. Recipe, which will make several wreaths, cannot be either halved or doubled.

COFFEE DOUGH

4 cups unsifted all-purpose flour
1 cup salt
¼ cup instant coffee powder
1½ cups warm water

Preheat oven to 300°F. Combine flour with salt. Dissolve coffee powder in warm water. Make a hole in the center of the flour-salt mixture and pour in 1 cup coffee-water. Mix thoroughly with fork or hands, adding more coffee-water if necessary. Dough should be smooth and satiny and neither crumbly nor sticky. Form into balls and place in plastic bags to prevent drying out. Use one ball at a time.

Making the wreath: Working on aluminum foil, form a ¼"-thick 6"-diameter ring with a 3¼"-diameter centered hole, for base of wreath. Referring to photograph, make ¼"-thick x ½" x 1½" leaves, cutting out shapes with a wet knife. To keep wreath in scale, make larger fruit shapes first. Fill in with smaller fruit shapes and nuts. To attach dough pieces to ring, brush with water and press shapes in place. Texture leaves and fruit with sharp point of a pencil or knife.

Bake wreath on foil for an hour, or until hard. When cool, peel away foil and apply two coats of shellac, front and back, to preserve.

Popcorn-and-peppermint Wreath

Cookie Wreath

Popcorn-and-peppermint Wreath

SIZE: Approximately 18" in diameter.

MATERIALS: 15½"-diameter x 2"-wide plastic-foam ring; 6 to 8 quarts unbuttered popcorn; 4 dozen round, flat, red-and-white peppermint candies; white glue; 6 yards ⅝"-wide red satin ribbon; thin flexible wire; 3 yards 1½"-wide red-and-white polka-dot ribbon; cocktail picks; pipe cleaner; colorless nail polish; waxed paper.

Cover work surface with waxed paper. Unwrap candies and brush colorless nail polish on all surfaces; put aside on waxed paper to dry. Place plastic-foam wreath on waxed paper and pour container of undiluted white glue into bowl; allow glue to thicken slightly. Dip picks halfway into glue and stud plastic-foam wreath liberally but not densely with picks so that about 1" projects out of ring; let dry.

Dilute ½ cup white glue with ½ cup water; mix well. Working with small amount (1½ quarts) at a time, pour diluted glue over some of the popcorn and mix well to coat thoroughly. Working quickly, begin spreading popcorn on wreath, covering front and sides. Prepare more popcorn as you work and build up wreath as shown in photograph. Set wreath aside to dry for a day or two.

Cut red satin ribbon into twenty-four 9" pieces and tie into small bows. Wire a pick to each bow. Also make loopy bow from polka-dot ribbon as in photograph; wire a pick to it.

When wreath is dry, use undiluted glue to attach coated candies. Dip bow picks in glue and push in place over wreath as in photograph; add polka-dot bow at top, slightly off center. Allow trimmed wreath to dry.

To hang, bend pipe cleaner in U shape and work tips into back of plastic foam at top. Pull out and dip tips of pipe cleaner in glue; reinsert in holes; let dry.

Cookie Wreath

MATERIALS: Glue dough (recipe and handling instructions follow); cookie cutters (refer to photograph for kinds you need); pizza pan; foil; frosting and food coloring or white glue and acrylic paint; decorative candies; ribbon. **Note:** Wreath is not edible.

Making and handling glue dough: For dough, you need ¼ cup each flour, cornstarch and white glue. Measure ingredients in a bowl. (For best results, use even measures.) Mix and knead until well blended. If mixture is too dry, add a drop or two of glue; if too moist, sprinkle with flour and cornstarch, a little at a time.

Divide up the clay-like ball according to your purpose: rolling it flat with a rolling pin to cut shapes with cutters; breaking off small amounts for hand shaping of strands or ropes.

Making the wreath parts: To make the outside boundary, make small "snake" strands with the dough. Keep your fingers moist and apply even pressure, stroking from center out to each end while rolling. Use palms to make strands smoother.

Make the two ropes by fitting one small piece to the next until you achieve the proper length; one rope is a long smooth strand and the other is two strands wound around each other. Wrap ribbon around these two pieces as shown in the photograph.

Cover a pizza pan with foil, grease lightly, and work ropes around the edge. Flour your cookie cutters, cut shapes from rolled dough, and press the cookies gently into the braid and onto each other, following the photograph for the correct placement.

If using frosting for the stripes on the cookies, simply apply it where you should, using food coloring if you want variety. Position candies on top. If using glue, apply a layer and let it dry, then another and another, building up until they form a strand. Paint with acrylic paint. With household cement, glue candies to the strand.

Make bow with centered hanging loop and glue it in place.

Pasta Wreath

SIZE: Approximately 18″ in diameter.

MATERIALS: Two 15″-diameter plastic-foam rings; two 1-pound bags unshelled walnuts; 1-pound box each jumbo, medium and small macaroni shells; 6 yards stiff lightweight florist's wire; white glue; 45 to 50 small seashells; orange shellac; 2 yards 2″-wide green satin ribbon.

To preserve nuts, punch or drill a small hole in each one. Dip quickly in boiling water, remove and let dry. Cut a 3″ wire stem for each walnut. Dip one end of wire into glue and insert in drilled hole in nut, leaving a 2″ stem.

Glue plastic-foam rings together. Make hanger loop by wrapping wire around rings several times, leaving ends to form loop; twist ends together.

Position wreath on two blocks on a newspaper-covered work surface. Dip walnut stems in glue and push into wreath every 2″, covering front and both inner and outer sides. Glue jumbo macaroni shells in spaces between nuts (the nuts will support macaroni and seashells). Allow to dry. Fill in remaining spaces with medium and small macaroni, overlapping macaroni until wreath is covered as in photograph. Glue seashells evenly spaced on wreath as shown. Allow wreath to dry overnight.

To finish wreath, brush on orange shellac; dry overnight. Make flat bow with streamers; wire in place.

Pasta Wreath

Original, Ingenious Gift Wraps and Cards

The gifts you give and the cards you send are not mere customary gestures. They are signs of how much you value the love or friendship of the person who receives them. You naturally want your gifts and greetings to be as individual and personal as possible. Our sentiments exactly, and the guiding thought behind our designs.

Quick-print Wrappings

Quick-print Wrappings

MATERIALS: One tube each red, green and iridescent gold acrylic artist's paint; package of small sponges (preferably 3"-square pot-scrubbing type with a darker rough side); scissors; ruler; pencil; brown paper; shopping bags, brown paper bags, purchased white paper bags (or make your own using a brown bag as a pattern); boxes; shallow dishes; rubber cement; hole punch; scrap cardboard and 1 yard gold cord for wrap No. 3; 1' of ¼" ribbon for No. 7.

General directions: Choose design you want to make and cut sponges accordingly (see specific directions below). In shallow dish, mix enough paint to fill bottom of dish with 1 or 2 drops of water, using a separate dish for each color. Make very light pencil guidelines on paper or bag to be printed. Hold sponge by the rough side and dip into paint. Make sure paint covers sponge printing surface completely. Print in series as shown in color photograph, dipping sponge for each application. If you want to change colors, use another sponge (or wash thoroughly before re-use). Let paint dry before using wrap.

Note: Numbers that follow refer to schematic layout.

1. Shopping bag is printed with 1⅞" red squares, using sponge with corners cut off, interspersed with ¾" green squares overprinted, when dry, with ½" gold squares.

2. Wine-bottle bag is printed with 3" red squares stamped on the diagonal, and green starbursts made by applying ½" x 3" edge of sponge in four crisscross impressions.

3. Drawstring bag is made from 14" x 17" sheet of paper printed with rows of 1¾" x 1¾" x 3" red and green triangles. Cut 5"-diameter cardboard circle. Fold under one long edge of paper 1½" and glue down. Punch small holes 1" apart, ¼" down from top of fold. Fold under other long edge 2½" for bottom; cut slits ¾" apart from edge to fold. Glue tabs to bottom of cardboard circle. Overlap short edges, then glue. Pleat top of bag evenly and

thread 1 yard gold cord through holes. Knot ends of cord.

4. Small bag is printed with red starbursts, made as for No. 2, overprinted with ½" gold squares after red dries. A single starburst was printed on white paper and cut out for tissue-paper decoration.

5. Paper covering large box is printed with series of diagonal lines created by ½" x 3" sponge edge.

6. Top paper on small box is printed with 1"-diameter red circles, surrounded by ⅜" green squares. Bottom is series of green and red ¾" squares. After printing, cut paper to fit top and bottom of box. Lap neatly over box edges and glue inside.

7. Cornucopia is made of double layer of white paper. Outer layer is first printed with same pattern as for No. 2, following directions for No. 4. Make cornucopia pattern following dimensions on diagram. Rubber-cement printed paper to plain sheet and cut out pattern. Cut slots for ribbon. Score all fold lines with spoon edge and ruler, then fold along scored lines and flatten each fold with back of spoon. Overlap outer straight edge over tab edge and glue in place. Insert ends of ¼" ribbon in slits from top and glue in place inside.

8. Flat box is wrapped in brown paper printed with diagonal sponge-edge lines in green and 1"-diameter circles in red.

QUICK-PRINT WRAPPINGS

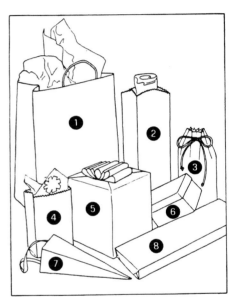

(schematic layout)

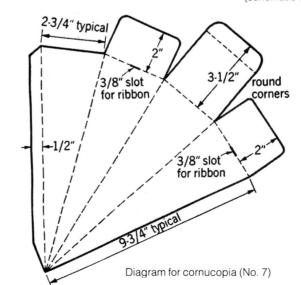

Diagram for cornucopia (No. 7)

WRAPPING A SQUARE PACKAGE

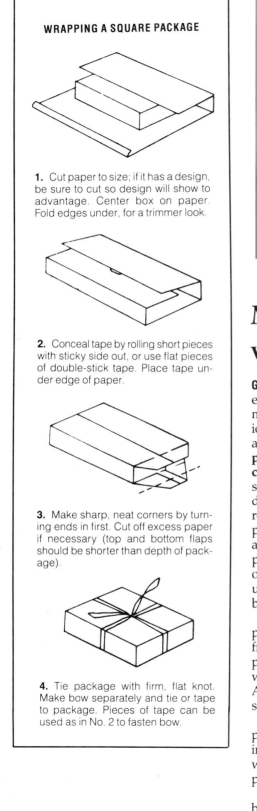

1. Cut paper to size; if it has a design, be sure to cut so design will show to advantage. Center box on paper. Fold edges under, for a trimmer look.

2. Conceal tape by rolling short pieces with sticky side out, or use flat pieces of double-stick tape. Place tape under edge of paper.

3. Make sharp, neat corners by turning ends in first. Cut off excess paper if necessary (top and bottom flaps should be shorter than depth of package).

4. Tie package with firm, flat knot. Make bow separately and tie or tape to package. Pieces of tape can be used as in No. 2 to fasten bow.

Cotton Swab Motifs, (left to right): Candle, Star, Tree, Geometric, Bird

Motifs to Make with Cotton Swabs

General directions: Cover boxed presents with solid-colored paper so white motifs will stand out. Motifs are variously made with **whole** cotton swabs as they come from the box, with **small pieces** cut with scissors, or with a **combination** of the two. Prepare a supply of the types required for the design of your choice, and pencil a rough sketch of it on the wrapped package (use photograph for guidance). If design details call for colored paper, glue these on first, then glue on the swab elements. White glue is used to attach all pieces; applicator bottle is convenient for the purpose.

Candle motif: Cut candle from white paper, ribbon, cloth, etc. Cut flame from pink paper, glow from yellow paper. Glue these in place, then trim with "light rays" of swabs, as shown. Apply glue lines first, then attach swab pieces.

Star motif: Cut star from yellow paper, glue in place, trim with swabs as in photograph (tint swabs in center with paint or dye). Note alternating pattern of swab tips.

Tree motif: Sketch tree on wrapped box, basic outline first, then branches. Cut swabs into appropriate pieces (mainly tips; some straight lengths).

Working an area at a time (basic shape first, then branches from the bottom up to permit overlapping), glue swabs in place. Add details (bird, swab tip "snowflakes").

Geometric motif: Sketch design on paper first, following photograph; cut a supply of long pieces and tips as shown; glue them in place.

Bird motif: Sketch two bird shapes on box, following photograph; cut long and short swab pieces and glue on to fill in bird shapes. (Glue underlying long pieces first.) Add paper wreath, trimming with swab tips. Add piece of cord, gluing only a few places: at ends, at birds' beaks and at cord bow tied at side of wreath.

Glue Dough Ornaments, "Appliquéd" Cards

Glue Dough Ornaments

MATERIALS: Dough (recipe and general handling instructions below); rolling pin; biscuit or cookie cutters (see photograph for examples); food coloring; fabric and ribbon remnants.

Making and handling glue dough: Mix together ¼ cup each white glue, flour and cornstarch in a bowl. For best results, use level measures. Mix and knead until well blended. If mixture is too dry, add a drop or two of glue; if too moist, sprinkle with flour and cornstarch, a little at a time.

Divide up the clay-like ball, roll it flat with a rolling pin and cut into stars, gingerbread men, lollipops, etc., with cookie and biscuit cutters or into candy canes by hand. If you want to tie the ornaments on packages, make a hole while dough is still soft with a toothpick or plastic straw. Leftover dough can be worked together just as you would cookie dough, then rolled out again or wrapped tightly in a plastic bag for another session.

Allow 12 to 24 hours for decorations to dry, the time depending on the thickness, turning once or twice, before painting.

Decorating dough figures: While dough figures are drying, fill gift boxes and wrap them in white or colored tissue paper or gift wrap. Cut strips of scrap fabric or ribbon and glue them to the packages. Bits of rickrack are good trim too.

To paint the glue dough ornaments, mix food color into a little glue in a small plastic cup or glue applicator (1¼-ounce size). Glue ornaments, as they are painted, to the packages. Use wooden tongue depressors for lollipop sticks, tying on a ribbon bow before gluing them down.

To make hanging ornaments: Use the same dough mixture as above, roll out dough and cut into shapes with knife or cookie cutters; make a hole, as above, for hanging ribbon or cord. Give Santa Claus three-dimensional look by adding extra pieces for his bag, giving him a curly beard by using a garlic press. Additional pieces can be pressed into place while dough is still wet. To be sure of a good hold, apply a little glue to joints. Let dry and paint with a mixture of white glue and food coloring or acrylic paint. To put "panes" in windows of house, cut out the windows, then lay the house on plastic wrap and dribble a mixture of glue and food coloring into the spaces. Let dry overnight and carefully peel wrap off.

"Appliquéd" Cards

MATERIALS: Scraps of fabric, ribbon, felt, yarn; white glue; blank notepaper or cards with envelopes (not necessary if cards will be gift tags); tracing paper; dressmaker's carbon paper.

Sketch seasonal patterns on tracing paper (for examples see photograph above) to conform to paper or card size. Glue fabric background, cut to exact size, to paper or card. Using dressmaker's carbon, trace patchwork pattern on fabric in as much detail as you feel is necessary. Cut, arrange and glue fabric or felt "patches," following pattern lines; glue border in appropriate color to edges. (For gift tags, choose colors to coordinate with wrapped package; punch hole for cord or ribbon tie.) Add other decorations, such as yarn bow, tree star, etc.

Crocheted Gift Tie
(shown with Yo-yo Santas in photograph on page 121)

MATERIALS: Scraps of knitting-worsted-weight yarn; aluminum crochet hook size G (or international hook size 4:50 mm); string.

Wrap string around package to determine desired length for tie. Make a chain this length plus 40 ch (20 ch at each end for curl). Work 3 sc in 2nd ch from hook, (3 sc in next ch) 19 times; sl st in each ch to last 20 ch, (3 sc in next ch) 20 times. Break off.

In the Bag

BLACK TRASH BAG

MATERIALS: 30-gallon black plastic trash bag, with twist closure; 8-gallon or larger white plastic trash bag; ¾"-wide red tape; white string; 2⅜" x 4¾" baggage tag; red and green felt-tip markers; tissue paper (optional).

Place gift in black trash bag. Fill in around gift with tissue paper or crumpled newspaper to give a rounded look. Close with twist closure.

Place white bag on flat surface. Mark off line 3" from top. Cover marked-off area with 3½"-long strips of red tape placed diagonally about 1½" apart; repeat on other side of bag. Cut bag on line; trim tape ends at top of bag. Cut one end open to make a long strip. Cut ends on an angle. Make bow and secure at center with wrap of red tape. Tape string to back of bow and tie to bag.

With markers, make decorative borders on baggage tag, using ruler for straight lines. Attach to bow with string.

CLEAR PLASTIC BAGS

MATERIALS: Jumbo and regular-size clear plastic food-storage bags with twist closures; red and green tissue paper; red and green narrow ribbon or green yarn with tassels (sold in gift-wrap departments); ¾"-diameter self-adhesive label dots; self-adhesive red foil stars; transparent tape.

In the Bag gift wrappings

Apply stars to label dots while backing is still on dots. Cover bag with dots about 1½" apart in staggered rows. At top, inside bag, cover outside dots with additional dots. Wrap gift in tissue paper, leaving excess showing at top. Line bag with matching paper. Place gift in bag and close with twist closure. Tie with co-ordinating ribbons or tasseled yarn.

Card Tricks

MATERIALS (for all cards): Stiff metallic acetate (available at art-supply stores); nylon monofilament; ⅞" x 2¾" heavy white paper tags (sold in packages of 20); ¼"-diameter gummed gold signal dots (sold in boxes of 200); 3¾" x 5¾" white envelopes. (**Note:** To remove fingerprints and smudges from acetate, use rubber-cement thinner.)

DISCO

Use materials required for all plus orange ¾"-diameter self-adhesive coding labels. Cut a 3"-diameter circle from metallic acetate and a 12" length of monofilament. Make a hanging loop at one end of monofilament. Attach circle to monofilament with a centered coding label; center a matching label on other side of circle. Attach tag to other end of monofilament with gummed signal dot.

CONSTELLATION

Use materials required for all plus gummed foil stars in ½", ¾" and 1¾" sizes. Cut a 14" length of monofilament. Make a hanging loop at one end and attach tag to other end with gummed signal dot. Stick together gummed sides of same-size stars on monofilament about 2" apart as shown in photograph (upper photo shows Constellation attached to Disco card).

DOILY

Use materials required for all plus 3½"-diameter metallic cocktail doilies, double-stick transparent tape and gold foil-wrapped string. Cut two 3½"-diameter circles of metallic acetate; cut one slit in each circle from the outer edge to center, then slip slits together to from ball-like shape as shown. Tape all four joints. Cut 11" length of gold thread, fold it over on one end to form a 3"-long loop, leaving a 5" tail, then secure base of loop to tape on one of the joints. Attach a tag to other end with a signal dot. Attach doilies with small pieces of dou-

ble-stick tape placed in the center of each half circle; smooth doilies into taped joints (each card requires four doilies).

ANGEL

Use materials required for all plus red cotton cord (such as crochet cotton) and double-stick tape. Enlarge angel pattern, following instructions on page 189. Use enlarged pattern to cut two pieces from metallic acetate in different colors. Tape pieces together with double-stick tape, matching shapes. Cut slits as shown. Poke a small hole in head with needle, then thread with a 10" length of red cotton cord. Make loop for hanging at one end and attach a tag with signal dot at other end. To make angel three-dimensional, slip slits together. (**Note:** Since you will be mailing Angel card flat, you should include brief how-to-put-together directions in envelope.)

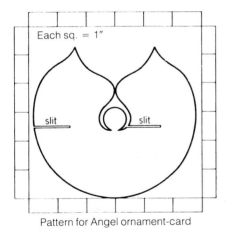

Each sq. = 1"

slit   slit

Pattern for Angel ornament-card

CARD TRICKS are simple cutout designs that open up to act as ornaments, fold flat (see below) to slip neatly into envelopes for mailing. Designs are, left to right: Disco, Constellation (attached to Disco), Doily, Angel and Tree.

TREE

Use materials required for all plus hole punch, ½" and ¾" gummed foil stars, glue and ½"-wide shiny transparent tape. Cut two triangles from acetate, both with two sides of 5¼" and base of 3¾". In one triangle cut a slit 2½" down from pointed top, in other triangle cut slit 2½" up from center of base. Slip slits together to form tree as shown in photograph. Punch out ornamental holes. Tape all four joints. In one joint, attach a 14" length of monofilament with a loop at one end and a tag at the other. Stick two ¾" stars together over monofilament at top of tree, then glue a smaller star to each side.

Stenciled Cards

MATERIALS: White or off-white blank cards or notepaper 4½" x 6¼" or larger; red and/or green blank cards or notepaper with matching envelopes (colored backing paper is optional; if you prefer to use white on white, trim about ½" from all edges of the white paper that bears the design); scarlet, yellow and kelly green liquid fabric dyes; waxed stencil paper; tracing paper; pencil; art-blade knife; dressmaker's carbon paper; scrap of cardboard (for working surface); size 1 or 2 artist's bristle brush (ideally, one for each color); black india ink and pen staff with #5 or #6 pen point (or corresponding-width felt-tip markers).

Cutting stencils: Enlarge motifs, following instructions on page 189 and adjusting pattern size, if necessary, to conform to size of paper you will be using. Transfer enlarged designs to tracing paper. Draw a guideline around the designs to represent the size of your card or notepaper. Cut rectangles of stencil paper to the sizes marked off by the guidelines. Place carbon paper on top of stencil paper, then center tracing on top and transfer motif. Working on cardboard surface, cut out design areas for each motif with knife.

Stenciling: Work on cardboard or cleanable surface. Place stencil over white card or envelope flap. Dip brush into liquid dye bottle and remove excess dye by wiping bristles against inside of bottle mouth. Brush dye onto paper with light strokes, working from edges toward center of open area and using color indicated by design. Stencil can be held in place with other hand or weighted with a book or other heavy object.

Let dry. Using pen and india ink or markers, add details as desired. Veins can be added to the holly leaves, stems to the berries and outlining to bow. Christmas tree can be outlined or decorated with stripes or V-shaped strokes down each branch. Shading or complete outline can be added to the star.

When colored designs are dry, mount them, using glue or rubber cement, on white or colored backing card or notepaper. (Designs on envelope flaps, of course, will not be backed.) At this stage, you can further embellish the designs if you wish—with marker, paper or fabric appliqués, etc.—and add special greetings or messages. You can also combine parts of these designs to create others.

STENCILED CARDS (from left): Guiding Star, Holly Branch, Christmas Tree

Each sq. = 1"

HOLLY STENCIL
(bow and berries, scarlet; stem and leaves, kelly green)

Each sq. = 1"

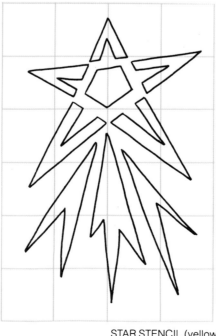

STAR STENCIL (yellow)

Custom Wraps

CHANUKAH PRESENT

MATERIALS: Hebrew-language newspaper; blue ribbon; transparent tape.

Wrap gift in sheet of newspaper. Tie with ribbon. Make a spiral bow and attach with tape.

BROWN-BAG-IT

MATERIALS: Brown paper bag to fit gift; red foil legal seals; red and green narrow ribbon; red and green felt-tip markers; hole punch; colored tissue paper (optional).

Using marker, outline nameplate on bag. (Bag shown is 3⅛" x 5⅛" x 10⅝" and the nameplate is 4½" x 3⅝".) Fill in outline with thick and thin lines, dots, dashes and curved

Following photograph, glue seal near each top corner of bag. Punch centered holes through seals. Cut 12" to 16" ribbons for handles. Use double knots to secure in holes. Line inside of bag with tissue paper if desired.

lines, alternating colors and leaving space in center for name. Write or print name.

CUSTOM WRAPS (from left): Chanukah Present, Brown-bag-it, Sunday Comics

SUNDAY COMICS

MATERIALS: Sunday comic pages; red balloon; green ribbon; self-adhesive ¾"-diameter green label dots; transparent tape.

Wrap gift in comics. Tie on ribbon with large bow, following photograph. As close as possible to gift-opening time, inflate balloon, cover with dots and attach to package with tape.

Bump Chenille "Ribbons" with Felt Dimensional Trims

MATERIALS: Gift-wrap paper, preferably in solid colors for contrast; bump chenille in various sizes and colors; felt in coordinated colors; scraps of posterboard; paper; pencil; scissors; glue.

Wrap gift box with paper, then wrap chenille around box as you would ribbon: at long edges, across corners, at both ends, crossing at right angles, etc. Use one, two or three

rows; for two or more, use contrasting colors and stagger or nest bumps for added interest. Fasten ends of each piece by twisting them together under the box.

Sketch and cut freehand patterns for felt ornaments—bell, snowflake, apple, star, etc. (**Note:** For other possibilities, see "Appliquéd" Cards, page 65.) Using pattern, cut three of each shape. Glue into three-layer stacks (this gives ornaments their dimensional effect, even more pronounced when gluing is confined to centers so edges "float free"). Add trim to ornaments if desired. Glue or tie to box. (Here too, it can be effective to glue only centers, leaving edges free.)

Each sq. = 1"

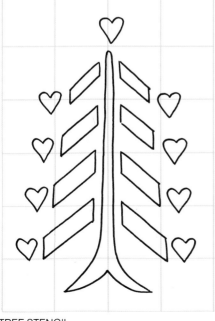

TREE STENCIL
(scarlet and kelly green)

DRESSING UP THE HOLIDAY HOUSE

*Surprising as it may seem, our home-decorating ideas were inspired by a line dear to the heart of every caroler: " 'Tis the season to be jolly." True, it is usually people who are said to be jolly—to be, as the dictionary puts it, "full of high spirits, cheerful and merry." But we can't imagine better words to describe a home's holiday atmosphere, or the designs we suggest for creating it. If you like the impact of a strong, single theme, look through **Vivid Impressions.** Or you might prefer a number of **Accents Small But Striking:** make-it-yourself table trees, ornamental clusters, ceiling and window displays. For your walls, there are **Hangings, Plaques and Pictures;** for "exterior decoration," **Inviting Outdoor Decor.** There's only one thing more fun than seeing Christmas all around, and that's the joy of knowing you've created the surroundings!*

Vivid Impressions

If you entertain a lot, or just find a coordinated theme powerfully appealing, fabrics can create mighty dramatic settings. Use colors explosively, as in Calico Christmas. Or keep contrasts quieter, as in the Gingham Ribbon scheme that follows. Garlands are also great attention-getters: traditional swirls of links like those shown here, or one of our Novel Noel Garlands (pages 76 to 79).

A CALICO CHRISTMAS

Patchwork-pattern Tree Base

MATERIALS: Sheet of ¼"-thick foam-core board; 1 yard of red fabric (A in diagram), ½ yard of green (B) and ¼ yard or scrap of red-and-white (C); fabric glue or spray adhesive.

Cut 4 rectangles from board, each 8" x 10". Cut 1"-wide strips of fabric A. Wrap and glue around all edges of board rectangles. Cut 8 rectangles, each 8" x 10", from A. Glue in place, one on each side of each board. Enlarge patchwork design (enlarging instructions, page 189) and cut out fabric pieces according to color key. Glue in place as shown. Cut 3" x 8" strips of fabric B. Glue to backs at 8" edges of rectangles, creating inside joints to form box shape from rectangles (no top or bottom). Let dry.

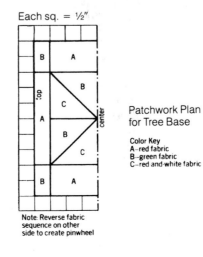

Each sq. = ½"

Patchwork Plan for Tree Base

Color Key
A—red fabric
B—green fabric
C—red-and-white fabric

Note: Reverse fabric sequence on other side to create pinwheel

Puffy Calico Trees

MATERIALS: Assorted scraps of calico (preferably reds, greens and whites); contrasting sewing thread; cotton or fiberfill stuffing; 18" length of ¼"-wide grosgrain ribbon (per tree).

Enlarge pattern (enlarging instructions, page 189) and cut on folded fabric, using pinking shears and placing center line on fold. Topstitch, leaving small opening for stuffing at top. Stuff lightly and close opening, catching ribbon loop in stitches. Make small ribbon bow and sew or glue in place.

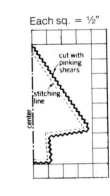

Each sq. = ½"

cut with pinking shears

stitching line

center

Calico Tree

Fabric-link Garlands

MATERIALS: Assorted scraps of calico fabric or ¼ yard each of several colors; stiff paper; fabric glue or spray adhesive.

Fold each piece of calico in half, right side out. Cut paper to approximate size of folded piece. Apply glue to each side, slip paper into fold and glue fabric to paper. With pinking shears, cut strips 1½" x 6" for large links and ⅞" x 5" for small. Stapling strips into links, make chain (use all large or all small strips in any chain).

Jar-and-goblet Candleholders

MATERIALS (for each candleholder): Preserving jar; short-stemmed water glass with foot that will fit securely inside top of jar; dried strawflowers (red) and baby's breath (white); one yard of 1"-wide ribbon (ribbon here is red with white dots); red candle.

Fit foot of glass into jar. Set candle in glass, first softening wax on candle bottom to secure. Tie a bouquet of dried flowers at front of jar by running red ribbon around it, then tying into a bow; notch ends.

Prequilted Place Mats and Table Runner

MATERIALS: 2 yards 36"-wide prequilted fabric (enough for 4 place mats and 1 runner); double-fold bias tape in contrasting color (12 yards for 4 mats, 8 yards for runner); matching sewing thread.

For place mats: Cut 4 rectangles (leave 12" x 72" uncut for runner), each 13" x 17¼". Round corners; place tape around edge and topstitch in place, overlapping ends.

For runner: Cut 12" x 72" rectangle. Round corners and finish as for place mats.

Crocheted Napkin Rings

MATERIALS: ½ ounce knitting-worsted-weight yarn (enough for one 3"-diameter ring); aluminum crochet hook size G (or international hook size 4:50 mm).

Ch 16. Join with sl st to form ring. **1st rnd:** *Ch 5, sc in next ch, ch 5, sc in same sc. Repeat from * around; join. Break off. **2nd rnd:** * Sc in next ch-5 sp, ch 3, (sc in same sp, ch 3) 3 times. Repeat from * around; join. Break off.

CALICO CHRISTMAS. Simple fabrics in basic colors, but a very merry mixture! **On and under the tree:** Patchwork-pattern Tree Base; Puffy Calico Trees; Yo-yo Santas; Fabric-link Garlands. **On the table:** Jar-and-Goblet Candleholders; Prequilted Place Mats and Runner; Crocheted Napkin Rings. Directions for all except Yo-yo Santas given here; Santa instructions, page 121.

GINGHAM RIBBON CHRISTMAS

Ribbon Bows

MATERIALS: Florist's wire; gingham ribbon in complementary colors (brown and beige used here).

Use stiff ribbon so that the bows will be perky and stay that way throughout the season. Experiment with the ribbon to determine the best size for the bow. As a rule of thumb, each loop of the bow should be at least as long as the ribbon is wide, and the tail of the bow slightly longer than the bow part. For instance, with ribbon 3" wide, allow at least 8" for each loop and about 5" for each tail. Each bow half is 13", so cut ribbon (angling the ends) 26" long for each bow.

To make the bow, find the center of the ribbon. Cross the two loops over the center. Twist wire around the center, leaving about 6" wire ends to use for attaching the bow to boughs. Fluff up the bow, and wire to the tree.

Greens-and-garland Chandelier

MATERIALS: Evergreen sprigs, florist's wire, ribbon.

Attach sprigs to chandelier with florist's wire. When the greens are in place, wrap a garland of the gingham ribbon around the greens as shown.

GINGHAM RIBBON CHRISTMAS ties tree and table gaily together with Ribbon Bows; Topiary Tree Centerpiece; Greens-and-garland Chandelier. Two-way table runners are simply ribbons in two widths crisscrossed to accommodate settings for four.

Topiary Tree Centerpiece

MATERIALS: Plastic-foam cone of desired centerpiece height (to buy or make—see Note below); florist's tape; toothpicks; florist's wire; superstrength glue; greens such as boxwood; gingham ribbon; fruits and nuts of your choice.

Anchor cone shape (it becomes the tree form) into a shallow bowl with florist's tape. (**Note:** Preshaped foam cones are available at florist shops. Or make your own by joining plastic-foam blocks to the desired height and cutting the joined blocks into cone shape with a sharp knife. To anchor one block to another, push toothpicks halfway into the base block, then press the top block down on the toothpicks. Use green foam or cover white foam with green tissue.)

Starting at the base, attach fresh boughs of boxwood to the entire tree by sticking the stems directly into the foam cone.

To decorate: Tree in photograph is encircled with a ribbon garland. You might wish, instead, to attach miniature bows (made the same way as the larger bows for the large tree). Wire the bows to the stem part of the boxwood, or attach the bows to toothpicks and press picks into cone.

Lady apples and other soft fruit are easily attached. Press a toothpick halfway into the fruit, then press the exposed part of toothpick into cone.

Nuts and other hard objects are attached by first gluing on florist's wire, then winding and gluing the wire onto toothpicks. You can cluster small nuts and berries, using one pick for each miniature bunch. Use superstick glue to attach the wire, reinforcing the bond with a small scrap of paper on the back of the nut. Allow this to dry, then wind the wire around a toothpick, and push pick into cone.

Detail of Topiary Tree

NOVEL
NOEL GARLANDS

Note: All of these garlands are basically collections of small ornaments tacked to lengths of ribbon. With the exception of the Pot-scrubber Wreath and Dress-parade Drum, which would be too large for this purpose, the ornaments could be used as tree decorations. The only change would be the addition of a hanging cord or ribbon. Two of the garlands, Loop-the-loop and Festive Festoon, feature "necklaces" that run along the ribbon from end to end.

Loop-the-loop

MATERIALS: Ribbon in two widths (about 2" for garland, 1" for small sprays) and contrasting colors; sewing thread. **For Frosty Necklace:** Plastic packing pellets; small gold beads; heavy-duty thread or nylon monofilament. **For Curtain-ring Ornament:** Self-stick metallic plastic or plastic tape; 2¾"-diameter plastic curtain ring; ¼"-wide paper ribbon. **For Pot-scrubber Wreath:** 10"-diameter wicker plate holder; thin wire; 13 pot scrubbers, mixed silver, gold, copper and bright-colored plastic; scissors or wire cutter; metal-foil cupcake holders.

FROSTY NECKLACE

On doubled heavy-duty thread or monofilament, string plastic packing pellets and gold beads, alternating them as shown.

CURTAIN-RING ORNAMENT

From self-stick metallic sheet or tape, cut 11 strips, each ½" x 4". Working a strip at a time and distributing them evenly, fold strips in half over curtain ring and press halves together; notch ends. Wind paper ribbon around ring between strips.

POT-SCRUBBER WREATH

Using scissors or wire cutter, snip 6"-diameter hole in center of plate holder. Push an 8" U-shaped length of wire through each of the pot scrubbers, flattening centers somewhat. Attach wire ends to back of plate holder. Fold cupcake holders in quarters; attach with wire between scrubbers, with wrappers opening toward center of wreath. Add ribbon bow.

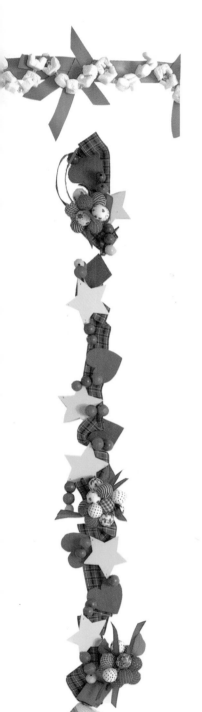

Festive Festoon

MATERIALS: Red-plaid ribbon; sewing thread. **For Berry Cluster:** Assorted red and green print fabrics; ¾"-diameter plastic-foam balls; pinking shears; co-ordinated sewing thread; small amounts of narrow red ribbon; synthetic leaves. **For Star-studded String:** ¹⁄₁₆"-thick balsa wood; mat knife; awl or large nail; ¾"-diameter wooden beads; red, yellow and green acrylic paints; nylon monofilament or heavy-duty thread. **For Dress-parade Drum:** Three plastic-foam circles, 1¼" thick and 8" in diameter; glue; plain paper; 3½"-wide velvet strips (or velvet ribbon in that width); ½"-wide gold ribbon; white pipe cleaners; pencil; two 12" lengths ¼"-diameter dowel; red acrylic paint; two small red pompons (buy, or see instructions, page 189).

BERRY CLUSTER

With pinking shears, cut thirteen 3"-diameter circles from assorted print fabrics. Working one circle at a time, gather edge with running stitch and insert plastic-foam ball. Tighten the stitches and secure; tack ribbon and leaves to base of cluster.

STAR-STUDDED STRING

Trace the star and the smaller of the two heart patterns on page 79; draw pattern for diamond 2¼" wide and 2½" high. Make a cardboard template of each pattern to use in transferring patterns to balsa wood. With knife, cut several of each pattern (they are used more or less at random; see photograph). Punch a hole in two corners of each piece with awl or large nail. Paint pieces (yellow stars, red hearts, green diamonds). String them, when dry, on monofilament or doubled heavy-duty thread. Knot ends but leave shapes loose so that they can be moved into any desired position when ornaments are arranged for tacking to ribbon.

DRESS-PARADE DRUM

Glue the three plastic-foam disks together. Glue a ¾"-wide paper strip around the circumference, then center and glue a 3½"-wide velvet strip over it, butting ends. Glue four X's of gold ribbon, as shown, to the outer surface of the drum, then glue two rows of the same ribbon to top and bottom edges. Wrap four pipe cleaners around a pencil; remove the coils and glue them as shown between the X's. For drumsticks, paint the two dowels red. When paint is dry, glue a red pompon to one end of each and glue drumsticks to top of drum.

Satin-ornaments Swag

MATERIALS: Pastel-plaid ribbon; sewing thread. **For Stocking and Padded Heart:** Satin and lace as specified; cotton or fiberfill stuffing; small pearls; lace and floral appliqués. **For Bell Frames:** Cardboard; spray adhesive; satin fabric; cotton or fiberfill stuffing; white glue; gold braid; small photograph or Christmas sticker; lace for bow. **For Snappers:** Satin fabric; 1"-wide and ½"-wide lace; ⅛"-wide satin ribbon; cotton or fiberfill stuffing; lace and floral appliqués. **For Shirred Lace Heart:** Thin wire; ⅝"-wide lace; floral appliqués. **For Lace Rosette:** 2½"-wide lace; ½"-wide ribbon.

STOCKING AND PADDED HEART

Trace larger heart and enlarge stocking pattern (see instructions, page 189). Cut two pieces each from satin fabric, adding ¼" seam allowance. (For lace-covered stocking, also cut two from lace; topstitch to right side of satin pieces and treat as a single piece.) With right sides facing, stitch pieces together, leaving opening for turning and stuffing. Clip corners; turn; stuff. Close opening, inserting 1¼"-wide lace strip for cuff of stocking. Sew on lace trims, pearls and appliqués as shown in photograph.

BELL FRAMES

Enlarge pattern (enlarging instructions, page 189). Cut two pieces from thin cardboard, cutting hole in front piece. Cut two pieces from satin, adding 1" seam allowance. **Back:** Spray one side of back cardboard with glue. Stick on one thin layer of stuffing; spray stuffing. Glue on 2nd layer; grade edges with scissors; spray. Cover with satin fabric; turn edges over cardboard; trim and glue in place, smoothing folds at edges. **Front:** Glue three layers to front cardboard, cutting out and grading sides and center. Cover with satin as for back. Cut slits radiating from center in fabric over hole; fold and glue to reverse side of cardboard. (Touch raw edges of slits with white glue to prevent fraying.) Tack gold trim to lower front, folding ends over edges. Glue photograph or Christmas sticker to back cardboard, aligning with hole. Glue front and back together. Tack lace bow to top front.

SNAPPERS

Cut 5¾" x 6" piece of satin; fold under ¼" on each short edge. Topstitch strips of 1"-wide lace under folds. Topstitch inner edge of ½"-wide lace about 1½" from each folded edge; topstitch ⅛"-wide satin ribbon over stitching. With wrong side out, stitch untrimmed edges together to form tube. Turn; gather satin at one end with running stitch; stuff; gather other end. Tie same satin ribbon in bow around gathers. Tack on appliqués.

SHIRRED LACE HEART

For 3½"-wide heart, pinch small loop at one end of 8½" length of thin wire. Run other end through 1½ yards of ⅝"-wide lace along edge, gathering lace tightly. Insert end of wire in loop; pinch closed. With joined ends at bottom, shape heart. Tack or glue floral appliqués at top.

LACE ROSETTE

Gather one edge of ½ yard of 2½"-wide lace and pull up to form circle. Sew ½"-wide ribbon bow to edge.

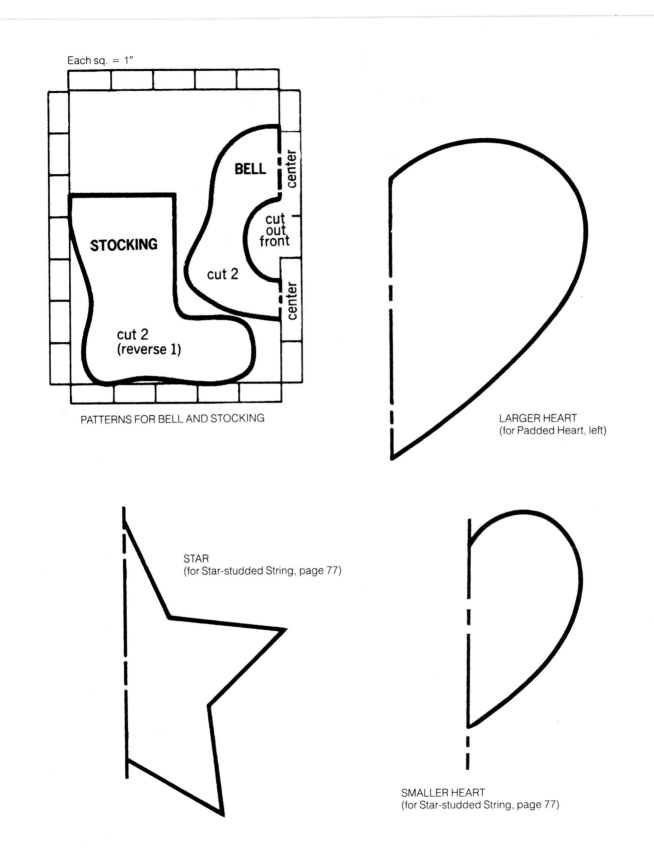

Each sq. = 1"

BELL

center

STOCKING

cut out front

cut 2

cut 2
(reverse 1)

center

PATTERNS FOR BELL AND STOCKING

LARGER HEART
(for Padded Heart, left)

STAR
(for Star-studded String, page 77)

SMALLER HEART
(for Star-studded String, page 77)

Accents Small But Striking

*Once you catch the holiday spirit, you won't want to stop with the big tree, masterpiece though it may be. Didn't the old carol advise us to "deck the halls"? Amen, we say, **and** the den and dining room! It's fun to spot some sparkle dancing on the ceiling or at a window . . . brightening a table or corner. Browse through the ideas, and prepare to be inspired!*

Crocheted Table Tree

MATERIALS: Knitting-worsted-weight yarn, 5 ounces emerald (color E), 2 ounces forest green (F), 1 ounce each dark gold (G) and red (R); aluminum crochet hook size H (or international hook size 5:00 mm), **or the size that will give you the correct gauge;** plastic-foam cone 12″ high x 5″ diameter at base (to buy or make—see Topiary Tree instructions, page 75).

GAUGE: 3 dc = 1″.

FOUNDATION: Starting at tip with E, ch 5, join with sl st to form ring. **1st rnd:** Ch 3, work 5 dc in ring; sl st in top of ch-3. **2nd rnd:** Ch 3, work 2 dc in next dc, (dc in next dc, 2 dc in next dc) twice; sl st in ch-3. **3rd rnd (lp rnd):** * Ch 6, sc in next 3 dc. Repeat from * around, ending ch 6; sc in last 2 dc; sl st in sl st at base of 1st lp (3 lps). **4th rnd:** Ch 3, dc in same place as sl st; * holding lp forward, skip next ch-6 lp, dc in next 2 sc, 2 dc in next sc. Repeat from *, ending dc in last 2 sc; sl st in ch-3. **5th rnd:** Repeat 3rd rnd (4 lps). **6th rnd:** Ch 3, * skip next ch-6 lp, dc in next 3 sc. Repeat from *, ending dc in last 2 sc; sl st in ch-3. **7th rnd:** Repeat 3rd rnd (4 lps). **8th rnd:** Repeat 4th rnd. **9th rnd:** *Ch 6, sc in next 4 dc. Repeat from *, ending sc in last 3 dc; sl st in sl st (4 lps). **10th rnd:** Ch 3, dc in same place as sl st, * skip next ch-6 lp, dc in next 3 sc, 2 dc in next sc. Repeat from *, ending dc in last 3 sc; sl st in ch-3. **11th rnd:** Repeat 9th rnd (5 lps). **12th rnd:** Ch 3, * skip next ch-6 lp, dc in next 4 sc. Repeat from *, ending dc in last 3 sc; sl st in ch-3. **13th rnd:** Repeat 9th rnd (5 lps). **14th rnd:** Repeat 10th rnd. **15th rnd:** * Ch 6, sc in next 5 dc. Repeat from *, ending sc in last 4 dc; sl st in sl st (5 lps).

16th rnd: Ch 3, dc in same place as sl st, * skip next ch-6 lp, dc in next 4 sc, 2 dc in next sc. Repeat from *, ending dc in last 4 dc; sl st in ch-3. **17th rnd:** Repeat 15th rnd (6 lps). **18th rnd:** Ch 3, * skip next ch-6 lp, dc in next 5 sc. Repeat from *, ending dc in last 4 sc; sl st in ch-3. **19th rnd:** * Ch 6, sc in next 4 sc. Repeat from *, ending sc in last 5 sc; sl st in sl st (7 lps). **20th rnd:** Ch 3, dc in same place as sl st, * skip next ch-6 lp, dc in next 3 sc, 2 dc in next sc. Repeat from *, ending dc in last 5 sc; sl st in ch-3. **21st rnd:** * Ch 6, sc in next 6 dc. Repeat from * around; sl st in sl st (6 lps). **22nd rnd:** Ch 3, * skip next ch-6 lp, dc in next 5 sc, 2 dc in next sc. Repeat from *, ending dc in last 6 sc; sl st in ch-3. **23rd rnd:** * Ch 6, sc in next 6 dc. Repeat from *, ending sc in last 5 sc; sl st in sl st (7 lps). **24th rnd:** Ch 3, * skip next ch-6 lp, dc in next 6 sc. Repeat from *, ending dc in last 5 sc; sl st in ch-3. **25th rnd:** Repeat 23rd rnd. **26th rnd:** Ch 3, dc in same place as sl st, * skip next ch-6 lp, dc in next 5 sc, 2 dc in next sc. Repeat from *, ending dc in last 5 sc; sl st in ch-3. **27th rnd:** * Ch 6, sc in next 7 dc. Repeat from *, ending sc in last 6 dc; sl st in sl st (7 lps). **28th rnd:** Ch 3, dc in same place as sl st, * skip next ch-6 lp, dc in next 6 sc, 2 dc in next sc. Repeat from *, ending dc in last 6 dc; sl st in ch-3. **29th rnd:** * Ch 6, sc in next 7 dc. Repeat from *, ending sc in last 6 dc; sl st in sl st (8 lps). **30th rnd:** Ch 3, * skip next ch-6 lp, dc in next 7 sc. Repeat from *, ending dc in last 6 sc; sl st in ch-3. **31st rnd:** Repeat 29th rnd. **32nd rnd:** Ch 3, dc in same place as sl st, * skip next ch-6 lp, dc in next 6 sc, 2 dc in next sc. Repeat from *, ending dc in last 6 sc; sl st in ch-3. Break off.

BRANCHES: 1st rnd: Starting with 1st lp of 1st lp rnd, with E, work as follows in each lp: Sc in lp, * ch 3, sc in 3rd ch from hook (p made), sc in same lp. Repeat from * twice more. Repeat in each lp around. **2nd rnd:** Repeat 1st rnd in each lp of next lp rnd. **3rd rnd:** With F, * hdc in next lp, (make p, hdc in same lp) 4 times. Repeat from * around. **4th rnd:** With E, repeat 3rd rnd. **5th rnd:** * Dc in next lp, (make p, dc in same lp) 5 times. Repeat from * around. Working as for 5th rnd, work 1 rnd each F and E. **8th rnd:** * Tr in next lp, (make p, tr in same lp) 6 times. Repeat from * around. Working as for 8th rnd, work 2 rnds F, 1 rnd E, 1 rnd F. **13th rnd: (Note:** To make dtr: Yo 3 times, insert hook in lp and draw lp through, (yo and draw through 2 lps on hook) 4 times): * Dtr in next lp, (make p, dtr in same lp) 7 times. Repeat from * around. **14th rnd:** With E, repeat 13th rnd. **15th rnd:** With F, repeat 13th rnd, sl st in top of 1st dtr. Break off.

CONES (make 5): With G, ch 6. With F, 5 sc in 2nd ch from hook and in each ch across. Break off.

BERRIES (make 5): With R, make lp on hook, (make p) 3 times, sl st in 1st ch. Break off.

Sew on cones and berries and slip tree over cone. For tighter fit, pad with tissue paper.

Children's Party Block Tree

MATERIALS: Plastic-foam cone about 11" high (to buy or make—see Topiary Tree instructions, page 75); plastic lazy Susan; 1¼"-square blocks; white glue; miniature decorations.

Glue plastic-foam cone to lazy Susan. Arrange and glue blocks around cone, providing "shelf space" as shown for decorations. Glue on decorations.

Crocheted Table Tree

Children's Party Block Tree

Yarn-wrapped-cord Christmas Box-tree

MATERIALS: 3½ ounces 4-ply hand knitting yarn in emerald; tapestry needle; prepackaged hank of ³⁄₁₆"-diameter cotton venetian blind cord (approximately 18 yards); ½" purchased pompons—8 red, 7 yellow and 35 white (or make your own, following instructions on page 189). **Note:** Unwind cord from hank as needed but do not cut.

Lower tree section: Cut a strand of yarn about 2 yards long; overlap 1" of yarn-end over 1" of cord-end and glue together. Thread other end of yarn into needle.

Wrapping cord: Wind wrapping strand closely around cord as shown in Fig. 1 for about ½". Insert needle under a wrapped strand on tip as shown in Fig. 2 and bring yarn through to start the spiral for base of tree. Wind strand about 10 times around cord, then with needle join to spiral as shown in Fig. 3. Continue to work in this manner until flat piece for base is 6" in diameter. (**Note:** To join additional wrapping strands, wind strand in use over cord and first ½" of new strand, drop working strand, pick up new strand and wrap for ½" over cord and end of previous strand; trim end of previous

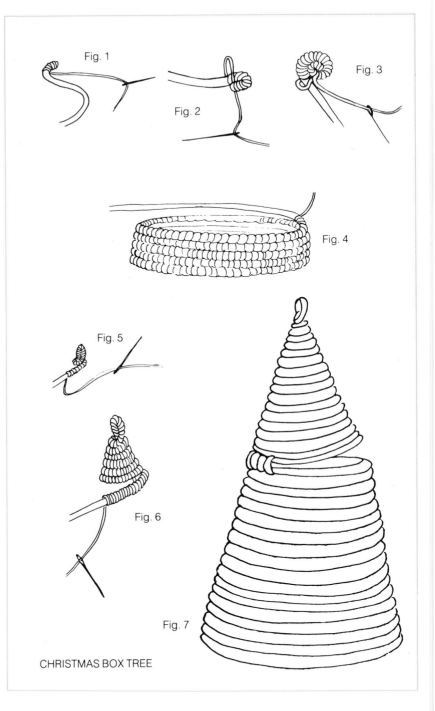

CHRISTMAS BOX TREE

strand.) Next, continue to work upward from base, gradually tapering sides of tree—see Fig. 4—until tree is 5¼" high and has an opening 3½" in diameter. Cut cord and secure strand.

Top section: Staring at center top—see Fig. 5— and working in same manner as before, taper top section—see Fig 6—working for 3½" and having 3½" diameter opening to match opening of lower section. Cut *cord*

only. Using wrapping strand, hinge top to lower section by sewing 1¼" of corresponding edges together—see Fig. 7. Cut strand.

Glue red and white pompons at random over entire tree. Make star for top by gluing six yellow pompons to form a circle and then gluing one pompon in center opening. Glue star to top of tree as shown.

Velvet Tree

MATERIALS: ½ yard 40"-wide green velvet; ½ yard 45"-wide green satin; 1½ yards ¼"-wide gold metallic ribbon; 11 yards thin wire; 12" x 20" block of plastic foam 1¼" thick; glue; rubber cement; 19 small gold balls; straight pins and T-pins.

From plastic foam cut 12" x 18" x 18" triangle for tree. Cut three 2" x 5½" pieces; glue to form 2"-high x 5½"-long x 3¾"-deep base. Center and glue tree to base. Cover base with satin. Pin metallic ribbon around base as shown.

PETALS: Cut 2" x 3½" cardboard rectangle. Round to oval, cut off ½" straight across at one end for 2" x 3" petal pattern. Make six petals at a time as follows: Cut 6" squares of velvet and satin. Cut six 3" lengths wire. Brush rubber cement on wrong side of each square. Place wires in 2 rows on satin (where centers of petals will be). Allow to dry, then cement velvet to satin with wires between. Cut six petals with wires running lengthwise through them. Cut petals as you need them. (Be sure velvet pile runs in same direction on all.)

To assemble: Insert straight pins in both corners of a petal, then into tree, starting about 1" up from base. Continue attaching petals in slightly uneven, overlapping rows across tree. Use T-pins to attach balls.

Velvet Tree

Candlelight Pine Tree

MATERIALS: 12' of 1 x 1 pine; 3' length ⅜"-diameter dowel; 16 heavy-aluminum fluted brioche cups (do not use tin); small pine cones; 3¼ yards 1"-wide red satin ribbon; thin wire; small red glass balls; open star-shaped metal cookie cutter; white glue; one ⅜" and sixteen 1" wood screws; doweling jig; drill and bits; 16 votive candles; crosscut saw; miter box; sandpaper; felt scraps.

Set miter box at 60° for all cuts. Mark off 1 x 1 and cut all pieces as follows: **For base and branches:** Cut with angles at both ends so that pieces are trapezoids; longest side is length given. **Base:** Two 10" pieces; **branches:** two 6¾", two 11½", two 15½" and two 20". **For cup holders and base feet:** 18 pieces with 1"-long sides and angles at both ends to form a parallelogram. Sand all pieces. Cut 26" dowel for trunk.

In all base and branch pieces, drill one ⅜"-diameter hole centered in longest side, using doweling jig.

Glue one foot to each end of long side of one 10" base piece, following photograph for placement. When dry, cut felt to fit bottom of each foot and glue in place. Glue felt strip to long side of other base piece. Form cross of two pieces (footed piece on top); glue dowel into holes.

Thread branches on dowel, starting with largest pair at bottom near base; longest side of each piece faces down. If fit is tight, rub soap on dowel. Space pairs of arms evenly along trunk, rotating on base to form tree shape. If fit is loose, glue in place and tighten with toothpicks wedged in place and broken off above branch.

Glue 1" cup holder to end of each branch so that angled end of branch and holder form a V shape. Drill centered pilot hole for 1" screw in top of each holder and centered clearance hole in bottom of each cup. Drill hole for ⅜" screw in top of dowel and clearance hole in cookie cutter.

Glue satin ribbon around edge of cookie cutter (do not cover screw hole). Wire cones and balls around

Candlelight Pine Tree

the dowel. Tie ribbon bows around holders. Screw on star, then cups; insert candles.

Caution: Do not leave tree unattended when lit or permit children to light candles.

Color-wrapped Foam Balls

MATERIALS: Plastic-foam balls in assorted sizes; scrap yarns in many contrasting colors; scraps of calico or other small-print fabric; ribbon in Christmas colors; white glue; baby's breath or small artificial flowers.

Yarn-wrapped balls in foreground: Using two strands (2 colors) at a time, wrap neat parallel rows around ball, gluing ends to ball to secure. Then change colors, and wrap in another direction to get an overlapping effect. Wrap about 6 times in each combination. Add yarn hanging loop.

Calico-wrapped balls in basket: Cover ball with fabric scrap; grasp ends and tie with ribbon. Tuck sprig of baby's breath into tied end. Add a ribbon hanging loop if you wish to use ball as an ornament.

Color-wrapped Foam Balls

Starshine Pendants

MATERIALS: 2" x 4" sheet light-diffuser plastic; jeweler's or coping saw; clear cement.

For lower star: Cut eight 2" x 8" x 8" triangles from plastic; sand edges. Arrange four triangles so that bases touch, forming open square at center; place remaining four in the same arrangement on top, rotated to form 8-pointed star. Cement together.

For upper star: Cut eight 2" x 8" x 8" triangles and eight 2" x 5" x 5" triangles from plastic. Place two large triangles base to base; place two more on top, perpendicular to first two. Cement. Do same with four smaller triangles. Cement first group to second to form 8-pointed star. Cement remaining four large triangles to points of small ones and remaining four small triangles to points of large ones (see photograph).

For either star, drill a ⅛"-diameter hole 3" from one point for insertion of hanging cord.

Starshine Pendants

Red Velvet Obelisks

(shown in photograph on page 90)

MATERIALS: Gold or silver glitter in applicator tube; illustration board; Sobo glue; transparent tape; ¾"- or 1"-diameter wooden beads (4 per obelisk); ⅓ yard red velveteen and ¼ yard satin (all white, or combination white and silver-gray as in photograph) for each obelisk; craft knife; fusible interfacing; small paintbrush; scissors; iron and pressing cloth.

For each obelisk: Enlarge pyramid pattern (enlarging instructions, page 189). Using enlargement, outline four triangles on illustration board. Cut out with craft knife. Mark four 4½" x 3¾" rectangles on illustration board. Also mark out three 4½" squares. Cut all out with craft knife. Place the four triangles on a flat surface, wrong side up, with long edges touching. Tape abutting seams. Bring last two long edges together with right sides facing outward and tape-tack in a few places. Place one of the squares as a base and tape-tack it to joined triangles. Place a bead of glue in each crack at corners and allow to dry. Make base in the same way—tape the short edges of the rectangles together and close them to form an open square. Use remaining squares as top and bottom of "box," gluing in same way as for top.

Cut a piece of velveteen large enough to completely cover the outside of pyramid part with about 1" extra to turn under. Mix 1 ounce of glue with 1 tablespoon of water. Coat one face of the pyramid with glue and water, brushing it on with paintbrush. Smooth velveteen on it. Repeat until entire pyramid is wrapped. Trim off excess fabric except at bottom edges. Slash corners, cutting off overlap, and glue fabric to underside of pyramid. Repeat for base box: Cut fabric to fit sides plus 1" to turn under. Glue to box. Cut square of fabric to fit top of box and glue it into place. Glue a wooden bead to each corner (see photograph). Let dry. Glue beads to base of pyramid and let dry.

Fuse interfacing to back of satin according to manufacturer's instructions. Make templates of enlarged patterns for shapes on front of pyramid and box. Use to cut out fused satin. Glue cut-out pieces in proper places on front of obelisk. Let dry. Outline edges and details with a single line of glitter.

PYRAMID PATTERN

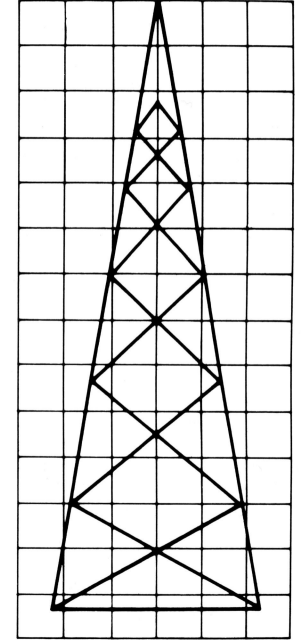

DIAGRAM OF RECTANGLE

Each sq. = 1"

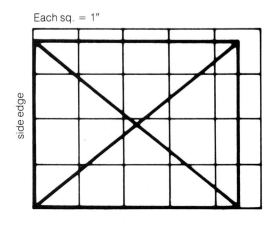

side edge

Tree of Paradise

MATERIALS: For tree: 8'-long 1"-diameter dowel; 6"-, 9"- and 12"-diameter plastic-foam balls; 1 bale real or artificial evergreens; 18 artificial apples; gold cord; T-pins; sheet moss; heavy wire; wire cutters; several yards brown grosgrain ribbon; cardboard paint bucket; plaster of Paris; heavy twine; white glue; large decorative container. **For 42 ribbon roses:** 126 yards 1½"-wide satin ribbon (or buy artificial roses); cornstarch; coated florist's wire (or it will rust); floral picks; tape; straight pins. **For 40 white dough hearts and stars:** Baking soda; cornstarch; thin gold cord; sandpaper; toothpick; heart and star cookie cutters.

Original tree was a topiary design in *The Trees of Christmas* by Edna Metcalf (Abingdon Press). You can make a smaller tree by scaling down all dimensions.

TREE: Cut dowel to desired height for tree minus 6". Sharpen one end. Mix plaster in paint bucket; insert flat end of dowel centered and perpendicular to ground.

Center bottom of largest foam ball on point of dowel; slide to within 2½' of bucket. Wrap just below ball with twine, securing with white glue. Repeat with medium and smallest ball, sticking the latter halfway onto dowel end. Wrap grosgrain between balls and secure with pins.

Cover all balls with sheet moss, securing with T-pins. Cut 4"-long tips from evergreen. Wrap bunches of tips with wire, leaving 3" wire ends for picks. Insert enough picks to cover balls, leaving space around dowel free for about 2" radius. Hang six apples from each ball as shown with gold cord. Pin to base of balls with wires bent in half.

RIBBON ROSES (as shown): Bring ½ cup cornstarch and 1½ cups water to boil, stirring occasionally; boil until mixture is gelatinous. Let cool.

Cut 3-yard ribbon and 10" florist's wire. Fold wire in half. Dip ribbon into mixture; fold in half lengthwise and insert one end into fold of wire. Turn wire, coiling folded ribbon around it to form a rose (folded edge at top).

Secure other end with straight pin. Let dry. Tape stem and base. Wire to pick; insert into tree. Make about 42.

WHITE DOUGH HEARTS AND STARS: Put 1 cup water in saucepan. Sift in and beat 1½ cups baking soda and 1 cup cornstarch, keeping mixture smooth. Mixture will become difficult to beat. Bring to low boil, stirring. Mixture will thin, then thicken rapidly. Stir until texture of mashed potatoes. Let cool a minute. Turn into plastic bag and close tight. Refrigerate ½ hour.

Remove dough from bag and knead until smooth, dusting with cornstarch. Roll out half the dough to ⅛" thickness. Cut out stars and hearts (about 20 of each) with cookie cutters. Place on waxed paper. Puncture hole near top edge. Allow to dry; to prevent curling, turn shapes over occasionally. Sand edges. Attach to tree with gold cord. Place tree in container and conceal the contents of the bucket with sheet moss.

Tree of Paradise

Wall Hangings, Plaques and Pictures

If you yearn to be creative—in ways that take very little skill, money or time—browse through our original works of holiday art. No matter how little space you have to spare, you're sure to find something to place proudly on your wall and, like your beloved ornaments, to cherish for many Christmases to come.

Crocheted Wall Tree

Crocheted Wall Tree

SIZE: 10" x 18".

MATERIALS (for one): Knitting-worsted-weight yarn, 2 ounces dark green, ½ ounce red, small amount white; aluminum crochet hook size G (or international hook size 4.50 mm), **or the size that will give you the correct gauge;** 15 small (½"-diameter) pompons in assorted colors (pompon instructions, page 189); 1½ yards gold cord; scraps gold and yellow felt; white glue.

GAUGE: 5 sts = 2".

Tree: Starting at lower edge above trunk with green, ch 52 to measure about 10". **1st row:** Dc in 6th ch from hook, * ch 1, sk next ch, dc in next ch; repeat from * across (24 sp); ch 4, turn. **2nd row:** Sk first dc and ch, dc in next dc, * ch 1, sk next ch, dc in next dc; repeat from * across, ch 1, skip next ch, dc in next ch (24 sp); turn. **3rd row:** Sl st across first dc, ch and dc; ch 4, sk next ch, dc in next dc, * ch 1, sk next ch, dc in next dc; repeat from * to last dc (22 sp—2 sp dec); ch 4, turn. **4th row:** Repeat 2nd row (22 sp). **5th row:** Repeat 3rd row (20 sp). Repeat 2nd and 3rd rows nine times more (2 sp), then repeat 2nd row once more. Fasten off.

Trunk: Mark off center 13 sts along starting chain at lower edge of tree. **1st row:** With red, sc in free lps of 13 marked sts; ch 1, turn. **2nd row:** Sc in each sc across; ch 1, turn. Repeat 2nd row six times more. Fasten off.

Decorations: Zigzag gold cord back and forth under stitches of tree to create "tinsel." Make two 3" candy canes by braiding two double strands white with one double strand red for 5"; knot ends. Bend to shape; glue in place. Glue on pompons. Cut 2½" and 1" gold felt stars and 2" yellow felt star; glue graduated sizes together and glue to top of tree.

Partridge Plaque

Partridge-in-a-pear-tree Plaque

SIZE: Octagon is about 18" x 18" at widest points.

MATERIALS: 1 square foot of ¼" plywood; 18" square of ⅛" plywood; 3' of ½ x 10 pine; 3' of 1 x 2 pine; 1" x No. 6 screws; 2 screw eyes; blue, tan, yellow, green, red and purple wood stains (or use food dyes, watercolor paints or diluted inks); spray shellac; craft torch (optional); wire brush; wood glue, or hot-glue gun (optional).

Note: For general guidance, see directions below for working with wood.

Enlarge plaque pattern (enlarging instructions, page 189); cut two pieces for plaque from ½ x 10 pine; glue edges of pieces together. Cut two strips of 1 x 2 pine; glue and screw to back, perpendicular to joint. Turn plaque so that strips are horizontal during assembly.

Sand plaque smooth. For optional burnt effect, scorch front with torch; brush away charred areas with wire brush. Stain blue. (If not scorching, just stain blue.) Sand until some natural wood shows through.

Cut design parts, following enlarged patterns and General Directions below. Stain all parts as shown. Position tree, following arrangement diagram and enlarged pattern. Arrange some leaves under and around

as well as on tree. Attach all to plaque with hot glue or wood glue. Complete placing and gluing of design parts, following diagram (photograph will also be helpful).

Coat completed plaque lightly with shellac. Attach two screw eyes to top of 1 x 2 strip for hanging.

General directions for working with wood: Enlarge patterns following instructions on page 189, preferably onto oaktag or manila file-folder paper.

Straight cuts or broad curves can be made with a saber or table saw. If making a number of the same item, you can mark one piece and stack on several others to cut at one time. Use a band or jig saw if possible. Separate and sand all pieces smooth.

Apply stain after sanding but before gluing. You can use either hot glue or dabs of wood glue to attach details to base; be sure to place glue dabs where they won't ooze.

89

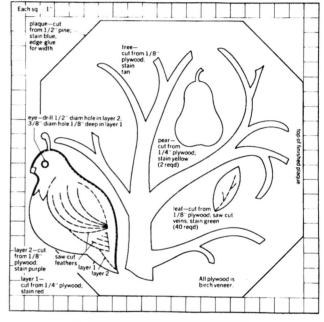

PLAQUE ARRANGEMENT DIAGRAM

PLAQUE PATTERN

Felt Tree of Hearts with Red Velvet Obelisks
(obelisk instructions, page 86).

Felt Tree of Hearts

SIZE: Backing panel is 36" x 27".

MATERIALS: 9" x 12" pieces of felt—11 red, 6 white, 5 yellow, 3 lime, 1 hot pink, 1 orange—and ¾ yard emerald felt; 2½ yards fusible web; 25 gold metallic chenille stems; quick-drying glue; needle; white or yellow thread; scissors.

To make hearts: Fuse red felt rectangles in pairs to make two-layer pieces. Cut odd piece in half and fuse these two pieces also. Enlarge all patterns (enlarging instructions, page 189). Using the larger of the two heart patterns and layered red felt pieces, cut out 21 hearts. Repeat with white, fusing pieces and cutting 21 hearts using smaller pattern. Glue white hearts, centered, on red ones. Let dry. Shape gold tinsel stems to outline white hearts and sew in place. Take small stitches across the stem about 1" apart.

To compose the tree: Cut emerald felt along center fold line. Place one of the 36" x 27" pieces on a flat surface. Place on it a line of six hearts with side edges touching and bottom points 7" above one 27" edge. Have the line centered, with the same amount visible at each side. Glue hearts in place. Repeat with subsequent rows as shown.

Fuse two of the lime rectangles, cutting odd piece in half and fusing the halves. Using enlarged leaf pattern, cut 63 leaves of fused lime. Glue three above each heart as shown. Save scraps for flower centers. Fuse all but one yellow felt piece in pairs. Cut star of yellow felt, using enlarged pattern. Cut pieces of gold tinsel stem to fit edges of star and glue them to edges (optional). Glue star to top of tree.

Using enlarged pattern for tree base, cut from fused yellow. Cut a 1½" x 8½" piece of fused red; glue it across base as band; let dry. Cut off excess at sides. Sew piece of gold tinsel stem above and below the band. Glue base with top edge touching bottom points of hearts. Using enlarged pattern of flower and center, cut flowers of single thickness yellow, orange and hot pink felt, placing colors as shown. Cut centers of scrap fused lime. Cover each corner of backing with a triangle of fused red felt. Each side of triangle extends 7" along edge of emerald backing.

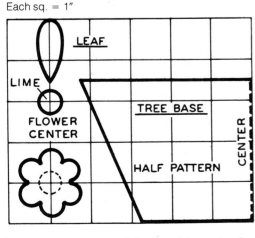

Each sq. = 1"

FELT TREE OF HEARTS (base and decorations)

LEAF

LIME

FLOWER CENTER

TREE BASE

HALF PATTERN

CENTER

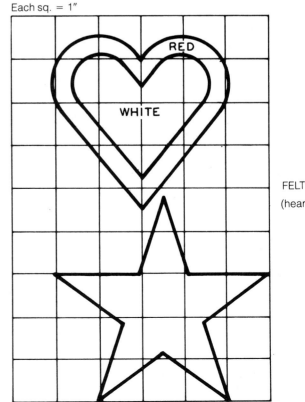

Each sq. = 1"

RED

WHITE

FELT TREE OF HEARTS
(hearts and star)

Madonna and Child Crayon-on-fabric "Painting"

SIZE: 10″ x 12″.

MATERIALS: 10″ x 12″ piece of white polyester-cotton fabric; clean white paper; dressmaker's carbon paper; fabric crayons; newspaper; iron; 10″ x 12″ piece of cotton batting; 10″ x 12″ fabric for backing; embroidery cotton in various colors; embroidery needle; strips of 1¼″-wide satin—two 10″ and two 12″ long—in two colors.

Enlarge design following instructions on page 189. Place dressmaker's carbon paper face down between sheet of clean white paper and enlarged design. Lightly trace over lines of drawing to transfer design to clean, gridless paper. Fill in all areas of design with fabric crayons, consulting photograph for color suggestions. (Crayon colors will not be very bright on paper but will come alive when ironed onto fabric.)

Following crayon package instructions, place several folded sheets of newspaper, topped with a sheet of clean white paper, on ironing board. Place the piece of white fabric on top of this padded surface. Lay the crayon design face down and centered on the fabric. Turn iron to cotton setting. Press with a steady, strong pressure over entire design until color becomes slightly visible through top sheet of paper. Check frequently by carefully lifting corner of design to make sure fabric is not scorching and color is transferring evenly. Once transferred to fabric made with synthetic fibers, color is permanent and washable.

Place a thin sheet of cotton batting between the fabric design and a piece of backing. With different colors of embroidery thread, embroider running stitches around parts of design to give a trapunto effect. Highlight facial features and hair, and give hands a clear outline around the shape and fingers. Sew strips of satin around picture as shown to cover edges of fabric and batting and to frame the design. Frame or hang as desired.

Madonna and Child "Painting"

MADONNA AND CHILD DESIGN

Inviting Outdoor Decor

One of the nicest of holiday customs is greeting guests at your door. What is even nicer is welcoming them as they arrive, with a gala and glittering sign of the hospitality awaiting them inside. Feel free to choose the display that is most to your liking; they are all warm and tasteful symbols of the neighborly season.

Off-the-door Spray

MATERIALS: Several large sprays of blue spruce; 1' x 6' piece of ½" hardware cloth; medium-gauge florist's wire; metal-cutting shears; various muted shades of artificial grape clusters; several "hens and chickens" cacti; 10 yards of 3"-wide pink velvet florist's ribbon; spray wax preservative; floral picks; picture hanger.

Cut hardware cloth for frame into a narrow 6' triangle shape, using metal-cutting shears. Following photograph, arrange and wire spruce sprays on frame. Wire grape clusters to spruce background. Spray cacti with wax preservative for protection; let dry. Insert a floral pick in each one and wire to arrangement. From pink ribbon, make nine or ten large loops, satin side out, with two long streamers wired together at center. Nestle bow to one side in greenery, securing to frame with more wire. Hang completed decoration to wall at side of door, using picture hanger.

Off-the-door Spray

Holly Door Tree

MATERIALS: 2' x 6' length of ¼" hardboard; dark green spray paint; several sprays of plain and variegated artificial holly with berries; artificial pears; metallic gold spray paint; staple gun; floral picks; florist's wire; red bird; two ¾" wood screws. **Note:** The tree in photograph is 5½' high and shown on an oversize door. Scale your tree to dimensions of your door.

Draw a freehand tree shape on ¼" hardboard; cut out, using saber saw. Spray with green paint; let dry. Working with old leather gloves to protect your hands, cut holly into 4" to 6" pieces. Staple holly to hardboard base, following tree shape and positioning pieces to resemble branches (see photograph). Spray-paint artificial pears gold; let dry. Insert floral pick in each pear and wire to holly tree. Attach tree to door with the wood screws, placed about 12" from top and bottom of hardboard. Wire bird to a branch.

Holly Door Tree

94

Velvet-and-holly Streamers

MATERIALS: 9 yards 3"-wide picot-edged, wired white velvet florist's ribbon; florist's wire; two large and four small artificial-holly wreaths; extra-long pushpins.

Make bow loops and streamers as shown in photograph, leaving longest streamer about 42" in length and wrapping streamers and loops with wire securely. Let streamers hang free and snip notches at ends as shown. Attach bows firmly to door with pushpins; add artificial-holly wreaths at intervals along streamers, attaching them securely with several pins concealed in greenery.

Apple Tree

Apple Tree

MATERIALS: 4 dozen pine cones; fifteen 3"-diameter plastic apples; 6 dozen stemmed artificial red berries; two bags unshelled mixed nuts; 24"-square piece ¼" pegboard; 6" x 10" woven wood basket; brown stain; red spray paint; two-part epoxy putty; florist's wire; floral picks; ⅝" x No. 6 sheet-metal screw; live greens.

To make pegboard tree, mark midpoint on one side, then draw cutting lines from midpoint to each corner on opposite side; cut out triangular shape. Also cut a 5" x 9" pegboard piece for tree trunk. Centering trunk along base of tree, overlap edges, with holes lined up, and glue and screw in place. Attach basket with glue and screws to bottom of trunk. Stain basket dark brown; let dry.

Push a floral pick into each apple; spray-paint red; let dry. To prepare nuts for tree, punch a small hole in each one, then dip quickly into boiling water to preserve them; put aside to dry. Insert and glue piece of florist's wire in each hole. Make clusters of three or four nuts each, with pine cones and berries, as shown in photograph. Following manufacturer's directions, prepare enough two-part epoxy and, inserting exposed point of floral picks into pegboard, attach apples firmly in place with a blob of adhesive. Fill in areas between apples with wired nuts, cones and berries as indicated in photograph. To hang tree, attach through pegboard with wood screw directly to the door; fill basket with live greens.

Velvet-and-holly Streamers

Beckoning Star

Gilded Leaves and Ornaments

MATERIALS: 2 wire coat hangers; florist's wire; assorted packages of craft leaves, about 75 in all (available where craft supplies or party favors are sold); about 35 wire-stemmed Christmas balls in assorted sizes; florist's tape; metallic gold spray paint.

Untwist coat hangers. From each, make one arm of spray by twisting ends for about 8" down from the top. Wire the hangers together at this point, leaving loop for hanging. To attach leaves and balls, begin at bottom end and tape stems and wires to framework with one continuous coil of tape. Spray all gold.

Bushel-basket Holiday Bouquet

Beckoning Star

MATERIALS: Two 30"-square pieces of corrugated cardboard; utility knife; gold foil gift-wrap paper; 6" plastic-foam dome; prewired artificial fruit; dried grasses; rubber cement; florist's wire; floral picks; metallic gold spray paint; picture hanger.

To begin drawing two stars 28" high x 24" wide, mark a centered 6" square between two sets of parallel lines on cardboard. Complete the stars, drawing four points for each. Cut out stars with utility knife; join with rubber cement. Cement gold paper to one side of star, carefully wrapping star points to achieve softened edges. Punch several holes through center of star and wire plastic dome to it. Insert picks in dome and mount artificial fruit, wrapping their wire stems around picks. Insert dried grasses directly into base of dome, wiring material first, if necessary. Spray-paint arrangement gold; let dry. Add picture hanger on back to mount on door.

Gilded Leaves and Ornaments

Bushel-basket Holiday Bouquet

MATERIALS: Bushel basket about 11½" in diameter, with handle; scrap of wood 11½" long; spray paint in both silver and metallic gold; dried baby's breath; 3 yards of 2½"-wide wired florist's ribbon in complementary color (russet used here); 1½ dozen assorted-size wired silver balls; wire.

Cut wood to fit vertically inside of basket and nail in place. Saw off back of basket (behind wood support). Spray basket silver and flowers gold. Cut 1-yard length of ribbon; tack each end to wood on basket; reinforce with wire through handle loops. Use as hanging loop, adding ribbon bow as shown. Insert flowers, fluffing out to conceal basket edges; wire balls to them.

SIGHTS TO DELIGHT THE CHILDREN

*Lots of people insist that Christmas belongs to children, and there's some truth in what they say. Youngsters do enjoy all the goings-on: the gifts they know are in store for them . . . the sing-along fun of Christmas carols . . . the magic change that decorations make in the house. But hard as the little ones try to join in, these are mostly adult activities. What kids would love dearly are some holiday "happenings" of their own, things that turn grownups into spectators. This section does just that, with two all-time young favorites. In **Sweet Spectaculars**, cookies, cake and candy become the most delectable creations: a farm scene, sumptuous houses, a gingerbread church, a candy bear and airplane. **Santa Claus and Friends,** too, features something sensational: a big, bright parade of Santa, sleigh and reindeer. But Santa also shows what a doll he can be—**and** a pillow **and** a package decoration and ever so much more!*

Sweet Spectaculars of Cookies and Candy

*Imagine a world that's all cookies and candy! It's every child's fantasy, and no longer a dream. The farm really **is** made of cookies, even the sugar-coated animals. So are the candy-studded buildings (with one sweet exception: White-cake Cottage). Our Gumdrop Bear and Candyland Airplane are **all** candy. For a finale: trims and tree shaped from a marshmallow-popcorn mixture.*

CHRISTMAS ON THE FARM. Endearing country scene, creatures and all, is made entirely of cookies. Instructions begin on page 100.

Christmas on the Farm

BARNYARD COOKIES

3½ **cups unsifted flour**
  1 **teaspoon ground cinnamon**
 ½ **teaspoon ground nutmeg**
 ½ **teaspoon ground cloves**
 ⅛ **teaspoon salt**
  1 **cup margarine**
 ⅓ **cup firmly packed brown sugar**
 ⅔ **cup dark corn syrup**
     Frosting (recipe below)

Preheat oven to 400°F. In small bowl, stir together flour, cinnamon, nutmeg, cloves and salt. In large bowl, using mixer at medium speed, beat margarine to soften. Beat in sugar; beat in corn syrup until well blended. Reduce speed to low; gradually beat in flour mixture until well mixed. Cover and refrigerate several hours.

Enlarge cookie diagrams, following instructions on page 189. Cut cardboard forms from paper patterns to use as cookie cutting guides.

On lightly floured surface, roll out one-half of the dough at a time to ¼" thickness. Place cardboard forms on dough. Using the point of a knife, cut dough following outline of cardboard forms. Cut 1 barn, 1 house, 1 mother, 1 father (larger figures), 1 daughter, 1 son (smaller figures), 1 sleigh, 1 horse, 2 cows, 2 pigs, 2 ducks, 2 chickens and 2 trees. Place on ungreased cookie sheets.

Insert wooden picks into base of each cookie before baking. (Picks will serve to secure cookies into plastic-foam base. They should not extend more than an inch.) For house and barn, use 3 picks; for sleigh, family figures, trees and animals, 2 picks; for ducks and chickens, 1 pick. Bake 8 to 10 minutes, or until edges are lightly browned. Cool on wire racks. To decorate, tint frosting as desired (keep covered).

Each sq. = 1"

DIAGRAMS FOR FARM BUILDINGS

DIAGRAMS FOR FARM FAMILY, ANIMALS, ETC.

Frost cookies following photograph. Make fence by gluing craft sticks (ice cream sticks) together as shown. Stand fence and farm scene cookies on plastic-foam base (approximately 18 x 24 inches). Trim edges of base with ribbon.

FROSTING

3 egg whites

1 pound confectioners' sugar

⅛ teaspoon cream of tartar

Food coloring

Beat ingredients together in small bowl, using mixer at low speed. Tint as desired, putting each color in a separate bowl. Some decorations will require piping.

Suggestion: Mix a second batch of dough for cookies to be baked later for eating. Cover and refrigerate until baking time. Then, on lightly floured surface, roll dough to ⅛" thickness and cut cookies, using cookie cutters or cardboard forms. Place on ungreased cookie sheets. Bake in 400°F oven 8 to 10 minutes, or until lightly browned around edges. Makes 6 to 8 dozen cookies (depending on size of cutters). Place in basket or other container in front of farm scene.

Christmas Cottage

COOKIE DOUGH

- 9 cups unsifted flour
- 3 teaspoons ground cinnamon
- 2 teaspoons ground ginger
- 1 teaspoon salt
- ½ teaspoon ground cloves
- 2 cups dark corn syrup
- 1½ cups firmly packed light brown sugar
- 1¼ cups margarine
- 2 squares (1 ounce each) unsweetened chocolate, melted
  Assorted candies for decoration
  "Window Glass" Mixture and Builder's Icing (recipes below)

In a large bowl, stir together flour, cinnamon, ginger, salt and cloves. In 3-quart saucepan, stirring occasionally, heat corn syrup, brown sugar and margarine over medium heat until margarine is melted. Stir into flour mixture until well blended. Place one-third of dough in another bowl. Stir chocolate into the one-third dough in second bowl; mix until blended.

Line four 15½" x 12" cookie sheets with foil. (See Note.) Divide chocolate dough in half and place halves on two of the cookie sheets. Divide light dough in half and place halves on two remaining cooking sheets. Before rolling out dough on cookie sheets, place damp cloth or paper towel under sheet to prevent sliding. Roll out each piece of light dough to 14½" x 11½" rectangle. Roll out each piece of chocolate dough to 11" x 9" rectangle. Refrigerate at least 30 minutes. Prepare "Window Glass" Mixture.

Note: You will need four 15½" x 12" cookie sheets for the cookie cottage. If you don't have or can't borrow four cookie sheets, roll out the dough to size on extra-wide foil and slide foil onto tray or large piece of cardboard to refrigerate. Then slide foil onto cookie sheet for baking.

"WINDOW GLASS" MIXTURE

Place 12" square of foil on heat-resistant surface. In small saucepan, stir together ¼ cup each granulated sugar and light corn syrup. Stirring constantly, bring to boil over medium heat. Cook at full rolling boil, without stirring, for 2 minutes. Remove from heat; stir in 3 drops of desired food coloring. Quickly pour onto foil. Let stand about 20 minutes, or until completely cool. Place in plastic bag; seal. Using hammer or mallet, crush fine. Store tightly covered in cool place.

BUILDER'S ICING

- 1 pound confectioners' sugar
- 3 egg whites
- ½ teaspoon cream of tartar

In large bowl, using mixer at low speed, beat ingredients together until well blended. Beat at high speed, scraping sides frequently, 7 to 10 minutes, or until knife drawn through mixture leaves a path. Keep covered with damp cloth at all times.

To make cardboard patterns: Enlarge patterns (enlarging instructions, page 189) on lightweight glossy cardboard. Place on board or several layers of newspaper and, using ruler and mat knife, or single-edged razor blade in holder, cut out pattern pieces and label each. Without cutting frames, cut out window-pane spaces.

To bake cookie sections: Preheat oven to 350°F. Dust pattern pieces well with flour. Remove one cookie sheet of light dough from refrigerator. Arrange pattern pieces for back, front, one wide side of chimney and three narrow sides of chimney on dough, leaving ½" between pieces. With sharp, pointed paring knife, using a ruler as a guide, carefully cut out each shape. Carefully remove each pattern piece after dough piece has been cut and remove all excess dough.

Bake 12 minutes. Remove from oven. Let cool about 2 minutes. Fill in window openings in dough with a layer of crushed "Window Glass" Mixture, being careful not to get candy on dough. Bake 5 to 7 minutes longer, or until edges begin to brown and cookies are set. Cool completely before removing from foil.

Remove remaining cookie sheet of light dough from refrigerator. Arrange pattern pieces for two sides of house, one wide side of chimney and one narrow side of chimney on dough, leaving ½" between pieces. Carefully cut out each shape. Remove pattern pieces and excess dough. Bake 17 minutes, or until edges begin to brown and cookies are set.

Remove one cookie sheet of chocolate dough from refrigerator. Arrange pattern pieces for one side of roof, door and four shutters on dough, leaving ½" between pieces. Carefully cut out each shape. Remove pattern pieces and excess dough. Bake 15 minutes, or until cookies are set.

Remove remaining cookie sheet of chocolate dough from refrigerator. Arrange pattern pieces for remaining side of roof and remaining four shutters on dough, leaving ½" between pieces. Carefully cut out each shape. Remove pattern pieces and excess dough. Bake 15 minutes, or until cookies are set.

Constructing the cottage: Cover an 18" x 12" piece of heavy cardboard with foil. In center, draw 9" x 6" rectangle to serve as guide for base of house. Set aside.

Decorate shutters as desired, using small amount of Builder's Icing to attach candies. Working with one shutter at a time, spread small amount of icing on backs of shutter pieces. Arrange each shutter in place next to window.

Spread icing along seam edges of two narrow chimney pieces and one wide chimney piece. Assemble three sides. Attach to one side wall piece. Set aside; let set about 5 minutes. Repeat with remaining two narrow chimney pieces and remaining wide chimney piece. Attach to other side wall piece. Set aside; let set.

On back piece of house, spread icing along inside edge of one side and bottom edge. On one side piece of house, spread icing along side and bottom edge. Following predrawn guidelines, carefully stand back and side wall pieces of house on cardboard base, placing edge of side wall against inside edge of back wall. Spread extra icing on inside seams for extra strength. Fill in any seam irregularities with icing. Back and side should stand alone.

On other side piece of house, spread icing on side edge that will form seam

CHRISTMAS COTTAGE, too, is "built" of cookies. Cutting diagrams for cottage parts are on page 104.

Each sq. = 1″

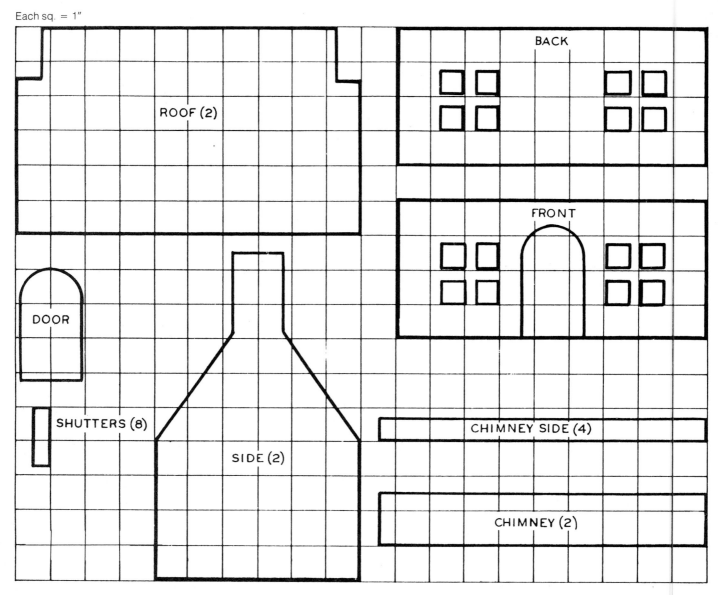

DIAGRAMS FOR PARTS OF CHRISTMAS COTTAGE

with back wall of house and bottom edge. Spread icing on inside edge of remaining side of back piece of house. Attach side piece to back and base, following predrawn guidelines. Spread extra icing on inside seam.

On front piece of house, spread icing on inside edges of both sides and bottom edge. Spread icing on side edges of both side walls. Attach front piece to sides. Spread extra icing on inside seams. Let set about 5 minutes.

To attach roof, spread icing along top edges of front wall and front half of side walls. Place one roof piece on front of house; hold or prop in place about 7 minutes, or until set. On roof pieces, spread icing along seam edges where roof pieces will meet. Spread icing along top edges of back wall and side walls. Place remaining roof section on back of house so that roof pieces form peak; hold or prop in place about 7 minutes, or until set.

Use icing to fill in any spaces along peak of roof and around chimney.

Decorate door as desired, using icing to attach candies. Spread icing along inside edge of hinge side of door piece. Attach to house with door slightly ajar. Decorate house as desired, using icing to attach candies.

Ginger-cookie House

Ginger-cookie House

GINGER-COOKIE DOUGH

- **1 cup shortening**
- **1 cup firmly packed brown sugar**
- **1 tablespoon each cinnamon and ginger**
- **1 cup dark corn syrup**
- **2 eggs**
- **5½ cups flour, divided**
- **1½ teaspoons baking soda**

In large bowl, cream shortening with brown sugar, cinnamon and ginger until fluffy. Beat in corn syrup and eggs until well blended. Mix 2 cups flour with the baking soda; beat into creamed mixture. Stir in remaining 3½ cups flour (working with hands if necessary to get a smooth dough). Wrap airtight; chill overnight. Makes 1 ginger-cookie house with trees and snowmen, and extra ginger cookies.

To make cookie-house parts: Cut enlarged patterns (enlarging instructions, page 189) from thin cardboard and label each piece. Preheat oven to 375°F.

On lightly floured surface with stockinette-covered rolling pin, roll out portions of dough to ³⁄₁₆" thickness. Dust pattern pieces with flour; place on dough; cut out with sharp knife. With large spatula, transfer large and small pieces of dough onto separate, lightly greased cookie sheets. Place patterns again on pieces cut from them and line up edges with edge of knife if necessary. Bake until lightly browned—12 to 15 minutes for large pieces, 7 to 8 minutes for small. About halfway through baking, check edges; push with knife blade if necessary to keep straight. Remove cookie sheets to wire racks. Loosen pieces with spatula while warm. Cool *completely* on the sheets before removing.

To assemble house: In addition to cookie parts, you will need 1 cup granulated sugar; about 4¼ ounces white icing (enough to fill tube equipped with writing tip); multi-colored sugar-coated chocolate or peanut-butter candies.

Melt sugar in large heavy skillet over low heat, stirring constantly to keep sugar from burning. Keep melted sugar over low heat and work quickly, using syrup as glue. (Be very careful not to touch hot syrup.) Dip short edges of house sides (pieces 4) in syrup; attach to house front (1) and back (9). Attach the shutters and doors (6 and 10). Next attach roof (2), one section at a time. Assemble chimney (3, 5, 7 and 8) and attach to roof. With icing, decorate house in desired pattern and attach candies to roof (photograph will give helpful guidance). Let house dry thoroughly; place on bed of cotton. Decorate tree and snowmen and arrange around house. Use any leftover dough for trees and snowmen, or bake in a sheet and let it serve as a platform for the house.

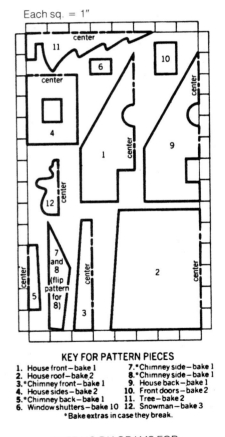

Each sq. = 1"

KEY FOR PATTERN PIECES

1. House front—bake 1
2. House roof—bake 2
3. *Chimney front—bake 1
4. House sides—bake 2
5. *Chimney back—bake 1
6. Window shutters—bake 10
7. *Chimney side—bake 1
8. *Chimney side—bake 1
9. House back—bake 1
10. Front doors—bake 2
11. Tree—bake 2
12. Snowman—bake 3

*Bake extras in case they break.

CUTTING DIAGRAMS FOR
GINGER-COOKIE HOUSE

Gingerbread Church

GINGERBREAD DOUGH

- 8 cups unsifted flour
- 2 teaspoons each ground cinnamon and ginger
- ½ teaspoon salt
- 1¾ cups dark corn syrup
- 1 cup firmly packed light brown sugar
- ¾ cup (1½ sticks) margarine

  "Window Glass" Mixture and Builder's Icing (see Note)

  Assorted candies for decoration

Note: For recipes, see Christmas Cottage, page 102. "Window Glass" here must be made in four colors, each separately mixed, crushed and stored.

In large bowl, using whisk or fork, stir together flour, cinnamon, ginger and salt. In 2-quart saucepan, stirring occasionally, heat corn syrup, brown sugar and margarine over medium heat until margarine is melted. Stir into flour mixture until well blended. Knead dough with hands until pliable, smooth and even in color. Divide dough into four equal parts. Wrap each fourth in plastic wrap until ready to roll out.

Line four 15½" x 12" cookie sheets with foil. (See Note.) Before rolling dough on cookie sheet, place damp cloth or paper towel under sheet to prevent sliding. Place one of the dough quarters on a cookie sheet. Shape dough into rectangle and flatten slightly. Roll out to 14" x 10" rectangle about ¼" thick. Repeat with second fourth of dough. Roll out each of the other two fourths of dough on separate cookie sheets to 13" x 11" rectangles. After dough has been rolled, refrigerate at least 30 minutes. **Note:** Dough can be rolled to size on foil and slid onto trays or large pieces of cardboard to refrigerate. To bake, slide foil with dough onto cookie sheet.

To make cardboard patterns: Enlarge patterns (enlarging instructions, page 189) on lightweight glossy cardboard. Label each piece. Place on board or several layers of newspaper and, using a ruler and mat knife, or single-edged razor blade in holder, cut out pattern pieces. Cut out door and side windows; set aside.

To make parts of church: Preheat oven to 350°F. Dust pattern pieces with flour. Remove 1 cookie sheet of 14" x 10" dough from refrigerator. Leaving ½" between pieces, arrange on dough pattern pieces for 2 side walls, belfry base and belfry sides. With sharp, pointed paring knife, using a ruler as a guide, carefully cut out each shape. Cut out windows in side walls. Carefully remove each pattern piece after dough shape has been cut and remove all excess dough.

Bake 12 minutes. Remove from oven. Let cool about 2 minutes. Using a variety of colors, each added separately, fill in windows in dough with thin, even layer of crushed "Window Glass" Mixture, being careful not to get candy on dough. Bake 5 to 9 minutes longer, or until edges begin to brown and cookies are set. Cool completely before removing from foil. If candy window sticks to foil, remove entire cookie piece with surrounding foil still attached and gently peel foil from back of cookie.

Remove second cookie sheet of 14" x 10" dough from refrigerator. Leaving ½" between pieces, arrange on dough pattern pieces for right and left door; four sides of spire and spire base; front, back and two sides of watch tower; step; and front and back of belfry. Carefully cut out each shape. Remove pattern pieces and excess dough.

Bake about 15 minutes, or until edges begin to brown and cookies are set. Cool completely before removing from foil.

Remove one cookie sheet of 13" x 11" dough from refrigerator. Leaving ½" between pieces, arrange on dough pattern pieces for one side of roof and back wall. Carefully cut out each shape. Remove pattern pieces and excess dough. Using 2" round cookie

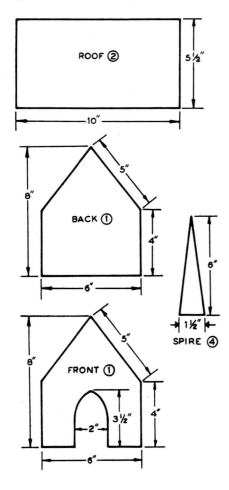

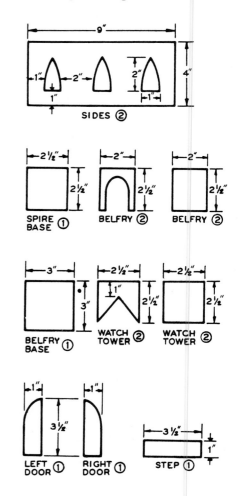

GINGERBREAD CHURCH in friendly holiday surroundings, with Santa Stocking Doll in back (instructions, page 122) and Elf Stocking Doll at right (instructions, page 124). For the unusual yarn-wrapped Christmas tree to the left, see page 82.

cutter, cut out space for rose window in back wall.

Bake 15 minutes. Remove from oven. Let cool about 2 minutes. Using a variety of colors, each added separately, fill in window opening in dough with a thin, even layer of crushed "Window Glass" Mixture. Bake 5 to 9 minutes longer, or until edges begin to brown and cookies are set. Cool completely before removing from foil. If candy window sticks to foil, remove entire cookie piece with surrounding foil still attached and gently peel foil from back of cookie.

Remove remaining cookie sheet of 13" x 11" dough from refrigerator. Leaving ½" between pieces, arrange on dough pattern pieces for remaining roof and front wall. Carefully cut out each shape. Remove pattern pieces and excess dough.

Bake about 15 minutes, or until edges begin to brown and cookies are set. Cool completely before removing from foil.

Constructing the church: Cover an 18" x 12" (or larger) piece of heavy cardboard with foil. In center, draw a 9" x 6" rectangle to serve as guide for base of church.

Assemble 4 sides of watch tower: Using small paring knife or spatula, spread small amount of Builder's Icing along side seam edge of front piece and adjoining seam of one side piece. Join two pieces. Spread icing along other side seam of front piece and adjoining seam of the remaining side piece. Join pieces. Spread icing along both side seams of back piece and adjoining seams of side pieces and attach. Four sides of watch tower should stand alone when joined. Set aside for about 5 minutes, or until icing is set. Add shoestring licorice to seams before icing sets.

Assemble 4 sides of belfry: Using Builder's Icing to join sides of belfry, assemble as watch tower above. Decorate with licorice; set aside.

Assemble 4 sides of spire: Using icing, assemble as above. For extra strength, spread additional icing on inside seams of spire. Decorate with licorice and with desired candy on point of spire. Set aside.

Decorate doors and front of church as desired, using small amount of

Builder's Icing to attach candies. Set aside.

Assemble 4 walls: On one side wall piece of church, spread icing along one side edge and bottom edge. On front wall piece of church, spread icing along inside edge of one side and bottom edge. Following drawn guidelines, carefully stand front and side wall pieces of church on cardboard base, placing edge of side wall against inside edge of front wall. For extra strength, spread extra icing on inside seams. Fill in any seam irregularities with icing. Joined front and side should stand alone. Decorate with licorice.

On other side wall piece of church, spread icing on bottom edge and side edge that will form seam with standing front wall piece. Spread icing along inside edge of unattached side of front piece. Following drawn guidelines on cardboard base, attach side piece to front wall. Spread extra icing on inside seams. Decorate with licorice.

On back wall piece of church, spread icing on bottom edge and inside edges of both sides. Spread icing on side edges of both standing side walls. Attach back piece to standing side wall pieces. Spread extra icing on inside seams. Decorate with licorice. Let set about 5 minutes.

Attach roof: Spread icing along top edges of one side wall and corresponding half of front and back walls. Spread icing on underside of one roof piece where roof will rest on walls. Place roof piece on iced side of church. Hold or prop in place about 7 minutes, or until set. On both roof pieces, spread icing along seam edges where roof pieces will meet. Spread icing along top edges of remaining side wall and corresponding half of front and back walls. Spread icing on underside of remaining roof piece where roof will rest on walls. Place roof piece on iced side of church so that roof pieces meet to form peak. Hold or prop in place about 7 minutes, or until set. Use icing to fill in any spaces along peak of roof.

Assemble steeple: Spread icing along bottom edges of assembled watch tower and place in position on peak of roof. Spread extra icing on inside

seams. Decorate with licorice. Let set about 5 minutes.

Spread icing along top edges of assembled belfry; place base of spire on top of belfry. Using icing, attach foil-wrapped candy kiss to underside of base of spire so that candy "bell" is visible in arch of belfry. Spread icing along bottom edges of assembled belfry; place on belfry base. Spread icing along top edges of watch tower; place assembled belfry on watch tower. Decorate with licorice. Let set about 5 minutes. Spread icing along bottom edges of assembled spire. Place on spire base. Decorate with licorice.

Finish assembly: Spread icing on underside of step; attach to cardboard base at front door opening. Spread icing along hinge sides of door pieces. Attach to church with doors slightly ajar. Decorate with licorice.

Decorate church with candies as desired, using icing to attach.

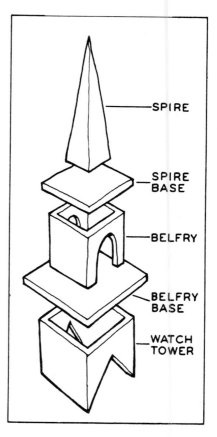

STEEPLE ASSEMBLY FOR GINGERBREAD CHURCH

White-cake Cottage

White-cake Cottage

FOR CAKE

3 **packages (18.5 ounces each) white-cake mix**

FOR FROSTING

1⅓ **cups white vegetable shortening**

2 **pounds confectioners' sugar**

2 **teaspoons vanilla**

4-6 **tablespoons milk**

FOR ASSEMBLY AND DECORATION

1 **can spreadable chocolate frosting**

2 **bags (1 pound each) multicolored chocolate candies**

Following cake mix directions, bake three white cakes in 7" x 11" cake pans. Cut each cake in half crosswise so that you have six 7" x 5½" cake layers. (**Note:** Only five layers are used, and parts of two of those are trimmed off to shape roof. You may wish to frost unused pieces as you frost the cottage to serve as a teatime treat or luncheon dessert.)

Mix creamy white frosting as follows:

With electric mixer, cream shortening in large mixing bowl. Add confectioners' sugar ½ cup at a time and continue to beat until all sugar is added. Beat in vanilla and enough milk to make the frosting of spreading consistency.

Assembling the cottage: Cover 13" square of heavy cardboard with heavy-duty aluminum foil. Assemble bottom of house by stacking three cake layers with creamy white frosting between them on foil-covered cardboard. (Remember that 7" sides are front and back of house.) To shape roof, stack two layers and trim at an angle to form peak. Spread frosting between roof layers. Place on top of house, spreading frosting between house and roof. Fill in any spaces with frosting to even sides and seams of house. Frost the front, back and sides and seams of house. Frost the front, back and sides with white frosting. Frost roof with chocolate frosting.

Decorating with candies: Use toothpick to mark door and window design on front of house following drawing. Fit pastry bag with fine plain tip; fill with chocolate frosting. Outline door and windows with chocolate frosting, adding all the dots and lines shown in drawing. Repeat marking and decorating on sides and back of house, using windows similar to those in drawing. Mark two windows on each side and three windows plus one attic window on back. Cut six yellow and six orange candies in half. Add whole and halved candies to house positioned as in drawing, with halved candies placed in each window as flowers. If frosting has set, apply dab of white frosting to house before pushing candies in place. With fine plain tip and chocolate frosting, decorate each halved candy with chocolate frosting dots. Using fine star tip and chocolate frosting, add row of stars to each corner of house (see drawing). Using large star tip and white frosting, add row off stars around bottom of house. While frost-

ing is still soft, insert green, yellow and orange candies in frosting. Using fine plain tip and white frosting, decorate slanting sides of roof with scallop design. Apply dab of white frosting to center of each scallop and push orange candy onto dab. Decorate peak of roof with white frosting lines and one orange candy. Add row of white frosting dots below last row of scallops. Using large star tip and chocolate frosting, outline roof.

Additional decoration (optional): If desired, decorate foil around cottage as follows: Add path of light and dark brown candies running from front door to edge of foil by dabbing white frosting on foil and putting one candy on each dab. With large star tip and white frosting, add border on each side of path; while frosting is still soft, insert green, yellow and orange candies in border. For grass, apply green candies to foil around house, using dabs of white frosting to attach candies to foil. If desired, make a second recipe of creamy white frosting, tint with green food color and spread on foil around house for grass. Make trees following recipe below (for tree pattern, see page 101 or page 105). Attach cookie trees to foil by applying large dollops of white frosting and inserting tree shapes in dollops. Apply yellow and orange candies to dollop at base of tree.

CHOPPED-CANDY COOKIE CUTOUTS

- 1 **package (17-ounces) sugar-cookie mix**
- ¼ **cup finely chopped multicolored chocolate candies**
- 1 **teaspoon grated orange peel**
- 2 **cups confectioners' sugar**
- 2-3 **tablespoons orange juice**
  Food coloring (if desired)
- ¾-1 **cup whole candies for decoration**

Preheat oven to 350°F. Prepare cookie mix according to package directions for butter cookies, using ¼ cup butter or margarine and 1 egg. Stir in chopped candies and orange peel. Wrap and chill. Roll out to ⅛" thickness on lightly floured surface. Cut into desired shapes. Place on ungreased cookie sheets. Bake 8 to 10 minutes, or until edges of cookies are lightly browned. Cool 1 minute; remove to wire racks to cool completely. Combine confectioners' sugar and 2 tablespoons of the orange juice; stir until smooth. Add enough of the remaining juice to form proper consistency for thin glaze. Tint with food coloring, if desired. Spread each cookie with glaze and decorate immediately. Makes about 4 dozen cookies, depending on pattern size.

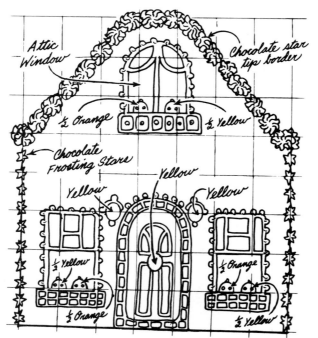

DECORATING THE
WHITE-CAKE COTTAGE

Gumdrop Bear

Gumdrop Bear

Note: For both candy sculptures — the Gumdrop Bear below and the Candyland Airplane that follows it — the candies shown in the photographed pieces may be slightly smaller or larger than the ones you are using,

since different candy companies make them in different sizes. Because of this, you may need more or fewer candies than called for in the directions.

MATERIALS: 24 assorted chocolate gold coins; 2 lollipops; 29 (approximately two 1-pound bags) jelly strings; 2 starlight mints; 3 black licorice buttons

(available in small 6-ounce packages); 1 small piece black string licorice; 1½′ ribbon, color of your choice; 3 pounds (approximately) assorted gumdrops; Icing Glue (see recipe); table knife. Plastic foam: 1″ slab, 24″ x 24″; 1½″ ball, cut in half; 5″ ball, cut in half; mat knife or single-edged razor blade in holder; cardboard mailing tube or paper towel roll, 1½" in diameter; masking tape.

Step 1: Enlarge pattern for bear body and arm, following instructions, page 189. Cut out pattern, trace onto foam slab, and use mat knife or single-edged razor blade to slice out two shapes for each pattern. Cut two 3" pieces of cardboard tube (for legs), cutting one end at a 45° angle.

Step 2 (assemble form): Tape two body forms together. Attach arms by pushing toothpick or 2" piece of lollipop stick into body form and straight-cut end of arm. (Note that ends are slanted so arms will extend down at an angle; you may wish to slant them even further.) Tape two pieces of cardboard tube, angled side in, onto either side, bottom front, of body form. Legs should jut out from body to provide a stable base. Tape hollow ends of legs. Place ½ of 5" foam ball on body so that bottom edge is almost resting on legs and forms a belly. To secure, insert a toothpick or 2" piece of a lollipop stick into body form and belly. Then tape over edges and around back of form. Place ½ of 1½" foam ball for snout on front of bear's face, slightly below center. Insert toothpick or piece of lollipop stick into snout and bear's face. Tape together securely.

Step 3: Prepare Icing Glue according to recipe that follows.

ICING GLUE

2 egg whites

½ teaspoom cream of tartar

3 cups confectioners' sugar

Beat egg whites until stiff. Stir in cream of tartar and confectioners' sugar, mixing until of thick icing consistency. May be kept several hours covered with a damp towel.

Step 4: Frost one leg and cover with gumdrops. **Note:** If candies slip, add more sugar to Icing Glue. Apply layer of Icing Glue to 2 large gold coins and place one at end of each leg for foot pad. Repeat for arms, but place 3 coins under each arm (instead of gumdrops).

Step 5: Frost belly. Tilt form backward to reach under belly. Work from bottom up, ending just below neck. Reserving white gumdrops, cover body front and belly with assorted gumdrops, "nesting" them as much as possible. Place assorted-size coins on their sides around neck.

Step 6 (face): To make eyes, place a dot of icing on back of two licorice buttons and apply each one to a gold coin. Use more icing to attach just above snout and far enough apart to fit two gumdrops in between. Place a third licorice button on center top of snout. Cut approximately 20 white gumdrops in half; cover snout with top halves. Working clockwise, cover face around snout with whole white gumdrops. Place bottom halves of gumdrops around edge of face. Insert a small licorice string smile just below button nose, as pictured. Secure lollipop ears to either side of top of head by gently pushing and twisting shortened sticks into foam. Working from one side to the other, place jelly strings around top of head.

Step 7: Cover the back and sides with frosting and compactly arranged gumdrops. At bottom of back, make a cluster of 10 jelly strings for a tail. Tie a bow and attach just above gold coin collar with a hairpin or short length of wire. Ice and apply 2 starlight mints below bow.

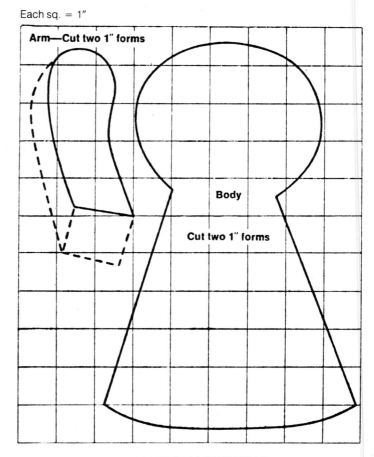

PATTERN FOR GUMDROP BEAR

Candyland Airplane

MATERIALS: 2 Tootsie Roll Pops; 12 ounces gumdrops; 4 large lollipops; 5 rolls candy wafers; 48 starlight mints; approximately 24 licorice pastels; 4 yards narrow ribbon; Icing Glue (recipe in Gumdrops Bear instructions, pages 111-112); table knife. Plastic foam: 5" x 10" piece 2" thick, or 2 pieces 1" thick; 5" x 12" piece of corrugated cardboard; mat knife or single-edged razor blade in holder; scissors; masking tape; hairpin.

Step 1: Enlarge pattern for body of plane and wings, following instructions on page 189. Cut out patterns, trace plane form onto foam and use knife or razor to slice out shape. (If using 1"-thick foam, cut two shapes and tape them securely together.) Cut wings from cardboard. Tape wings to plane sides, about 1" from front.

Step 2: Prepare Icing Glue (see left).

Step 3: Turn plane upside-down and use Icing Glue to frost underside of a wing. Start with the outer edge of wing and slightly overlap candy wafers, repeating this pattern from front to back of wing. Repeat on other wing.

Step 4: Ice bottom of plane and arrange starlight mints in rows of twos. Repeat on top of plane.

Step 5: Ice one side of plane and place one large lollipop, with stick broken off, above and to the front of wing for a cockpit. Place a second lollipop, also without its stick, under and to the front of wing for a wheel. Fill in rest of side with gumdrops in staggered rows. Repeat on other side of plane.

Step 6: Frost top of wings. Decorate same as undersides (refer to Step 3). Apply a dot of icing to each licorice pastel and arrange around the edge of each wing, as shown in photo.

Step 7: Frost and cover front of plane with staggered gumdrops. Tape Tootsie Roll Pops together. Cover sticks with ribbon: Starting midway between lollipops and leaving a tail of about 5", wrap ribbon at an angle around sticks to one candy and in opposite direction to other. Go back to center and tie tails in a bow. With excess ribbon, tie more bows in same place. Attach "propeller" to front of plane with a hairpin.

Candyland Airplane

Each sq. = 1"

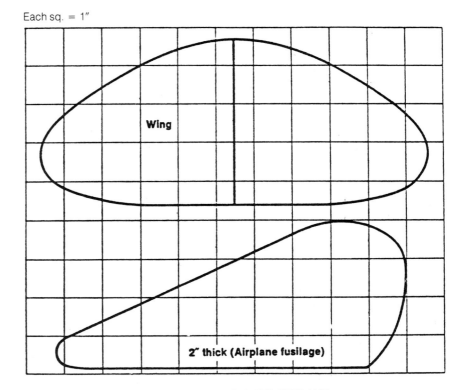

Wing

2" thick (Airplane fusilage)

PATTERN FOR CANDYLAND AIRPLANE

Marshmallow-popcorn Tree and Garland Trims

POPCORN-MARSHMALLOW BASE

- 2 pounds marshmallows (divided in 4 equal parts, ½ pound each)
- 8 tablespoons butter (2 tablespoons for each ½ pound of marshmallows)
- 3 quarts popped corn (for each ½ pound of marshmallows)

  Food coloring

Note: Recipe calls for 4 saucepans (one for each ½ pound of marshmallows). If you do not have that many, work a batch or two at a time, washing pans between batches. If you do work multiple batches, it is best to melt batches one at a time in any case, so marshmallows will stay malleable.

Place ½-pound portions of marshmallows in 4 separate saucepans; melt each with 2 tablespoons butter. Add food coloring (different color to each) and blend. Pour contents of each saucepan over 3 quarts popped corn; stir to mix and coat. When coated corn is cool enough to handle, lightly grease palms of hands and shape mixture into balls or other shapes as described below. Place on cookie sheet, waxed paper, foil, etc.

Popcorn balls: Mold balls of various shapes, sizes and tints. Insert a floral pick in each ball, letting about ½" extend from the top. Attach cord or ribbon to pick for hanging. Decorate and trim as desired (see photographs for some variations: hollowed-out balls with candy canes inserted; candy-studded balls with ribbon wrappings, streamers and bows; etc.).

Ice cream cones: Mold single and double dips from the colored popcorn mixture. Attach to store-bought cones with melted marshmallows.

Cupcakes: Shape the colored popcorn-marshmallow mixture into small cupcake liners or paper nutcups. Drizzle tops with tube frosting. Decorate with sprinkles.

Marshmallow-popcorn trims on tree

Marshmallow-popcorn trims on window garland

Candy Tree

BASE AND DECORATIONS

5 **quarts popped corn**

½ **cup butter or margarine**

1 **package (16 ounces) marshmallows**

Toothpicks

About 2 pounds assorted soft candies such as gumdrops and jellied candies, preferably red, green and multicolored

Measure popped corn into large bowl. In Dutch oven or heavy saucepot, melt butter over low heat. Add marshmallows; heat and stir until melted and smooth. Drizzle over popped corn, stirring to mix and coat. When cool enough to handle, with lightly greased palms, shape mixture into a ball. Remove ball to large cookie sheet greased or lined with foil; shape with hands into a firm cone about 11 inches high. Spear two or more candies on each toothpick; insert in desired pattern, covering cone partially or totally, as you wish.

CANDY TREE is based, too, on a marshmallow-popcorn mixture, here shaped into a cone.

Santa Claus and Friends

*If children had their way, Santa wouldn't drive off after his stop on Christmas Eve. He'd stay for the whole holiday. Now, with your help, he can: on display with sleigh and reindeer . . . as a pillow or doll . . . perched on a gift package . . . peering down from a wall. He and Mrs. Claus make fine ornaments, too. See them (**and** an elf and a reindeer) among the **Cunning Little Creatures** in the tree-trimming section that opens the book.*

Star-shaped Santa Pillow

SIZE: About 15" square.

MATERIALS: ¼ yard 45"-wide red polka-dot fabric makes 2 pillows; scraps green print, yellow polka-dot, white and pink fabrics and blue felt; cotton or fiberfill stuffing.

Enlarge pattern, following instructions on page 189. Cut out pieces for front and back, adding ¼" seam allowance, with the following exceptions: Cut out mustache, mouth and beard for front as one piece, omitting seam allowance at upper and lower edges; cut out mouth, omitting seam allowance; cut out face, mustache, mouth and beard section as one piece from white for back, omitting seam allowance at lower edge.

Lap mustache over face allowance and beard over body allowance; machine-appliqué over raw edge with zigzag stitch. Outline mustache and machine-appliquéd mouth in the same manner. For back, lap and machine-appliqué lower edge of head piece to body.

Turn under long raw edges of all "fur" cuffs and topstitch to face and hat, to body and hands and to body and feet. Turn under long raw edges of belt and topstitch. Repeat with buckle. Cut out felt eyes and nose and blanket-stitch in place. Stitch "pom-pon" to hat.

With right sides facing, stitch front to back, leaving opening for turning. Turn right side out, stuff and sew opening closed.

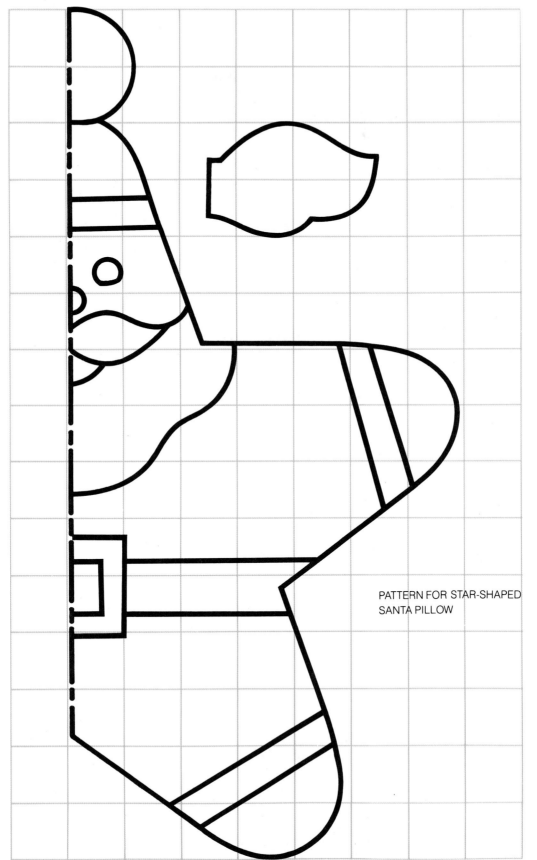

PATTERN FOR STAR-SHAPED
SANTA PILLOW

Santa, Sleigh and Reindeer

Note: Dimensions shown are finished sizes.

MATERIALS: 4½' of 1 x 10 clear pine, ¾" thick; saber or table saw; jig saw; drill; sandpaper; acrylic artist's paints for staining; fine-point felt-tip pen; wood glue; finishing nails; 6' of bead chain.

Follow dimensions to cut tongue and 5 crosspieces from clear pine. Following enlarged patterns (enlarging instructions, page 189); see also general directions below), cut out all other parts from pine with a jig saw. Drill holes in antlers and Santa's hand for bead chain. Sand all parts and round edges. Stain all pieces as in photograph (leave Santa's face unstained) with acrylic colors. Brush on liberally but neatly and wipe off immediately with paper towel. Draw in details with felt-tip pen.

Using glue and finishing nails, at-

tach Santa to center of crosspiece and assemble sleigh. Glue antlers to reindeer, and reindeer to tongue 2½" apart. Glue and nail tongue to sleigh.

String bead chain through antlers and Santa's hand.

General directions for working with wood: Enlarge patterns that require it, preferably onto oaktag or manila file-folder

paper. Lay out pattern part (or parts) and mark with pencil on the wood.

To cut: Several matching parts can be clamped together and cut as one with a jig saw; clamped matching parts can also be drilled at one time. Make straight cuts with saber or table saw.

To stain: Apply stain after sanding but before gluing.

Each sq. = 1"

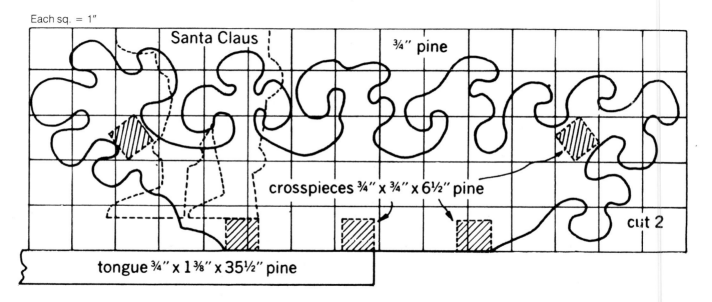

Santa Claus   ¾" pine

crosspieces ¾" x ¾" x 6½" pine

cut 2

tongue ¾" x 1⅜" x 35½" pine

Santa, Sleigh and Reindeer display is about 44″ long.

Each sq. = 1″

All patterns ¾″ pine

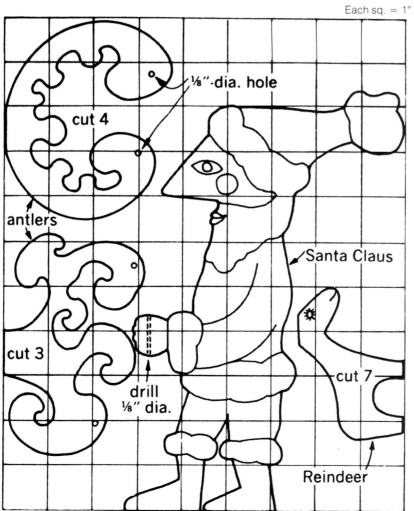

¼″-dia. hole

cut 4

antlers

cut 3

drill ⅛″ dia.

Santa Claus

cut 7

Reindeer

120

Quilted Wall Santa

MATERIALS: 1″ x 12″ x 20″ sheet of plastic foam; 1″-diameter plastic-foam ball; pencil; toothpicks; clear glue; straight pins; 12″ x 2¾″ piece of black velvet ribbon or fabric; 3 yards plaid ribbon or comparable amount of fabric scraps; ½ yard contrasting ribbon or comparable amount of fabric; cotton or fiber-fill stuffing; ornament for hat; small sharp knife; red and flesh-colored acrylic paints; scrap of red velvet ribbon or fabric; small piece of gold paper; chenille stem.

Enlarge pattern (enlarging instructions, page 189) and pin to plastic-foam sheet. Cut out basic Santa shape with knife. Round and smooth all edges with a scrap of the foam. Edges must be well-rounded to wrap materials smoothly and cover the foam for a finished look.

With pencil, press into foam to mark off inner shapes, following pattern. Cut ribbon or fabric swatches for various areas (see photograph), making them about ¼″ larger than the actual area to be covered (more at outer edges where excess will be pinned back—see below). Place a swatch on the foam and press edges down into lines marked with pencil, using a craft knife, seam ripper or table knife. (You might want to experiment until you find the tool that is most comfortable to work with.)

Place a second swatch next to the first and press edges into foam, using the groove where the swatches meet (the equivalent of a seam line). Continue until all foam is covered except the face area. Be sure no edges show. To finish, wrap the ribbon or fabric at outer edges around to the back of the shape and secure to foam with straight pins. Use contrasting ribbon or fabric to "quilt" the feet.

Paint the facial area with flesh-colored paint and let dry. Cut out the eyes from black velvet ribbon or fabric and glue to face. Cut out and glue on mouth of red velvet ribbon or fabric. Paint the foam ball with red acrylic paint; when dry, insert toothpick into it and press pick in position for nose.

Cut batting into 2″ strips and place around the ankles, arms, coat and hat for trim, securing strips with straight pins. Use 1″ strips of batting to shape a fluffy beard. Cut 1½″ strips of black velvet and glue to figure to form belt and trim. Cut belt buckle from square of gold paper and glue to belt. Attach an ornament to hat with a straight pin. To equip Santa for hanging, insert a chenille stem into the back of the figure.

Each sq. = 1″

PATTERN FOR QUILTED WALL SANTA

Large and small Yo-yo Santas. Instructions for crocheted tie (around box) are on page 66.

Yo-yo Santas

LARGE SANTAS

MATERIALS: 3 yards red and 1 yard green dotted-Swiss fabric; ½ yard flesh-colored fabric; ¼ yard white acrylic plush fabric; 2 small white pompons (from ball fringe); cotton or fiberfill stuffing; red and blue embroidery threads; green and red sewing threads; dressmaking shears.

To make yo-yos, see detail in illustration. Cut circles to required sizes; sew with running stitch and pull up as shown, then flatten to yo-yo shape. Set aside. Enlarge patterns (see diagrams on grid), following instructions on page 189, and cut hand and foot parts. Stitch pairs, with right sides facing, as indicated by dotted lines; turn and stuff. Set aside. Join body yo-yos in sequence given.

Cut circle for head; insert ball of stuffing and gather open end with running stitches. Embroider blue eyes and red nose and mouth as shown in diagram. Stitch head to body top. Join arm yo-yos as shown and stitch to body. Sew hands to ends of arms. Join leg yo-yos and attach to bottom of body. Join feet to bottom of legs.

Cut fabric hat as shown; with right sides facing, sew in cone shape; leave bottom open and turn right side out. Sew on two pompons (glued together) at tip. Sew hat to head. Cut beard and hatband from plush. Stitch beard in place. Cover bottom of hat with hatband; sew in place.

SMALL SANTAS

MATERIALS: ½ yard red and ¼ yard green dotted-Swiss fabric; white cotton pompons (cut from ball fringe); ¾"-diameter and 1"-diameter wooden beads; per Santa, 8" of ¼"-wide grosgrain ribbon; felt-tip markers; fabric glue; cotton or fiberfill stuffing; matching sewing thread; dressmaking shears.

See detail in Large Santa diagram to make yo-yos. For smallest ornament, make 6 red and 1 green yo-yos, all about 2" in diameter. For larger ornament, make same number and color but all about 4" in diameter. Stack yo-yos with green in center; stitch together. Sew small bead to top of small yo-yos, large bead to larger yo-yos. Mark a face on bead; glue on a stuffing beard, following photograph. Make hat, following directions for Large Santa's hat but using 2½"-diameter and 5"-diameter half-circles respectively. Fold under raw edge; stitch in place, then glue hat on head. Make hanging loop of 8" ribbon and sew or glue in place at back of head.

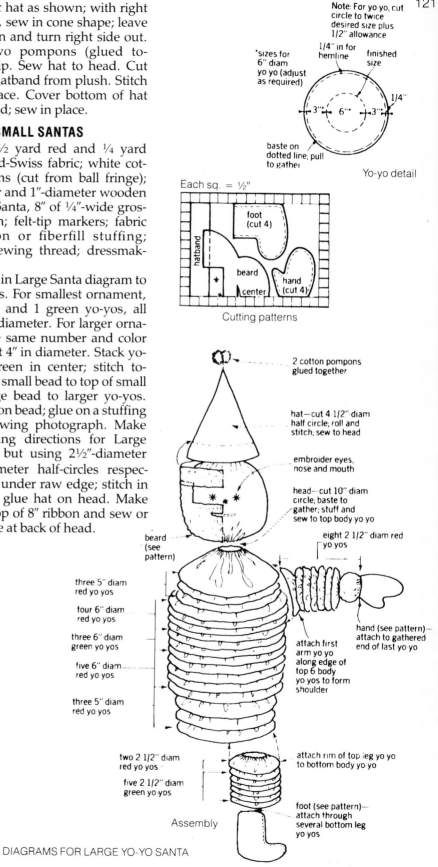

121

Note: For yo-yo, cut circle to twice desired size plus ½" allowance

Yo-yo detail

Each sq. = ½"

foot (cut 4)
hatband
beard center
hand (cut 4)

Cutting patterns

2 cotton pompons glued together

hat—cut 4 1/2" diam half circle; roll and stitch; sew to head

embroider eyes, nose and mouth

head—cut 10" diam circle; baste to gather; stuff and sew to top body yo yo

eight 2 1/2" diam red yo yos

attach first arm yo yo along edge of top 6 body yo yos to form shoulder

hand (see pattern)—attach to gathered end of last yo yo

beard (see pattern)

three 5" diam red yo yos
four 6" diam red yo yos
three 6" diam green yo yos
five 6" diam red yo yos
three 5" diam red yo yos

two 2 1/2" diam red yo yos
five 2 1/2" diam green yo yos

attach rim of top leg yo yo to bottom body yo yo

foot (see pattern)—attach through several bottom leg yo yos

Assembly

DIAGRAMS FOR LARGE YO-YO SANTA

Santa Stocking Doll

Santa Stocking Doll

MATERIALS: 4-ply knitting-worsted-weight yarn: 3½ ounces each white and red, 1 ounce black; 1" x 15" piece black felt for belt; sharp-pointed large-eyed needle; nylon stocking; tan thread for sewing; cotton or fiberfill stuffing; waterproof red and black felt-tip markers.

Cutting nylon stocking: Following inch measurements on cutting diagram, and making cuts on stocking only where indicated by broken lines, cut out parts of doll.

Assembling and stuffing: With running stitches, stitch nylon piece for head at one end as shown in diagram and draw this end closed (Fig. 1); then stuff head and shape piece to measure about 5" across and 5" high. With running stitches, draw other end of head closed (Figs. 2 and 3). Cut a 1½" square of nylon for nose and with running stitches gather outer edges together and stuff before closing entirely—see diagram. Sew to head. Stuff and sew body same way as for head, shaping piece to measure about 8" x 6". Following diagrams, sew and stuff arms to measure about 7" long by 1¾" across, legs 7" long by 2" across. Sew and stuff a scrap piece of nylon into a triangular shape for hat to measure about 4" high and 3½" across base. Then, using sharp-pointed needle and red yarn, take short stitches in nylon, leaving ½" loops all over parts of the body where red is shown on photo. With white yarn, sew loops on wrists, leaving part of the nylon uncovered at the ends of arms for hands. Sew black loops on lower part of leg for boots; sew white loops above boots for 1". Sew ½" white loops to head for hair, continuing to make loops around face for beard, lengthening the loops to about 1½" around chin. Sew red loops on hat. With black marker, draw features on face; tint cheeks and mouth with red marker. Color nose red. Make white yarn mustache and eyebrows as shown. Sew arms, legs and head to body. Sew on hat.

Belt: Place 1" x 15" piece of black felt around center of body and sew short ends together at back.

Pompons (make 3): Cut two cardboard circles each 1½" in diameter. Cut a hole ¾" in diameter in center of each circle. Cut three strands of white yarn each 3 yards long. Thread the strands into large-eyed yarn needle and double over. Placing cardboard circles together, draw yarn through center opening and over edge until yarn is used up. Slit yarn around outer edge between the circles. Double a ½-yard yarn length and slip between the circles. Tie securely around strands, knotting ends. Remove cardboard and trim pompon evenly. Sew two pompons to front of body and the third to top of hat as shown.

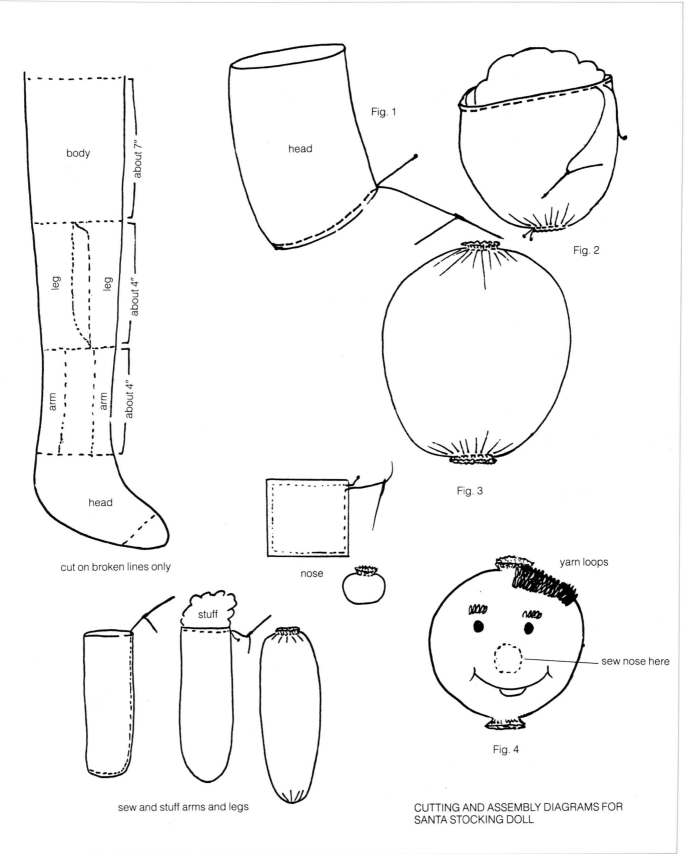

body

about 7"

leg leg

arm arm

about 4"

about 4"

head

cut on broken lines only

head

Fig. 1

Fig. 2

Fig. 3

nose

sew and stuff arms and legs

stuff

yarn loops

sew nose here

Fig. 4

CUTTING AND ASSEMBLY DIAGRAMS FOR
SANTA STOCKING DOLL

Elf Stocking Doll

Elf Stocking Doll

MATERIALS: 4-ply knitting-worsted-weight yarn, 3½ ounces emerald, and Persian-type needlepoint-and-crewel yarn, 2 (12-yard) pull skeins copper; small piece brown felt for shoes; 16 pink purchased pompons 1½" in diameter (or make pompons, following instructions on page 189); 1½ yards 1"-wide pink satin ribbon; nylon stocking; tan thread for sewing; cotton or fiberfill stuffing; sharp-pointed large-eyed needle; waterproof red and black felt-tip markers; white glue.

Cutting nylon stocking: Following the inch measurements on diagram and making cuts in stocking only where indicated by broken lines, cut out parts of doll.

Assembling and stuffing: With running stitches, stitch nylon piece for head at one end as shown in diagram (Fig. 1). Draw this end closed; then stuff head (Fig. 2) to measure about the size of a baseball. With running stitches, draw other end of head closed and secure ends; stitch a small circle in the nylon head piece and gather stitches together to form nose (Fig.3). Stuff and sew body as for head, shaping piece to measure 4" across and 6" high. Following diagrams, sew and stuff arms to measure 6" long by 1" across and legs 5" long by 1½" across. Stuff and sew a scrap piece of nylon into a triangular shape for hat to measure about 3½" high and 3" across base. Then, using sharp-pointed needle and emerald yarn, take short stitches in the nylon, leaving ½" loops all over body and hat; make same loops on arms and legs, leaving 1" of the nylon uncovered for hands and feet. With black marker, draw features on face, then tint cheeks and nose with red marker (Fig. 4). With copper yarn, work ½" yarn loops on head (Fig. 5). Sew arms, legs and head to body.

From brown felt, cut two shoes (see diagram). Fold in half on fold line, having pointed ends meet. Sew seam along dotted line. Fit shoes on feet of doll and sew one to each foot around the upper edge.

Ruffles: Cut two 7" lengths of pink ribbon for ankles and two 5" lengths for wrists. Work a running stitch down center of ribbons lengthwise and gather to form a ruffle. Sew ruffles in place around ankles and wrists. Cut two 15" lengths of ribbon for neck. Holding the two lengths together, work a running stitch through both thicknesses along one long edge; gather as above to form ruffle and sew in place around neck.

Sew hat in place on top of head as shown. Glue five pompons down center front of body; glue eight pompons around base of hat and one to tip; glue a pompon to the point of each of the shoes.

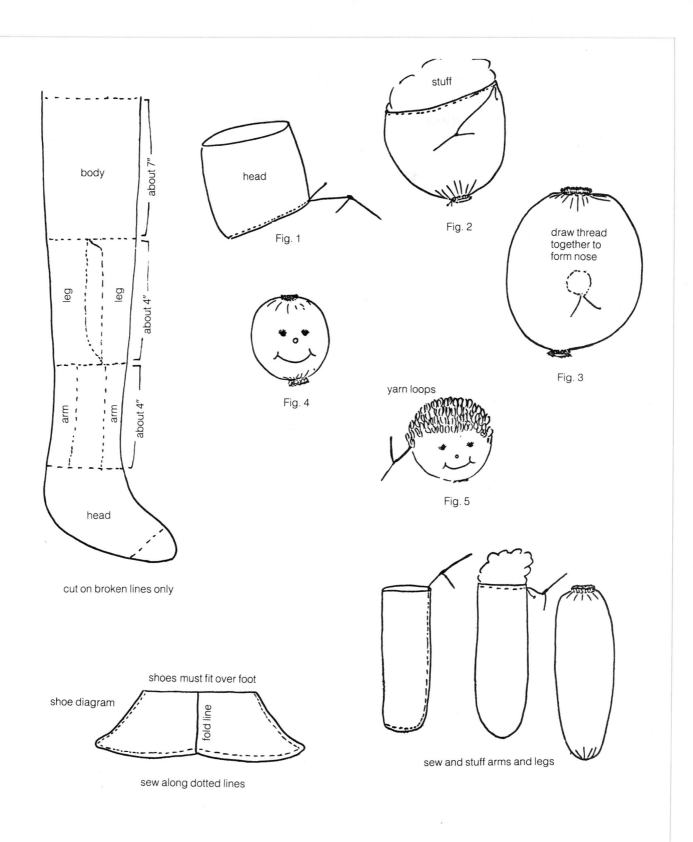

body

about 7"

leg   leg   about 4"

arm   arm   about 4"

head

cut on broken lines only

head

Fig. 1

stuff

Fig. 2

draw thread together to form nose

Fig. 3

Fig. 4

yarn loops

Fig. 5

shoe diagram   shoes must fit over foot

fold line

sew along dotted lines

sew and stuff arms and legs

CUTTING AND ASSEMBLY DIAGRAMS
FOR ELF STOCKING DOLL

HAPPY HO-HO'S. Note three separate versions—left, center and right.

Happy Ho-ho's

MATERIALS (for one): ¼ yard 36" velour or other red fabric; scraps of white and pink felt, white yarn, black and red embroidery floss; cotton or fiberfill stuffing; cardboard.

Left Ho-ho: Enlarge six patterns, including mustache from center Ho-ho (enlarging instructions, page 189). Cut red front and two backs, adding ¼" seam allowances and reversing backs when fabric has right and wrong sides. With right sides together and matching X and Y edges, stitch backs to front; stitch center back seams; leave opening at bottom for turning. Turn, stuff very firmly and slipstitch opening. Cut and sew on pink face. Cut white beard, mustache and 1½" x 9½" cap band. Sew on beard, then cap band, folding band lengthwise and trimming any excess. Satin-stitch yarn over beard and band. Sew on mustache and satin-stitch with yarn. Using floss, outline-stitch eyes; satin-stitch nose and mouth. Make a 1" pompon (instructions, page 189), and sew to cap.

Center Ho-ho: Enlarge five patterns, including face from left Ho-ho. Cut two red fronts and two red backs. Stitch center seams of fronts and backs, reversing one of each when fabric has right and wrong sides. Seam at sides X, leaving bottom open. Turn; stuff very firmly. Cover a 1⅜"-diameter cardboard disk with fabric; sew to bottom opening. Complete same as first Ho-ho.

Right Ho-ho: Enlarge seven patterns, including face and mustache from other Ho-hos; cut two red fronts and two red backs. Assemble same as center Ho-ho except match arm edges X. Sew fabric-covered cardboard disk to bottom and complete same as others.

Each sq. = 1"

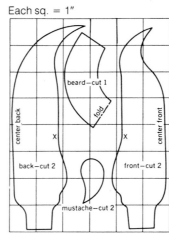

center Ho-ho

Each sq. = 1"

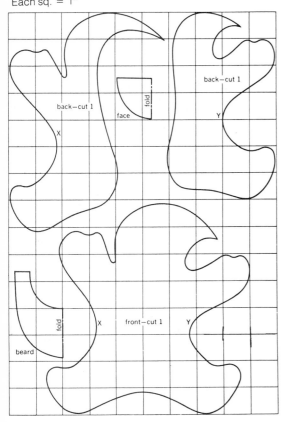

left Ho-ho

right Ho-ho

Each sq. = 1"

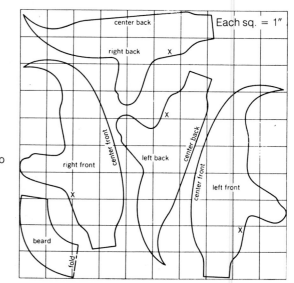

Coffee-can Santa Card Holder

Coffee-can Santa Card Holder

MATERIALS: 2-pound coffee can; white Bristol board; red, pink, white, blue and black felt; green and white yarn; white glue.

Cut top and bottom from can. Wrap with alternating green and white yarn. From Bristol board cut an 18"-diameter circle. Cut slit from edge to center and shape into cone; cut slits around edge. Glue slit edge into can. Trim with 2" width of red felt. Enlarge hand and face patterns (following instructions on page 189). Cut out felt pieces and glue on. Make conical hat from half of a 7"-diameter circle of red felt and glue in place. Trim with felt and yarn as shown. Make pompon of mixed yarns (instructions, page 189); glue to hat.

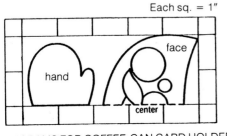

Each sq. = 1"

DIAGRAMS FOR COFFEE-CAN CARD HOLDER

Shoebox Santa Card Holder

SIZE: 12¼" tall.

MATERIALS: Shoebox about 6" wide; lightweight cardboard; scraps red, white, light and dark green, dark brown, gold, peach and blue felt; ¼ yard green polka-dot fabric; scraps red polka-dot fabric and white baby rickrack; small white purchased pompon (or make your own using directions on page 189); masking tape; white glue and spray adhesive.

Cut box in two parts 4¼" from one end; use only smaller part. From box top, cut 4¾" piece; tape to box section to form fourth side. Upend box so that open end becomes top. Cut green fabric to fit around box. Spray with adhesive and wrap around box. Glue rickrack around edges.

Enlarge Shoebox Santa pattern, following instructions on page 189. Trace shape on cardboard and cut out. Cut separate inner pieces of pattern from felt and fabric, following photograph (broken lines indicate underlap on sleeves). Using spray adhesive for large pieces and white glue for small, apply pieces to cardboard shape. Glue to box.

Each sq. = 1"

DIAGRAMS FOR SHOEBOX CARD HOLDER

Shoebox Santa Card Holder

FOODS AT THEIR MOST FESTIVE

*Christmas is a time for giving, for sharing, for generous personal gestures. And nothing beats foods, with their warmth and individuality, for expressing that outgoing spirit. There's thoughtfulness in the very name **Make-aheads for Holiday Giving,** and abundant variety among the foods: preserves and pickles, candies and confections, baked goods, even gifts for dedicated gourmet cooks. You'll find rich rewards for everyone in **Best of the Season's Baking,** which begins with breads, cakes and pastries and ends merrily with a Christmas Cookie Spree featuring cookie recipes of every conceivable kind. **Easy-does-it Party Foods** helps lavishly with entertaining, contributing ideas for patés, dips and spreads, hors d'oeuvres hot and cold, and, to go with them, all sorts of breads and crackers and some sensational holiday beverages.*

Make-aheads for Holiday Giving

Get an early start on presents from your kitchen and you can have a gift for everyone on your list—without ever going near a crowded store! First make up the list, then go through the recipes deciding who is to get what. Choose those that best fit your schedule, skills and budget, and of course individual tastes. You'll have no trouble—the selection is more than ample.

PICKLED VEGETABLES

SICHUAN CUCUMBERS

4   **medium cucumbers (2½ pounds)**
1   **tablespoon salt**
1   **teaspoon black peppercorns**
½   **teaspoon crushed red pepper**
2   **tablespoons oil, preferably peanut**
1   **tablespoon white vinegar**
1   **tablespoon sugar**
2   **large cloves garlic, crushed**

Wash cucumbers; scrape lightly to remove wax. Halve lengthwise; with teaspoon scoop out seeds. Cut in ¼"-thick slices. Place in bowl; sprinkle with salt; toss well and let stand at room temperature 2 hours. Meanwhile heat peppercorns in small skillet until they release a fragrant aroma. Remove from heat; cool, then crush and mix with red pepper, oil, vinegar, sugar and garlic. In colander or sieve, drain cucumbers well, squeezing lightly to release water. Return to bowl; add sauce mixture. Toss well. Pack into jars; cover and let stand at room temperature at least 3 hours. Chill. Makes 4½ pints (9 cups).

HOT ONION PICKLES
(shown on page 134)

2   **cups white vinegar**
½   **cup sugar**
1   **tablespoon mustard seed**
1   **tablespoon prepared horseradish**
2   **large bay leaves, crushed (1 teaspoon)**
¼   **teaspoon crushed red pepper**
4   **to 6 medium onions, preferably red, sliced ¼" thick and separated into rings (4 cups)**

In large saucepan, bring to boil all ingredients except onions, stirring to dissolve sugar. Simmer 5 minutes. Stir in onions. Bring just to boil, stirring gently (do not cook). Pour into bowl. Cover; refrigerate 2 days, stirring occasionally. Makes about 3 cups. Will keep refrigerated about 2 months.

SWEET ONION PICKLES

Simmer as above 1 cup each sugar and cider vinegar, ½ cup dill-pickle brine or water and 1½ teaspoons whole mixed pickling spices. Add onions and continue as above.

ALL WINNERS AS GIFTS, and a sampling of good things to come. **Clockwise from top:** Lemon-molasses Cookies on tree, page 162. Trail Snack Mix, page 183; Prune Liqueur with Tipsy Prunes, page 140; Individual Fruitcakes, page 149; Salad-dressing Mix, page 136; Quick Stollen, page 145; Low-calorie Cheese Spread, page 178; Chocolate-pecan Fudge, page 142; Orange-flavored Vinegar, page 136; Fennel Loops, page 182; Gingersnaps (in box), page 160; Pickled Herring, Swedish-style, page 180; **In center:** Whole-wheat and Oatmeal Crackers, page 183; Apricot-rhubarb Jam, page 137.

ONIONS MONEGASQUE
(shown in photograph on pages 138-139)

⅛ teaspoon crumbled saffron threads

1 tablespoon hot water

1 pound small white onions (about 2 dozen)

Water

⅓ cup each dry white wine and cider vinegar

¼ cup oil, preferably olive

2 cups water

1 teaspoon salt

½ teaspoon pepper

⅛ teaspoon ground turmeric

1 small bay leaf

1 tablespoon tomato paste

½ cup golden raisins

Soak saffron in hot water; set aside. To peel onions easily, place in large saucepan with water to cover; bring to boil. Drain, then rinse immediately with cold water; slip off skins. In large skillet combine wine, vinegar, oil, 2 cups water, salt, pepper, reserved saffron and liquid, turmeric and bay leaf; add onions; bring to boil; cover and simmer about 10 minutes, or until onions are just crisp-tender. Blend in tomato paste and raisins. Simmer 5 minutes, or until raisins are puffed. Cool in the liquid. Remove bay leaf. Spoon with liquid into gift jars; refrigerate. Makes about 4 cups.

MARINATED GREEN PEPPERS
(shown on page 134)

1 cup each oil, water and white-wine vinegar

1 tablespoon each salt and sugar

1½ teaspoons mustard seed

½ teaspoon celery seed

3 large cloves garlic, sliced thin

6 medium (about 2 pounds) green peppers, seeded and cut in ¾" strips (6 cups)

2 medium onions, sliced very thin and separated into rings (1⅓ cups)

In large saucepan, bring oil, water, vinegar, salt, sugar, mustard and celery seed, and garlic to boil. Add peppers. Return to boil; boil gently 2 minutes, or just until peppers are crisp-tender. Remove from heat; stir in onions. Spoon into small hot sterilized jars. Cover airtight and refrigerate at least 1 week before serving. Will keep in refrigerator several months. Makes about 6 cups.

FRUIT CHUTNEYS AND PICKLED FRUITS

CRANBERRY-PEACH CHUTNEY

2 cans (29 ounces each) peaches, drained and chopped (4 cups)

2 cups (8 ounces) cranberries

1½ cups cider vinegar

1 cup raisins

1 cup chopped onion (1 large)

1 cup packed brown sugar

½ cup chopped almonds

2 teaspoons each salt and curry powder

1 teaspoon cinnamon

½ teaspoon ground cloves

½ teaspoon ground ginger

8 small hot peppers or 1 teaspoon crushed red pepper (optional)

In large saucepan, combine all ingredients except peppers. Over medium heat, bring to boil, stirring often. Reduce heat, cover and simmer, stirring occasionally, 30 minutes. Ladle hot mixture into hot sterilized jars to within ¼" of top. Add a pepper to each (⅛ teaspoon crushed red pepper). Seal and process in boiling-water bath 10 minutes. Cool on rack. Makes 8 cups.

HOT MINCEMEAT CHUTNEY

1⅓ cups prepared mincemeat (half a 28-ounce jar)

¼ cup minced onion

¼ cup chopped green pepper

1 teaspoon hot-pepper sauce

Mix all ingredients well. Spoon into sterilized jars. Cover and chill. Makes 1⅔ cups.

RELISHES

CRANBERRY CATSUP

- 1 bag (16 ounces) cranberries, chopped fine or ground
- 1¾ cups sugar
- ⅓ cup cider vinegar
- 1½ teaspoons cinnamon
- ¾ teaspoon each allspice and pepper
- ½ teaspoon salt

In medium saucepan, stirring occasionally, bring all ingredients to boil. Reduce heat; simmer uncovered, stirring, 5 minutes, or until mixture is thick. Cool slightly; store covered. Will keep refrigerated several weeks. Makes 3 cups.

PICKLED PEARS

- 2 tablespoons mixed pickling spice
- 2 cinnamon sticks, each about 4" long
- 3 cups sugar
- 2½ cups water
- 1½ cups white vinegar
- 12 firm ripe Seckel pears (about 3 pounds), peeled
- 4 thin slices lemon

Tie pickling spice in cheesecloth bag. In large saucepan or Dutch oven, combine spice bag, cinnamon sticks, sugar, water and vinegar. Bring to boil, reduce heat and simmer 10 minutes. Add pears and lemon slices and simmer gently about 10 minutes, or until just tender. Discard spice bag and cinnamon sticks. Carefully remove pears and pack in hot sterilized jars, leaving ¼" headspace. Heat syrup to boiling. Pour over pears, leaving ¼" headspace. Seal. Process 15 minutes in boiling-water bath. Store at least 1 week before serving.

ZUCCHINI RELISH WITH MINT

- ½ cup oil
- 5 medium zucchini (2½ pounds), cut in ¼"-thick slices (9 cups)
- 4 to 5 cloves garlic, halved
- 2 tablespoons red-wine vinegar
- ¾ teaspoon salt
- ⅛ teaspoon pepper
- 2 tablespoons dried or 3 tablespoons minced fresh mint

Heat oil in heavy skillet; quickly fry zucchini a small amount at a time until just tender and light brown. With slotted spoon, remove to bowl, sprinkling each layer with a few pieces of garlic, some vinegar, salt, pepper and mint. Toss lightly. Cover bowl. Let stand at room temperature or in refrigerator several hours for flavors to blend. Discard garlic before serving. Will keep refrigerated up to 2 weeks. Makes about 3 cups. **Note:** For milder flavor, remove garlic after shorter period.

BEAN-CORN RELISH

(shown in photograph on pages 138-139)

- 2 medium onions, sliced (1 cup)
- 1 medium-size sweet red pepper, quartered, seeded and cut crosswise in ¼" strips
  Boiling water
- 2 cups white vinegar
- ½ cup sugar
- 2 teaspoons coarse salt
- 1 teaspoon dry mustard
- 1 teaspoon each mustard and celery seed
- ¼ teaspoon hot-pepper sauce
- 1 can (16 ounces) red kidney beans, well drained
- 1 can (12 ounces) whole-kernel corn, drained

Add onions and red pepper to boiling water; cook 2 minutes. Drain; rinse in cold running water; set aside. In 4-quart Dutch oven or saucepot over medium heat, bring vinegar, sugar, salt, mustard, mustard and celery seed, and pepper sauce to boil. Reduce heat and simmer 3 minutes. Add beans, corn and onion-pepper mixture. Bring to boil; reduce heat and simmer 3 minutes. Ladle hot into 3 hot sterilized 1-pint jars. Pour boiling liquid into jars to cover vegetables, leaving ¼" headspace. Remove air bubbles; clean edges of jars and seal. Process in boiling-water bath 5 minutes. Cool on wire rack or folded towel. Store in cool dry place at least 1 week before serving. Serve chilled. Makes three 1-pint jars (6 cups).

SPICED PLUM RELISH OR SAUCE

- 1 **jar (12 ounces) plum preserves (1 cup)**
- ⅓ **cup dry white wine**
- 1 **tablespoon grated orange peel**
- 2 **tablespoons orange juice**
- 1 **teaspoon ginger**
- ½ **teaspoon cinnamon**
- ⅛ **teaspoon cloves**

Stir all ingredients together until well blended and smooth. Pour into sterilized jars; cover tightly and store in refrigerator. Makes 1½ cups.

SWEET TOMATO RELISH

- 2 **cans (16 ounces each) stewed tomatoes, broken up**
- 1 **jar (15 ounces) applesauce**
- 2½ **cups sugar**
- ¼ **teaspoon cinnamon**
- 2 **tablespoons grated orange peel**
- ¾ **cup orange juice**

In large heavy saucepan, combine all ingredients. Stir over medium heat until sugar dissolves. Bring to boil; reduce heat and simmer, stirring often, until thick (about 216° on candy thermometer). Spoon into hot sterilized jars. Seal and process in boiling-water bath 10 minutes. Cool on rack. Makes about 4 cups.

GENEROUS OFFERINGS, four for giving, two for parties. **Lined up in back, foods to put by for gifts:** Seasoned Amandine Topping, page 136; Corn Relish, page 135; Hot Onion Pickles, page 130; Marinated Green Peppers, page 132. **Up-front party specialties:** Italian Antipasto, page 180, and Carrot Paté, page 178.

CORN RELISH
(shown at left)

- 3 cups finely shredded cabbage
- 1 tablespoon salt
- 1 cup each sugar and cider vinegar
- 2 tablespoons mustard seed
- 1 tablespoon flour
- 1 teaspoon turmeric
- 1 medium onion, minced (½ cup)
- 1 jar (5 ounces) pimiento, drained and chopped
- 2 cans (12 ounces each) whole-kernel corn, drained

Spinkle cabbage with salt; let stand 1 hour. Drain well. In saucepan, blend sugar, vinegar, mustard seed, flour and turmeric. Bring to boil, stirring. Stir in cabbage, onion and pimiento. Reheat to boiling. Remove from heat. Stir in corn. Spoon into hot sterilized jars. Cover and refrigerate. Will keep refrigerated several months. Makes about 6 cups.

GIFTS FOR GOURMETS

BASIC TOMATO SAUCE

- ⅔ cup chopped onion
- 3 large cloves garlic, halved
- ½ cup oil, preferably olive
- 3 cans (16 ounces each) tomatoes, broken up
- 1 can (29 ounces) tomato purée
- 1½ tablespoons mixed Italian herbs
- 1 tablespoon salt
- 1 teaspoon pepper
- 1 tomato can of water (16-ounce size from tomatoes above)
- 16-ounce tomato can of water
- 1½ teaspoons sugar

In large Dutch oven or saucepot, sauté onion and garlic in hot oil 5 minutes, or until onion is tender and golden. Add remaining ingredients; stir to blend. Bring to boil over moderate heat; reduce heat and, stirring occasionally, simmer 1½ hours, or until thick. Discard garlic. Makes 8 cups. **To can:** Ladle hot into clean hot jars, leaving 1" headspace. Process in boiling-water bath 45 minutes for pints and half-pints. **To freeze:** Ladle into freezer containers, leaving 1½" headspace. Seal and freeze.

PARSLEY PESTO
(shown in photograph on pages 138-139)

- 1¼ cups oil, preferably olive, divided
- 2 cups packed parsley leaves, preferably flat leaf, thick stems removed, divided
- ¼ teaspoon peppercorns
- ⅔ cup shelled walnuts
- ½ cup grated Romano or Parmesan cheese
- 4 large cloves garlic
- ½ teaspoon salt

In blender or food processor, whirl ½ cup oil, 1 cup parsley and the peppercorns until smooth. Add walnuts, cheese, garlic and salt; whirl until blended. Add remaining 1 cup parsley gradually and alternately with ½ cup oil; whirl until smooth. Pour into 2 clean half-pint jars; spoon 2 tablespoons oil over top of each to preserve color and flavor. Can be refrigerated, covered tightly, up to 1 month. Bring to room temperature before serving. Makes 2 cups. **To freeze:** Pour into freezer containers, leaving 1" headspace; seal and freeze. **Note:** To prepare by hand, with knife chop parsley, nuts and garlic fine. Mix with remaining ingredients, substituting ¼ teaspoon fresh-ground pepper for peppercorns.

ENGLISH MINT SAUCE
(shown in photograph on pages 138-139)

2 tablespoons hot water

1 teaspoon sugar

1 jar (12 ounces) dried mint flakes, crushed (5 tablespoons)

¼ cup cider vinegar

Dash of salt

Stir water and sugar together until sugar dissolves. Stir in remaining ingredients. Store covered in cool place. Makes ½ cup.

SEASONING PACKETS

½ cup dried parsley flakes

¼ cup each dehydrated onions and freeze-dried chopped chives

¼ cup thyme

2 tablespoons marjoram

1 tablespoon whole cloves

1 teaspoon black or white peppercorns

6 small bay leaves, broken

Mix all ingredients well. Cut double layers of cheesecloth into twelve 6" squares. Place 2 tablespoons seasoning mixture in center of each square. Bring up sides of cheesecloth and tie tightly with colorfast string. Pack in airtight container and store in cool, dry place. Use as bouquet garni when cooking soups, broths, stews, poached fish, etc. Each packet will season about 2 quarts liquid. Makes 12.

SEASONED AMANDINE TOPPING
(shown on page 134)

2 tablespoons butter or margarine

1 package (6 ounces) sliced almonds (2 cups)

½ teaspoon seasoning blend (salt, pepper, onion and garlic powders), or season to taste

Melt butter in roasting pan while preheating oven to 325°F. Add almonds and seasoning blend; stir to mix. Toast, stirring 3 times, 15 minutes, or until golden brown. Cool, then pack airtight and store in cool, dry place. Sprinkle over cooked fish or vegetables. Makes about 2 cups.

SALAD-DRESSING MIX
(shown on page 131)

½ cup dried parsley flakes

¼ cup freeze-dried chopped chives

1 tablespoon dillweed

¼ teaspoon salt

⅛ teaspoon pepper

Mix all ingredients well. Pour into spice jars or make packets, wrapping 2 tablespoons mix in plastic wrap or small plastic bags. To use as dressing, combine 2 tablespoons mix with 1 cup plain yogurt or sour cream. For use as dip, mix with smaller quantities same ingredients. Chill at least 2 hours for either use. Makes about 1 cup dressing, ½ to ¾ cup dip.

ORANGE-FLAVORED VINEGAR
(shown above)

1 cup each white vinegar and dry vermouth

Peel from 1 medium orange, cut in thin strips (orange part only)

Combine all ingredients in 2½-cup jar or bottle. Cover tightly and let stand at room temperature 10 days, shaking occasionally. Combine with oil for salad dressing or use instead of lemon juice as a complement to fish or chicken. Makes 2 cups.

JAMS, CONDIMENTS, TOPPINGS

CANDIED CRANBERRIES
(shown in photograph on pages 138-139)

1 cup sugar
⅛ teaspoon each salt and baking soda
⅓ cup water
2 cups fresh or frozen cranberries

In 3-quart saucepan, combine sugar, salt, baking soda and water. Cook, stirring, until sugar is dissolved. Add cranberries and simmer about 5 minutes, or until cranberries are tender but still hold their shape (watch carefully). Cover and cool at room temperature. Put in 2 sterilized screw-top ½-pint jars; divide syrup evenly between jars; seal. Store in refrigerator. Makes 2 cups.

CARROT-ORANGE DESSERT TOPPING

1 tablespoon grated orange peel
2 tablespoons grated lemon peel
4 cups water, divided
3 cups shredded carrots (3 large)
⅔ cup orange juice
3 tablespoons lemon juice
4 cups sugar
⅛ teaspoon salt

In 3-quart saucepan, cook orange and lemon peels in 2 cups water 15 minutes. Add carrots and remaining 2 cups water. Cook 10 to 15 minutes, or until carrots are barely tender. Add orange and lemon juices, sugar and salt. Boil until syrup reaches 220° on candy thermometer. Pour into hot sterilized jars, leaving ¼" headspace. Seal jars and process in simmering-water bath 10 minutes. Makes 4½ cups.

PEACH-ORANGE CONSERVE
(shown in photograph on pages 138-139)

1 medium orange
1 medium lemon
2 cans (16 ounces each) sliced peaches or whole peeled apricots, well drained
1½ cups sugar
1½ cups orange juice
Juice from lemon
⅓ cup slivered or chopped almonds or other nuts

With vegetable peeler, cut five 3" x 1" strips peel from both orange and lemon. Place on top of each other and cut crosswise into ⅛"-wide strips. In 3-quart heavy saucepan, combine peaches, sugar, orange juice, juice from lemon (3 tablespoons) and 2 tablespoons mixed peel strips. Bring to boil and, stirring often, cook rather briskly 20 to 25 minutes, or until thickened. Stir in almonds. Spoon into 3 sterilized ½-pint jars; seal with ¼"-thick layer melted paraffin. Store in cool dark place. Makes about 3 cups.

FIG BUTTER

1 package (12 ounces) dried figs, preferably small dark type, stems removed
3 cups water
1 small lemon, sliced thin
¾ cup packed brown sugar

In 3-quart heavy saucepan over medium heat, bring figs, water and lemon to boil. Reduce heat, cover and simmer 30 minutes, or until figs are tender. Remove from heat; cool slightly. Pour mixture into food processor and process until smooth; or purée half at a time in blender or with food mill. Return mixture to saucepan; add sugar and stir over low heat about 10 minutes, or until of spreading consistency. Spoon into 3 sterilized ½-pint jars. Seal with ¼"-thick layer melted paraffin. Store in cool dark place. Makes 3 cups.

APRICOT-RHUBARB JAM
(shown on page 131)

8 ounces (1½ cups) dried apricots
1½ cups water
4 cups frozen cut rhubarb (1 pound)
Peel of 1 large lemon, cut in julienne strips
3 cups sugar

In heavy 3-quart saucepan over medium heat, bring apricots and water to boil. Cover and simmer about 20 minutes, or until tender. Drain if any liquid remains. Add rhubarb, peel and sugar; heat, stirring, to simmering. Cook over low heat, stirring often, about 40 minutes, or until mixture has thickened (will thicken even more after cooling). Ladle into hot sterilized jars; seal. Refrigerate. Makes 4 cups.

SHARE THE BOUNTY OF THE SEASON with those you love. **On the windowsill, left to right:** Onions Monegasque, page 132; Bean-corn Relish, page 133; Candied Cranberries, page 137; Spiced Cranberry Glögg, page 188; Raisin Topping, page 140. **Below window, on green platform, left to right:** Mulled Wine Mix (with bottle of wine), page 188; Spiced Cider, page 188; Blueberry Liqueur, page 188; Old-fashioned Pomanders (hanging), page 28; Brandied Figs, page 140; Crocked Fruitcakes, page 149; Blueberry Syrup, page 140; Peach-orange Conserve, page 137; Parsley Pesto, page 135; Herbed Feta-cheese Cubes, page 180. **In the foreground, clockwise from the wall:** Holiday Coffee Wreath (hanging), page 147; Pull-apart Parmesan-garlic Bubble Loaf (against wall), page 182; Raisin Brioches (in basket), page 146; English Mint Sauce, page 136; Fruitcake Layered with Almond Paste, page 149; Pecan Rusks, page 157; Old-time Steamed Prune Bread, page 148; Quick-mix Panet-tone, page 146; Crisp Rye Crackers, page 183; Olive-cheese Pastry Wheels, page 186; Cheese "Apples," page 179; Ham-chicken Spread, page 179; Truffles, page 142; Sesame Crunch, page 142; Parmesan Rounds, page 183.

PRUNE LIQUEUR WITH TIPSY PRUNES
(shown on page 131)

1 cup packed dark-brown sugar
2 teaspoons vanilla
3 cups vodka
1 package (16 ounces) unpitted prunes

In 6-cup glass jar, stir together brown sugar, vanilla and vodka. Add prunes; cover tightly and store in dark place at room temperature at least 7 weeks, shaking jar once a week. Drain off liqueur and pour into decanter. Serve prunes separately as dessert with walnuts or ice cream. Makes 3 cups liqueur and about 67 flavored prunes.

BRANDIED FIGS
(shown in photograph on pages 138-139)

1 package (12 ounces) dried figs
1½ cups water
½ cup brandy
¼ cup packed brown sugar
Peel from 1 small lemon, cut in thin strips
3 tablespoons lemon juice

In heavy saucepan, combine figs, water and brandy. Bring to boil; reduce heat, cover and simmer 30 minutes, or until figs are tender and almost doubled in size. Add sugar and peel. Simmer 5 minutes, or until sugar is completely dissolved. Stir in lemon juice. Pour into hot sterilized pint glass jar with tight-fitting lid. Store in cool place. Makes about 2 cups.

BLUEBERRY SYRUP
(shown in photograph on pages 138-139)

1 quart (4 cups) fresh or frozen blueberries
½ cup water
1 teaspoon cinnamon
1 teaspoon whole cloves
Peel from 1 small lemon, cut in strips
2 cups sugar

In 3-quart heavy covered saucepan, simmer blueberries, water, cinnamon, cloves and peel 25 minutes. Strain through very fine sieve or several layers cheesecloth. Pour about 1¼ cups liquid into saucepan. Add sugar and, stirring occasionally, simmer uncovered 10 minutes, or until of syrup consistency. Pour into hot sterilized bottles or jars; seal airtight. Store in refrigerator. Makes 2 cups.

RAISIN TOPPING
(shown in photograph on pages 138-139)

½ cup raisins
¼ cup packed brown sugar
¼ cup each brandy and white grape juice

Combine all ingredients in 1-cup glass jar with screw lid. Cover and shake to mix. Store at room temperature 2 weeks, shaking jar occasionally. Makes 1 cup.

CANDIES AND CONFECTIONS

PEANUT BUTTER-CHOCOLATE FUDGE PINWHEELS
(shown at right)

1 cup (6 ounces) peanut-butter-flavored chips
1 can (14 ounces) sweetened condensed milk, divided
1 cup (6 ounces) semisweet-chocolate pieces
1 teaspoon vanilla
½ cup chocolate sprinkles

In medium saucepan over low heat, cook peanut-butter chips with half the condensed milk (about ⅔ cup), stirring occasionally, just until smooth. Remove from heat. Line a cookie sheet with foil; lightly grease a 12" x 10" area. With metal spatula, spread peanut-butter mixture evenly to cover greased rectangle. When mixture has cooled slightly, pat gently with hands to distribute more evenly. Let cool 30 minutes. In clean saucepan, cook chocolate with remaining condensed milk over low heat until melted and smooth. Remove from heat; stir in vanilla; cool slightly. Spread evenly over peanut-butter layer; let cool 30 minutes. Lifting long side of foil, gently roll both layers together, jelly-roll fashion. Roll log in chocolate sprinkles, pressing gently so they adhere. (Do not handle too long or chocolate will melt.) Wrap tightly in plastic wrap. Store in cool place up to 2 weeks. Bring to room temperature before cutting in ¼"-thick slices. Makes about 48.

CHRISTMAS SWEETS, packaged for giving. **From left:** Stuffed Apricots, page 143; Bourbon-praline Sauce, page 143; Peanut Butter-Chocolate Fudge Pinwheels, page 140. "Foamy beer" look-alike in glass mug at top actually is Beer Cheese, found on page 178.

CHOCOLATE-PECAN FUDGE
(shown on page 131)

- 8 squares (1 ounce each) semisweet-chocolate, coarsely chopped
- 8 squares (1 ounce each) unsweetened chocolate, coarsely chopped
- 1 jar (7½ ounces) marshmallow cream
- 2 cups coarsely chopped pecans
- 1 can (13 ounces) evaporated milk
- 4 cups sugar
- 2 tablespoons butter or margarine
- ¼ teaspoon salt
- 1 tablespoon vanilla

Place chocolate, marshmallow cream and pecans in large bowl; set aside. In large heavy saucepan, combine milk, sugar, butter and salt. Bring to boil, stirring; boil slowly 9 minutes. Pour at once over chocolate mixture; add vanilla. With wooden spoon, stir vigorously until chocolate is melted and mixture creamy. Pour into buttered 15" x 10" x 1" pan or waxed paper-lined tray. Smooth top. Chill until firm. Cut in 1" squares. Makes about 150.

WALNUT-RUM CONFECTIONS

- 2 cups walnut halves, chopped fine
- 30 round buttery crackers
- ⅔ cup confectioners' sugar
- 5 tablespoons rum (see Note)
  Semisweet-chocolate pieces (about 50)

In food processor or blender, whirl walnuts and crackers until very fine. (Or crush crackers fine in plastic bag with rolling pin; chop nuts fine with knife.) Mix well in large bowl with sugar. Add rum; blend well with wooden spoon or hands. (Mixture will be crumbly; press firmly to shape.) Place rounded half-teaspoonful of mixture in palm of hand; roll gently into 1" ball. Press chocolate piece on top of each. Let stand 12 to 24 hours. Makes about 50.

TRUFFLES
(shown in photograph on pages 138-139)

- 1 cup (6 ounces) semisweet-chocolate pieces
- 2 tablespoons butter or margarine
- ¼ cup water or light rum
- ½ cup plus 2 tablespoons confectioners' sugar, divided
- 2 tablespoons cocoa, divided
- 2 teaspoons instant coffee powder

In small heavy saucepan over low heat, stirring occasionally, melt chocolate and butter in water until mixture is smooth and shiny. Remove from heat; beat in ½ cup confectioners' sugar, 1 tablespoon cocoa and the coffee powder until well blended, scraping mixture from sides of pan occasionally. Chill 2 hours, or until firm. Place level measuring-teaspoonfuls mixture in small mounds on piece of waxed paper. Sift together remaining 2 tablespoons confectioners' sugar and 1 tablespoon cocoa. Dipping hands occasionally in sifted mixture, shape mounds into balls; roll balls in mixture. Place in single layer on waxed paper; chill overnight. Pack airtight; store in cool place for 2 weeks before serving. Makes about 36.

BUTTERMILK PRALINES

- 3 cups sugar
- 1 cup buttermilk
- 3 tablespoons light corn syrup
- 1 teaspoon baking soda
- ⅛ teaspoon salt
- 2 cups pecan halves, lightly toasted and coarsely chopped
- 2 tablespoons butter or margarine
- 2 teaspoons vanilla

In a large saucepan or Dutch oven, combine sugar, buttermilk, corn syrup, baking soda and salt. Bring to boil over medium heat, stirring to dissolve sugar. Cook, stirring occasionally, about 40 minutes, or until syrup reaches 234° on candy thermometer (soft-ball stage). Remove from heat; let stand 5 minutes. Stir in pecans, butter and vanilla. Beat with wooden spoon until mixture starts to thicken and lose its gloss. Working quickly, drop by teaspoonfuls on waxed paper. Let stand about 30 minutes, or until set. Store in airtight container in cool, dry place. Makes about 60.

SESAME CRUNCH
(shown in photograph on pages 138-139)

- 2 cups sesame seed (10 ounces)
- 1 cup each light corn syrup and sugar
- ⅓ cup water
- 2 tablespoons margarine or butter
- 1 teaspoon baking soda

On 15" x 10" jelly-roll pan, toast sesame seed in preheated 350° oven 15 minutes, or until light brown. Place seed in 3-quart saucepan with syrup, sugar, water and margarine. Wipe out jelly-roll pan; grease well; set aside. Over medium heat, stir sesame-seed mixture until it boils. Cook without stirring until candy thermometer registers 266°, or a small amount dropped in cold water forms ball that holds its shape. Stir in baking soda. Turn out on pan. With greased spatula or wooden spoon, spread quickly to ¼" thickness. Cool. Break into pieces. Makes 1¾ pounds.

SWEETMEATS FEATURING FRUIT

STUFFED APRICOTS
(shown below)

1 can or package (7 or 8 ounces) almond paste, cut in small pieces

1 tablespoon almond-flavor liqueur or lemon juice

12 ounces jumbo dried apricots

¼ cup sugar

In small bowl, cream almond paste with liqueur until smooth and creamy. Pat a *level* teaspoonful of almond mixture into middle of each apricot. Bring up sides of fruit, stretching gently to almost cover filling. Roll in sugar to coat. Dry overnight on rack in cool spot. Store airtight in cool place up to 2 weeks. Makes about 48.

STUFFED DATES

½ cup walnut halves, toasted and chopped fine

¼ cup packed brown sugar

2 tablespoons finely chopped candied orange peel

1 tablespoon frozen orange-juice concentrate

1 container (10 ounces) pitted dates, split lengthwise

¼ cup granulated sugar

Mix the walnuts, brown sugar, orange peel and orange-juice concentrate until blended and evenly moist. Stuff heaping half-teaspoonful into each date. Roll in granulated sugar to coat; pack airtight. Makes about 32.

DRIED FRUIT-NUT ROLLS

4 ounces each dried apricots, raisins, currants and pitted dates (about ¾ cup each)

1¼ cups pecan halves, toasted, divided

2 tablespoons frozen orange-juice concentrate

In food processor, whirl the apricots, raisins, currants, dates, 1 cup pecans and orange-juice concentrate until well blended. Or, using coarse blade, force fruits and nuts through food grinder, then mix well with concentrate. Shape in two 8"-long rolls. Chop remaining ¼ cup pecans fine. Roll fruit rolls in pecans; wrap tightly with plastic wrap. Ripen at room temperature at least 3 days before serving. Serve cut in ¼" slices. Makes about 74.

DESSERT SAUCES

BITTERSWEET CHOCOLATE-RUM SAUCE

1 cup each cocoa and sugar

¼ teaspoon salt

¾ cup hot water

2 tablespoons butter or margarine

3 tablespoons dark rum

2 teaspoons vanilla

In small heavy saucepan, stir together cocoa, sugar and salt. With whisk, gradually beat in water until smooth. Add butter; stir over medium-low heat about 10 minutes, or until slightly thickened. Remove from heat; stir in rum and vanilla. Cool, then pour into 1-pint glass jar; cover and store in cool place. Serve warm or cold over ice cream, plain cake or fruits. Makes 1⅔ cups. **Note:** To heat in glass jar, remove lid and set jar in saucepan of simmering water. Heat, stirring occasionally, about 20 minutes, or until warm.

BOURBON-PRALINE SAUCE
(shown on page 141)

½ cup butter or margarine

½ cup each firmly packed brown sugar and heavy cream

¼ cup molasses

¼ cup bourbon

¾ cup pecan halves

In medium saucepan over medium heat, melt butter. Add sugar and cream; stir with whisk or wooden spoon until sugar dissolves. Add molasses; cook and stir about 5 minutes, or until sauce thickens and is a dark caramel color. Remove from heat; stir in bourbon and pecans. Pour into gift jars; cool. Cover. Refrigerate up to 2 weeks. Makes about 2 cups. **Note:** To reheat, remove lid and place jar in saucepan of simmering water, stirring occasionally, about 20 minutes, or until warm.

Best of the Season's Baking

It's an exciting moment when you begin your annual round of holiday baking. And the fun never stops: stirring up batter, chopping up fruits and nuts, adding frosting or glaze or colorful trims. Children thrive on all the activity, even when they're only watching. And how they love the results! If they have a first love, it's cookies, and this section concludes with pages and pages of those.

BREAKFAST AND TEA BREADS

ALMOND KRINGLE
(shown at right)

4 cups flour, divided
½ cup sugar
1 teaspoon salt
2 packages active dry yeast
1 cup milk
1 cup butter or margarine, divided (½ cup kept firm)
2 eggs
Almond Paste (recipe below)
1 egg white
1 egg yolk beaten with 1 tablespoon water
¼ cup sliced almonds

Preheat oven to 375°F. In large bowl, mix well 1½ cups flour and the sugar, salt and yeast; set aside. In small saucepan, heat milk and ½ cup butter until very warm (120° to 130°). Gradually stir into flour mixture. Beat with electric mixer at high speed 5 minutes. Beat in 2 eggs. Stir in remaining 2½ cups flour to make medium-stiff dough. Chill overnight.

On floured surface, roll dough to an 18" x 12" rectangle. Thinly slice remaining ½ cup butter and distribute over two-thirds of dough to about ½" from edges. Fold unbuttered third over a buttered third. Fold again over remaining third. Press edges to seal. Cover; chill 30 minutes. On floured surface, roll again to an 18" x 12" rectangle. Fold in thirds, seal and cover; chill 30 minutes. Repeat three more times. Prepare Almond Paste. Spoon half on a 20"-long piece of waxed paper; cover with second sheet. With rolling pin, roll paste to a 19" x 9" rectangle. Chill very well. Repeat with rest of paste. Roll dough to 20" square. Cut in half, making 2 rectangles. Peel top sheet of paper from one paste rectangle. Invert paste onto dough rectangle. Carefully peel off top paper, using metal spatula to loosen if necessary. Starting with long side, roll dough. Brush seam with egg white; pinch to seal. Bring ends of roll toward center, forming a B. Place seam side down on greased cookie sheet. Repeat with remaining dough and paste. Cover; let rise in warm, draft-free place 45 minutes. Brush lightly with egg-yolk mixture; sprinkle with almonds. Bake 20 minutes, or until rich golden brown. Cool on rack. Makes 2 loaves, 12 servings each.

ALMOND PASTE

Combine 2 cups very finely chopped blanched almonds, 2 cups confectioners' sugar, 2 egg whites and ¼ teaspoon almond extract. Makes about 2 cups.

QUICK STOLLEN
(shown on page 131)

2½ cups flour

¾ cup sugar

4 teaspoons baking powder

½ teaspoon salt

½ teaspoon ground cardamom (optional)

½ cup firm butter or margarine

1 cup creamed cottage cheese

1 egg

2 tablespoons light rum

½ teaspoon vanilla

½ cup chopped pecans

¼ cup mixed candied fruits

¼ cup raisins

2 tablespoons butter or margarine, melted, divided

Pecan halves, candied cherry halves (optional)

2 tablespoons sugar blended well with ¼ teaspoon vanilla

Preheat oven to 325°F. In large bowl, combine flour, sugar, baking powder, salt and cardamom. Cut in firm butter until mixture resembles coarse crumbs; set aside. In small bowl, beat cottage cheese, egg, rum and vanilla until well blended. Stir in pecans, fruits and raisins. Add to flour mixture and mix until moistened. Form into ball. On lightly floured surface, knead slightly, about 10 turns. Roll to 10" x 8" oval. Lightly crease dough just off-center parallel to 10" side. Brush dough lightly with melted butter. Fold smaller section over larger on crease. Place on baking sheet lined with brown paper. Bake about 50 minutes, or until golden brown. Brush top lightly with remaining melted butter; decorate with pecan and cherry halves, if using; sprinkle with sugar-vanilla mixture. Cool on rack. Store airtight at room temperature. Makes 1 loaf, about 20 slices.

BAKED BEAUTIES in the best of holiday taste. **Clockwise from top left:** Soft Caraway Pretzels, page 182; Almond Kringle, page 144; Party Pumpernickel Braids, page 182; Bran Date-nut Loaves, page 148. **On the tree:** Lemon-Molasses Cookies, page 162.

RAISIN BRIOCHES
(shown at right)

¼ cup warm water (105° to 115°)

1½ teaspoons active dry yeast

3 tablespoons sugar, divided

2 cups flour, divided

3 eggs

½ cup butter or margarine, melted and cooled

1 tablespoon dark rum

¾ teaspoon salt

¼ cup raisins

1 tablespoon milk

Preheat oven to 375°F. In large bowl, combine water, yeast and 2 tablespoons sugar. Let stand about 3 minutes to dissolve yeast. Add ½ cup flour and beat until blended. Cover and let rise in warm, draft-free place about 30 minutes, or until dough has doubled. Add eggs, butter, rum and salt; beat until blended. Add remaining 1½ cups flour and the raisins; beat until blended. Cover bowl with plastic wrap; refrigerate overnight. Punch down and, on lightly floured surface, knead until smooth. Shape three-fourths of dough into 12 smooth balls. Place in greased muffin tins. Cut deep cross in top of each. With remaining dough, shape 12 pear-shaped knobs; fit tapered ends firmly into crosses. Let rise uncovered in warm, draft-free place about 45 minutes, or until doubled. Brush with milk; sprinkle with remaining 1 tablespoon sugar. Bake 18 to 20 minutes, or until golden brown. Unmold on rack. Serve warm or cold. Freezes well. Makes 12.

QUICK-MIX PANETTONE
(shown at left)

1 package (13¾ ounces) hot-roll mix

¾ cup warm water (105° to 115°)

½ cup sugar

¼ cup butter or margarine, softened

2 eggs

1 egg yolk

2 teaspoons grated lemon peel

½ cup flour (about)

½ cup raisins, preferably golden

¼ cup each chopped almonds and candied lemon peel

1 tablespoon butter, melted

Confectioners' Icing (optional; recipe below)

Whole almonds and candied cherries for garnish (optional)

Preheat oven to 375°F. In small bowl, stir yeast from mix into the water; let stand until dissolved. In large bowl, cream sugar and butter. Beat in yeast (mixture may appear curdled). Beat in eggs, yolk and the grated peel. Stir in roll mix and ½ cup flour; blend well. Add raisins, almonds and candied peel. Cover dough and let rise in warm, draft-free place about 1½ hours, or until doubled. Punch down; knead on well-floured surface until no longer sticky, working in more flour as needed. Pat into round; place in well-greased 8″ layer-cake pan. Fasten a foil collar around rim of pan to extend 2″ above edge. Let rise again about 1 hour 15 minutes, or until doubled. Brush with melted butter. Bake 40 minutes, or until loaf sounds hollow when tapped. (Top may crack during baking.) Remove from pan; cool on rack 20 minutes. While still warm, pour Confectioners' Icing over; garnish with whole almonds and candied cherries, if using. Serve warm or at room temperature. Store leftovers tightly wrapped at room temperature. Makes 1 loaf, about 16 slices.

CONFECTIONERS' ICING

Stir 1 tablespoon milk into 1 cup confectioners' sugar until smooth.

HOLIDAY COFFEE WREATH

4⅓ cups flour (about), divided
⅓ cup plus 2 tablespoons sugar
1 teaspoon salt
1 teaspoon ground cardamom
2 packages active dry yeast
½ cup butter or margarine
½ cup each water and milk
½ cup raisins
2 eggs, slightly beaten, divided
2 tablespoons chopped almonds or other nuts

Preheat oven to 375°F. In large bowl, combine 1 cup flour, ⅓ cup sugar, the salt, cardamom and yeast. In small saucepan, melt butter; add water, milk and raisins; heat to 120°. Add to flour mixture; beat with mixer at medium speed 2 minutes. Remove 2 tablespoons beaten eggs; reserve. Add remaining eggs and 1 cup flour; beat at high speed 2 minutes. Stir in enough flour to make a soft dough. Turn out on floured surface and knead 8 to 10 minutes, or until smooth and elastic. Place in greased bowl; turn to grease top. Cover and let rise in warm, draft-free place 1 hour, or until dough has doubled.

Punch dough down; turn out on lightly floured surface and, using more flour if necesssary, knead until smooth and elastic. Cut dough in 3 equal pieces. Shape each into a 30"-long rope. Braid ropes loosely; transfer braid to lightly greased baking sheet and shape into wreath, pinching ends firmly together. Place a 6-ounce custard cup, greased on outside, upside-down in hole in center. Cover and let rise in warm, draft-free place about 45 minutes, or until dough has doubled.

Brush with the reserved egg; sprinkle with mixture of remaining 2 tablespoons sugar and almonds. Bake 25 to 30 minutes, or until golden and done. Remove to rack to cool. Serve or wrap airtight and store in cool place or freeze. Best eaten within 1 week. Makes 12 servings.

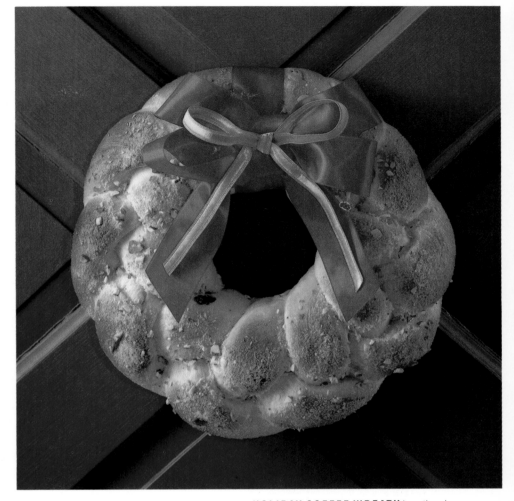

HOLIDAY COFFEE WREATH has the decorative look and generous size (makes 12 good-sized servings) to do the honors at a seasonal get-together with friends or neighbors. If you're feeling ambitious, these make wonderful gifts.

BRAN DATE-NUT LOAVES
(shown on page 145)

⅔ cup hot water
1 cup whole-bran cereal
1 cup finely snipped dates
1⅓ cups flour
⅔ cup sugar
½ cup chopped walnuts
2 teaspoons baking soda
1 teaspoon cinnamon
¾ teaspoon salt
2 eggs, slightly beaten
2 tablespoons oil
15 walnut halves (optional)

Preheat oven to 350°F. Mix water, cereal and dates; let stand until most of the water is absorbed. In large bowl, combine flour, sugar, walnuts, baking soda, cinnamon and salt. Stir in cereal mixture, eggs and oil just until combined. Spoon into five greased 4½" x 2½" loaf pans; spread smooth. Place three walnut halves on top of each. Bake 25 minutes, or until pick inserted in center comes out clean. Cool in pans on racks 5 minutes. Gently loosen sides with spatula. Turn out on racks to cool completely. Wrap airtight to keep up to 5 days. Serve with butter or cream cheese if desired. Makes 5 loaves of about 8 slices each.

OLD-TIME STEAMED PRUNE BREAD
(shown in photograph on pages 138-139)

1 package (12 ounces) pitted prunes, snipped in small pieces
Water
1½ cups flour
1 cup packed brown sugar
1 teaspoon each baking powder and baking soda
½ teaspoon salt
1 cup each bran flakes and chopped walnuts
1 egg, slightly beaten
1 cup sour cream
½ cup molasses
3 tablespoons butter or margarine, melted
1 tablespoon grated orange peel

Place prunes in medium saucepan with water just to cover. Bring to boil; reduce heat, cover and simmer 10 minutes. Remove from heat; set aside. In large bowl, mix well flour, sugar, baking powder, baking soda and salt. Stir in cereal and nuts. In medium bowl, beat together egg, sour cream, molasses, reserved prunes and their liquid, butter and orange peel. Stir into dry ingredients until blended. Divide batter evenly between two well-greased 1-pound coffee cans or among four 1-pound vegetable or fruit cans. Cover tops with double layer of foil; tie covering securely with string. Place cans on rack in large kettle. Add enough water to come halfway up sides of cans. Cover; bring to boil, reduce heat and simmer 4 hours, or until loaves are dark brown. With tongs, lift cans from water; remove foil. Cool on rack 15 minutes; remove breads from cans (open bottom and use bottom piece to push loaf out). Wrap airtight; store up to one month in refrigerator (flavor improves on standing). Makes 2 large loaves (sixteen ¼" slices each) or 4 small loaves (eight ½" slices each).

SPICE RING

1 tablespoon fine dry bread crumbs
2 cups flour
2 teaspoons cinnamon
1 teaspoon baking soda
½ teaspoon cardamom seed, crushed, or 1 teaspoon ground cardamom
½ teaspoon salt
2 eggs
2 cups packed brown sugar
¾ cup sour cream
½ cup butter or margarine, melted and cooled
Confectioners' sugar (optional)

Preheat oven to 325°F. Grease well a 2-quart fluted tube pan; sprinkle with crumbs; shake out excess; set aside. Stir together flour, cinnamon, baking soda, cardamom and salt; set aside. In large bowl, beat eggs and sugar until light and fluffy. Beat in sour cream and butter until well blended. Stir in flour mixture just until smooth. Turn into prepared pan. Bake 50 minutes, or until pick inserted in center comes out clean. Cool in pan on rack 10 minutes. Invert on rack; cool completely. Wrap airtight and store in cool place overnight or longer. Will keep up to 10 days in airtight storage or can be frozen. Sprinkle with confectioners' sugar before serving. Makes 20 slices.

FRUITCAKES

FRUITCAKE LAYERED WITH ALMOND PASTE
(shown in photograph on pages 138-139)

- 1 cup finely chopped mixed candied fruits
- ½ cup currants
- ¼ cup brandy or light rum
- 1 can (8 ounces) or 1 package (7 ounces) almond paste, cut in half
- 1½ cups butter or margarine, softened
- 1 cup granulated sugar
- 6 eggs
- 3½ cups flour
- Confectioners' sugar

Preheat oven to 350°F. At least a day before baking cake, combine candied fruits, currants and brandy in covered container; marinate at least 24 hours. Shape each piece of almond paste in a square. Roll out each to 9" square on pastry cloth lightly sprinkled with confectioners' sugar; set aside. Grease a 9" square baking pan; line bottom with waxed paper; grease again; set aside. In large bowl, cream butter; gradually add sugar; cream until light and fluffy. Add eggs one at a time, beating well after each addition. Stir in flour alternately with marinated fruits. (Most liquid should be absorbed; if not, do not add more than 2 tablespoons.) Spread enough batter (about 1 cup) in prepared pan to cover bottom. Top with square of almond paste. Spread half the remaining batter over almond paste; top with remaining square almond paste. Cover with remaining batter. Bake 1 hour, or until golden brown and pick inserted in center comes out clean. Cool in pan on rack 10 minutes. Unmold; peel off waxed paper. Turn top side up; cool completely before wrapping airtight. Can be refrigerated up to 6 weeks. Before serving, dust with confectioners' sugar. Cut in quarters, then ¼"-thick slices. Makes about 72 slices.

CROCKED FRUITCAKES
(shown in photograph on pages 138-139)

- 1 package (12 ounces) pitted prunes, snipped in small pieces
- 1 package (8 ounces) chopped dates
- 3 cups raisins
- 1 cup dry white wine
- 1 cup rum
- ½ cup butter or margarine, softened
- ½ cup each sugar and light corn syrup
- 3 eggs
- 2½ cups flour
- 1 teaspoon each baking powder, cinnamon and ginger
- 1 teaspoon vanilla
- 1 cup chopped nuts

Preheat oven to 300°F. In medium bowl, combine prunes, dates, raisins, wine and rum; cover and let stand in cool place 2 days, stirring occasionally. In large bowl, beat butter, sugar and corn syrup until well blended. Add eggs; beat until smooth. In medium bowl, mix well flour, baking powder, cinnamon and ginger. Add to butter mixture, beating just until moistened. Stir in fruit mixture, vanilla and nuts. Spoon about 1⅓ cups batter into each of six 1½-cup well-greased cheese crocks (see Note). Bake 1 hour 15 minutes, or until pick inserted in center comes out clean. Cool on rack 30 minutes. Remove from crocks; cool on rack. Return to crocks; can be refrigerated up to one month. Makes 6 cakes of 4 servings each. **Note:** Cake can also be baked in: two 9" x 5" x 3" loaf pans (1 hour 45 minutes), two 6-cup crocks (2 hours 15 minutes) or four 3-cup crocks (1 hour 30 minutes).

INDIVIDUAL FRUITCAKES
(shown on page 131)

- 1 cup flour
- 1 teaspoon allspice
- ½ teaspoon cinnamon
- ¼ teaspoon salt
- ½ cup butter or margarine
- ¼ cup packed brown sugar
- 2 eggs
- ¼ cup seedless black-raspberry preserves
- 1 cup currants soaked overnight in ⅓ cup brandy
- 1 cup mixed candied fruits
- 1 cup pecan halves, coarsely chopped (see Note)
- 1 tablespoon grated lemon or orange peel
- 15 candied cherry halves or pecan halves (optional)
- ⅓ cup brandy (about)

Preheat oven to 325°F. Combine flour, allspice, cinnamon and salt; set aside. In large bowl, cream butter and sugar until fluffy. Add eggs; beat with mixer at high speed 3 minutes. Blend in preserves. Stir in flour mixture. Fold in currants, fruits, pecans and grated peel. Spoon into 2"-midget-size foil baking cups set in muffin pans. Top each with candied cherry half, if using. Bake 20 minutes. Cool completely. Spoon about ½ teaspoon brandy over each. Store in airtight container. Makes 30. **Note:** Walnuts may be substituted for pecans.

SUMPTUOUS CHOCOLATE DESSERTS

DOUBLE CHOCOLATE TORTE

- 6 eggs, at room temperature
- 1 cup sugar
- 1 teaspoon vanilla
- ½ cup unsifted all-purpose flour
- ½ cup cocoa
- ½ cup butter or margarine, melted
  Cream Filling (recipe below)
  Chocolate Cream Frosting (recipe below)

Preheat oven to 350°F. Grease and flour three 8" layer cake pans. Beat eggs until light and fluffy in large mixer bowl. Gradually add sugar; continue beating until very thick. Blend in vanilla. Thoroughly combine flour and cocoa; gradually fold into egg mixture. Fold in melted butter until well blended. Divide batter evenly between prepared pans. Bake 15 minutes, or until top springs back when touched lightly. Cool in pans 5 minutes. Remove from pans; cool completely. Prepare Cream Filling. Spread one layer with pink filling, another with green. Stack all three, ending with plain layer on top. Prepare Chocolate Cream Frosting. Frost top and sides: refrigerate until serving time.

CREAM FILLING

Whip 1 cup heavy cream with ¼ cup confectioners' sugar. Tint half of the cream pink, the rest pale green.

CHOCOLATE CREAM FROSTING

- ¼ cup butter or margarine
- ½ cup cocoa
- 1 teaspoon vanilla
- ⅓ cup light cream or milk, heated slightly
- 2½ cups confectioners' sugar

Combine butter, cocoa, vanilla, half of the cream or milk and 1½ cups confectioners' sugar in small mixer bowl; beat until smooth. Gradually add remaining sugar and cream or milk. Beat until of spreading consistency.

CHOCOLATE DESSERTS of great elegance, for the times when only something lavish will do. **Clockwise from the top** (with recipes complete on these pages): Double Chocolate Torte; Chocolate-almond Napoleons; Chocolate-orange Eclairs.

CHOCOLATE ALMOND NAPOLEONS

2 packages (10 ounces each) frozen patty shells, thawed

Chocolate almond Filling (recipe below)

Vanilla Frosting (recipe below)

Chocolate Frosting (recipe below)

Preheat oven to 450°F. Press 4 shells together; roll out on lightly floured board into a 15" x 9" rectangle. Place on ungreased baking sheet; prick with fork. Place in 450° oven; immediately reduce oven temperature to 400°. Bake about 15 minutes, or until golden brown. Cool on wire rack. Repeat with remaining patty shells, making three rectangles. When pastry layers are completely cooled, carefully trim sides so layers are the same size. Prepare Chocolate almond Filling. Spread two layers with filling; stack all three, ending with plain layer on top. Prepare Vanilla Frosting and Chocolate Frosting: spread top with Vanilla Frosting. Drizzle with Chocolate Frosting or pipe on stripes. Refrigerate at least 1 hour. Just before serving, cut in half lengthwise; cut each half into 8 pieces. Makes 16 servings.

CHOCOLATE ALMOND FILLING

1 envelope unflavored gelatin

¼ cup cold water

½ cup sugar

¼ cup cocoa

¼ cup cornstarch

Dash salt

2 cups milk

3 egg yolks, slightly beaten

1 teaspoon almond extract

½ cup heavy cream

Sprinkle the gelatin over the cold water to soften. Combine sugar, cocoa, cornstarch and salt in medium saucepan. Gradually stir in milk and egg yolks. Cook over medium heat, stirring constantly, until mixture boils. Stir in softened gelatin: boil and stir 1 minute. Remove from heat; add almond extract. Press plastic wrap onto surface; chill. Whip cream; fold into chilled mixture.

VANILLA FROSTING

Combine 1¼ cups confectioners' sugar, 1 tablespoon light corn syrup, ¼ teaspoon almond extract and 1½ tablespoons hot water. Beat until of spreading consistency.

CHOCOLATE FROSTING

Melt ¼ cup butter or margarine in small saucepan. Remove from heat; stir in ½ cup cocoa.

CHOCOLATE ORANGE ECLAIRS

1 cup water

½ cup butter or margarine

¼ teaspoon salt

1 cup unsifted all-purpose flour

4 eggs

Chocolate orange Filling (recipe below)

Chocolate Glaze (recipe below)

Preheat oven to 375°F. Heat water, butter and salt to rolling boil in medium saucepan. Add flour all at once; stir vigorously over low heat about 1 minute, or until mixture leaves side of pan and forms a ball. Remove from heat; add eggs, one at a time, beating until smooth after each addition. After last egg is added, beat until smooth and velvety.

For each eclair, using spatula, spread about ¼ cup of mixture into rectangle 5" x ½" onto a greased cookie sheet. Bake about 40 minutes, or until puffed and golden brown. Cut a slit in side of each eclair and bake 10 minutes longer. Cool on wire rack. Prepare Chocolate orange Filling. Slice top from each eclair; fill each shell. Replace tops; set aside. Prepare Chocolate Glaze; spread some onto top of each eclair. Makes about 12.

CHOCOLATE ORANGE FILLING

1 cup sugar

½ cup cocoa

⅓ cup cornstarch

¼ teaspoon salt

3 cups milk

3 egg yolks, slightly beaten

1½ teaspoons vanilla

½ cup heavy cream

2 tablespoons orange-flavor liqueur

Combine sugar, cocoa, cornstarch and salt in heavy saucepan; gradually stir in milk and egg yolks. Cook over medium heat, stirring constantly, until mixture boils; boil and stir 1 minute. Remove from heat; add vanilla. Pour into bowl; press plastic wrap onto surface. Chill. Whip cream with liqueur until stiff. Fold into chocolate mixture.

CHOCOLATE GLAZE

Melt 2 tablespoons butter in small saucepan over low heat; add ¼ cup cocoa and 3 tablespoons water and continue to heat, stirring, until mixture thickens. Do not boil. Remove from heat; blend in 1¼ cups confectioners' sugar and ½ teaspoon vanilla. Using whisk if necessary, beat until smooth and of spreading consistency.

Christmas Cookie Spree

HAND-SHAPED OR PRESSED COOKIES

NO-BAKE COCOA-BOURBON BALLS
(shown above)

1 cup each finely crushed vanilla
   wafers (30 to 36), confectioners'
   sugar and chopped pecans

2 tablespoons each cocoa and light
   corn syrup

¼ cup bourbon, rum or brandy

Granulated sugar, additional
   chopped pecans or cocoa

In medium bowl, stir together crumbs, confectioners' sugar, pecans and cocoa. Add corn syrup and bourbon; mix well. With wet hands, shape into 1" balls. Roll in granulated sugar, chopped pecans or cocoa as desired. Store airtight in cool place. Makes about 36.

STRASBOURG COOKIES
(shown above)

- **1 cup butter or margarine, softened**
- **½ cup confectioners' sugar**
- **1 teaspoon vanilla**
- **2½ cups flour**
- **¼ cup fruit jelly (about)**

Preheat oven to 325°F. In large bowl, cream butter, sugar and vanilla until fluffy. Gradually stir in flour until well blended. Let stand 30 minutes. On lightly greased cookie sheet, press dough with thumb through a number 7 star-shape piping tip (tube), held at right angles to the sheet, into 1½"-wide rosettes 1" apart (see Note). Make a small indentation in center of each rosette; fill with dab of jelly. Bake 15 minutes, or until cookies are firm to touch and golden on bottom. Remove to rack to cool. Store loosely covered in cool place. Makes about 68.
Note: If desired, shape dough in two 10"-long rolls. Brush rolls with 1 beaten egg and roll in mixture of 2 tablespoons each sugar and chopped nuts. Cover and chill overnight. Slice ¼" thick; place ½" apart on lightly greased cookie sheet. Bake as above. Makes about 68.

A SEASONAL SAMPLER of cookie techniques and tastes. **From left to right:** Walnut Crescents, page 154, surrounded by Checkerboard Cookies, page 164, and alternating Coconut Macaroons, page 158, and Mexican Wedding Cookies, page 156; No-bake Cocoa-bourbon Balls and Strasbourg Cookies, below; Rolled Wafers and Lizzies, page 159.

WALNUT CRESCENTS
(shown on page 152)

- 1 cup butter or margarine, softened
- ½ cup confectioners' sugar
- 2 teaspoons vanilla
- ¼ teaspoon salt
- 1¾ cups flour
- 1 cup chopped walnuts
- ½ cup granulated sugar

Preheat oven to 300°F. In large bowl, cream butter, confectioners' sugar, vanilla and salt until fluffy. Stir in flour and walnuts until well blended. Cover and chill 30 minutes, or until firm enough to handle. Break off small pieces dough and on lightly floured surface roll with hands into finger-thick strips. Cut in 2" lengths; taper ends, then shape in crescents. Place 1" apart on ungreased cookie sheet. Bake 18 to 20 minutes, or until firm to the touch. While still warm, roll in granulated sugar. Place on racks to cool. Store airtight in cool place. Makes about 60.

SPRITZ COOKIES

- 2¼ cups flour
- ¼ teaspoon salt
- 1 cup butter or margarine, softened
- ⅔ cup sugar
- 1 egg
- 1 teaspoon vanilla
  Maraschino cherry halves or slivers, silver dragées or colored sugar for decoration (optional)

Preheat oven to 400°F. Mix flour and salt well; set aside. In large bowl, cream butter and sugar until light. Beat in egg and vanilla until fluffy. Stir in flour mixture until well blended. (Chill dough if too soft to hold shape.) Force dough through cookie press to form ½"-diameter cookies ½" apart on ungreased cookie sheets. Decorate as desired. Bake 7 to 10 minutes, or until light golden around edges. Remove to racks to cool. Store loosely covered in cool place. Makes about 75.

CRISP OATMEAL COOKIES

- 1½ cups packed brown sugar
- ¾ cup shortening, melted
- ⅓ cup buttermilk
- ½ teaspoon salt
- ¾ teaspoon vanilla
- 1¼ cups flour
- ¾ teaspoon baking soda
- 3 cups quick oats

Preheat oven to 375°F. Mix all ingredients well. Shape in 1" balls. Place 1" apart on greased cookie sheets. Press with wet spatula to ⅛" thickness. Bake 10 to 12 minutes, or until light brown and crisp. Remove to racks to cool. Store loosely covered in cool place. Makes about 80.

SPICY RAISIN CHEWS

- 2 cups flour
- 2 teaspoons cinnamon
- 1 teaspoon ground cloves
- ½ teaspoon each baking powder, baking soda, salt and fresh-ground pepper
- 1 cup finely chopped almonds
- 3 eggs
- 2 cups packed brown sugar
- 1 package (15 ounces) raisins, ground (see Note)
- 2 tablespoons citron, ground or chopped fine
  Confectioners' sugar

Preheat oven to 375°F. Stir together flour, cinnamon, cloves, baking powder, baking soda, salt, pepper and almonds; set aside. In large bowl, beat eggs and brown sugar until thick and fluffy. Add raisins and citron; beat to mix well. Stir in flour mixture until well blended (dough will be sticky). Wrap airtight; chill 2 hours, or until easy to handle.

Between floured palms, shape rounded teaspoonfuls dough in balls. Place 1" apart on well-greased cookie sheets. Bake 10 minutes, or until lightly browned and firm on bottom. Cookies will be soft and moist inside. Remove to racks to cool slightly. While still warm, roll in confectioners' sugar. Return to racks to cool thoroughly. Store airtight in cool place. Makes about 80. **Note:** Use food grinder for raisins or process a half box at a time in food processor fitted with metal blade, using quick on/off turns.

MOLASSES-SPICE COOKIES

2¼ cups flour
2 teaspoons baking powder
1 teaspoon each cinnamon and ginger
½ teaspoon cloves
¼ teaspoon salt
¾ cup butter or margarine, softened
1 cup packed brown sugar
1 egg
¼ cup molasses
Granulated sugar

Preheat oven to 375°F. Stir together flour, baking powder, cinnamon, ginger, cloves and salt; set aside. Cream butter and brown sugar until light and fluffy. Beat in egg and molasses. Stir in flour mixture until well blended. Chill several hours.

Shape in walnut-size balls; roll in granulated sugar. Place 1″ apart on lightly greased cookie sheets. Press flat with bottom of glass. Bake 12 minutes, or until lightly browned around edges. Store loosely covered in cool place. Makes about 48.

COCONUT-OATMEAL COOKIES

1 cup plus 2 tablespoons flour
1 teaspoon baking powder
½ teaspoon baking soda
½ cup butter or margarine, softened
1 cup packed brown sugar
1 teaspoon vanilla
½ teaspoon salt
1 egg
1 cup quick or old-fashioned rolled oats
1¼ cups or 1 can (3½ ounces) flaked coconut
Colored sugar (optional)

Preheat oven to 375°F. Stir together flour, baking powder and baking soda; set aside. In large bowl, cream butter, brown sugar, vanilla, salt and egg until fluffy. Stir in oats, coconut and flour mixture until well blended. Chill several hours, or until firm enough to handle.

Shape in 1″ balls. Place 2″ apart on lightly greased cookie sheets. Dip fork tines in flour and press crisscross pattern on balls, flattening to make 1½″ round cookies. Sprinkle with colored sugar if desired. Bake 10 minutes, or until brown. Remove to rack to cool. Store loosely covered in cool, dry place. Makes about 60.

PECAN BUTTER BALLS

2 cups flour
¼ cup granulated sugar
½ teaspoon salt
1 cup butter or margarine, softened
2 teaspoons vanilla
2 cups finely chopped pecans
3 tablespoons confectioners' sugar

Preheat oven to 325°F. In medium bowl, stir together flour, granulated sugar and salt; add butter and vanilla; blend with wooden spoon to a soft, smooth dough. Add pecans; mix well. Shape in 1″ balls. Bake on ungreased cookie sheets 25 minutes, or until firm and lightly browned on bottom. Remove to racks set over waxed paper. While still warm, sift confectioners' sugar over tops. Cool completely; store airtight in cool place. Makes about 48.

MEXICAN WEDDING COOKIES
(shown on page 152)

1 cup butter or margarine,
   softened

Confectioners' sugar
   (as specified)

1 teaspoon vanilla

¼ teaspoon salt

2 cups flour

Preheat oven to 375°F. In medium bowl, cream butter, ½ cup confectioners' sugar, vanilla and salt until fluffy. Stir in flour until well blended. Chill 30 minutes, or until firm enough to handle. Shape into 1″ balls. Place 1″ apart on ungreased cookie sheet; bake 12 to 15 minutes, or until light golden. Remove to rack (close together) set over waxed paper. While still warm, dust heavily with confectioners' sugar; cool. Store airtight in cool, dry place. Just before serving, dust cookies with additional confectioners' sugar. Makes about 48.

CHERRY BONBONS

½ cup butter or margarine,
   softened

¼ cup confectioners' sugar

½ teaspoon vanilla

1 cup flour

¼ cup finely minced nuts

½ pound red candied cherries
   (1½ cups)

Confectioners' Sugar Frosting
   (recipe below)

Sliced red candied cherries
   (optional)

Preheat oven to 350°F. In large bowl, cream butter, sugar and vanilla until light. Stir in flour and nuts until well blended. Cover and chill 30 minutes, or until firm enough to handle. On lightly floured surface, shape in 1″-thick rolls. Cut in ½″-thick slices. Turn cut side up; place cherry in center of each slice. With lightly floured hands, shape in balls, covering cherries completely with dough. Place 1″ apart on ungreased cookie sheet; chill 15 minutes. Bake 15 to 20 minutes, or until lightly browned. Remove to racks to cool.

To frost, set cookies on rack over waxed paper. Spoon frosting over cookies, allowing it to run down sides. (Scrape up dripped frosting and reuse.) Decorate with sliced cherries, if using. Store airtight in cool place. Makes about 24.

CONFECTIONERS' SUGAR FROSTING

In small bowl, mix well 1 cup confectioners' sugar, 1 to 1½ tablespoons water and ¼ teaspoon vanilla (optional) until smooth and of appropriate consistency to use as described.

RASPBERRY-ALMOND COOKIES

½ cup butter or margarine,
   softened

⅓ cup sugar

½ teaspoon vanilla

¼ teaspoon salt

1 egg, separated

1 cup flour

¾ cup finely chopped blanched
   almonds

3 tablespoons seedless raspberry
   jam (about)

Preheat oven to 300°F. In small bowl, cream butter; beat in sugar, vanilla, salt and egg yolk until light and fluffy. Stir in flour until well blended. Cover and chill 30 minutes, or until firm enough to handle. Divide in thirds. On lightly floured surface, shape in 1″-thick rolls. Cut rolls in ¾″ slices; roll each into a ball. In saucer, slightly beat egg white. Dip each ball in egg white, then roll in almonds. Place 1″ apart on ungreased cookie sheet. With floured index finger, make deep indentation in center of each. Fill with ¼ teaspoon jam. Bake 20 minutes, or until golden. Remove to racks to cool. Store loosely covered in cool place. Makes about 36.

DROPPED COOKIES

MELT-IN-MOUTH COOKIES

- ¾ cup flour
- 1 teaspoon baking powder
- ½ cup butter or margarine, softened
- 1 cup packed light-brown sugar
- 1 egg
- 1 teaspoon vanilla
- ½ cup finely chopped nuts

Preheat oven to 400°F. Stir together flour and baking powder; set aside. In large bowl, beat butter, sugar, egg and vanilla until light and fluffy. Beat in flour mixture until smooth. Stir in nuts. Drop by level measuring teaspoonfuls 2" apart on nonstick cookie sheets or cookie sheets lined with foil and then greased. Bake 5 to 6 minutes, or until flat and lightly browned. Remove from oven; cool 1 minute. Remove carefully (cookies will be soft) with thin metal spatula to wire racks. Cool completely. Store loosely covered in dry place. Makes about 72.

PECAN RUSKS
(shown above)

- 1½ cups flour
- 1½ teaspoons baking powder
- ¼ teaspoon salt
- ½ cup butter or margarine, softened
- ¾ cup sugar
- 1 teaspoon vanilla
- 2 eggs
- 1 cup chopped pecans

Preheat oven to 375°F. Mix well flour, baking powder and salt; set aside. In large bowl, cream butter, sugar and vanilla until light. Beat in eggs until well blended and fluffy. Stir in pecans and flour mixture until well blended. Using two teaspoons, spoon dough onto greased cookie sheet in four ½"-thick 1" strips, placing strips 3" apart. Bake 12 to 14 minutes, or until edges are light brown. Remove from oven; turn off heat. Cut strips diagonally in ¾" slices. Turn slices cut sides up on cookie sheet, slightly separated from each other. Place sheet in oven with door ajar about 15 minutes to dry slices slightly. Remove to racks to cool. Makes about 48.

BRANDY-GLAZED MINCEMEAT MOUNDS

- 2 cups flour
- ½ teaspoon each salt, baking soda and nutmeg
- 1 teaspoon cinnamon
- ⅔ cup butter or margarine, softened
- ⅔ cup packed dark-brown sugar
- 1 egg
- 1 cup mincemeat
- ¼ cup sour cream
- 1 cup coarsely chopped pecans
  Brandy Glaze (recipe below)
  Slivers of candied cherries or pecan pieces (optional)

Preheat oven to 400°F. Stir together flour, salt, baking soda, nutmeg and cinnamon; set aside. In medium bowl, cream butter and sugar until light; beat in egg. Stir in flour mixture until blended. Stir in mincemeat, sour cream and pecans. Drop by heaping teaspoonfuls to form mounds 2" apart on greased cookie sheets. Bake 10 minutes, or until lightly browned on bottom; remove immediately to rack placed over waxed paper. While still hot, spoon ½ teaspoonful Brandy Glaze on each. Press cherry slivers on each. Store airtight. Makes about 48.

BRANDY GLAZE

In medium bowl, mix together ¼ cup each milk and brandy and 1 teaspoon vanilla. Gradually blend in 3 cups confectioners' sugar until the mixture is smooth.

COCONUT MACAROONS
(shown on page 152)

- **2 egg whites**
- **⅛ teaspoon salt**
- **½ cup sugar**
- **½ teaspoon each vanilla and almond extract**
- **2 cups packed flaked coconut**
- **15 red candied cherries, halved (optional)**

Preheat oven to 300°F. Grease large cookie sheet well. Dust with flour; shake off excess; set aside. In small bowl, beat egg whites until foamy; add salt and beat until soft peaks form. Gradually add sugar 1 tablespoon at a time and beat until very stiff. Fold in extracts and coconut until well blended. Place rounded teaspoonfuls 1" apart on prepared cookie sheet. With fingers dipped in cold water, smooth mounds. Top each with cherry half. Bake 20 minutes, or until surface feels firm (inside should be slightly moist). Cool on sheet, then with flexible spatula remove to rack to cool completely. Store airtight. Makes about 30.

NOELS

- **1¼ cups flour**
- **¼ teaspoon baking powder**
- **½ teaspoon baking soda**
- **⅓ cup butter or margarine, softened**
- **¾ cup packed brown sugar**
- **1 egg**
- **1 teaspoon vanilla**
- **½ cup sour cream**
- **1 package (8 ounces) pitted dates (about 36)**
- **36 walnut halves**
- **Easy Icing (recipe below)**
- **Colored sprinkles (optional)**

Preheat oven to 400°F. Stir together flour, baking powder and baking soda; set aside. In medium bowl, cream butter and sugar until light and fluffy. Beat in egg and vanilla until blended. Stir in flour mixture alternately with sour cream until blended. Stuff dates with walnut halves; using two forks, roll each in dough until well covered. Drop 2" apart on ungreased cookie sheets. Bake 10 minutes, or until golden brown (cookies will still be soft to touch). Immediately remove to racks. When cooled, spread with Easy Icing. Decorate with sprinkles if desired. Store airtight. Makes about 36.

EASY ICING

In small bowl, stir together 2 tablespoons melted butter, 1 tablespoon milk, 1 teaspoon vanilla and 1 cup confectioners' sugar until smooth.

NO-BAKE PEANUTTY DROPS

- **½ cup packed brown sugar**
- **½ cup light corn syrup**
- **¾ cup chunky peanut butter**
- **1 teaspoon vanilla**

In medium saucepan, over medium heat, bring to boil sugar and corn syrup; stir until sugar is dissolved. Remove from heat; fold in remaining ingredients until well blended. Drop by heaping teaspoonfuls onto waxed paper. Cool until firm. Store airtight. Makes about 36.

LIZZIES
(shown below)

1½ cups raisins

¼ cup bourbon or orange juice

¾ cup flour

¾ teaspoon each baking soda and cinnamon

¼ teaspoon each nutmeg and ground cloves

2 tablespoons butter or margarine

¼ cup packed light-brown sugar

1 egg

2 cups pecan halves or broken walnut halves

4 ounces citron, diced

8 ounces candied cherries (1½ cups)

Confectioners' sugar (optional)

Preheat oven to 325°F. Stir together raisins and bourbon; let stand 1 hour. Mix flour, baking soda and spices; set aside. In large bowl, cream butter until fluffy; beat in brown sugar, then egg. Stir in flour mixture. Add raisin-bourbon mixture, pecans and fruits; mix well. Drop by teaspoonfuls about 1″ apart on greased cookie sheets.

With wet fingers, press fruit and nuts into batter to form compact ball. Bake about 15 minutes, or until edges are lightly browned. Remove cookies at once to cool on racks. Before serving, sprinkle with confectioners' sugar if desired. Store airtight in cool, dry place with waxed paper between layers. Makes about 60. **Note:** Recipe can be doubled.

ROLLED WAFERS
(shown below)

½ cup butter or margarine, softened

½ cup sugar

1 teaspoon vanilla

2 egg whites

⅔ cup flour

Preheat oven to 400°F. Grease cookie sheet; trace six 3½″ circles 1″ apart; set aside. In small bowl, cream butter, sugar and vanilla until fluffy. Beat in egg whites until well blended. Stir in flour until just blended. Place 1 rounded teaspoonful batter in each circle. With small spatula, spread batter to fill circle (will be very thin). Bake on middle rack in preheated oven 4 to 5 minutes, or until edges are light brown. Immediately, with wide flexible spatula, loosen one cookie at a time; turn bottom side up and roll tightly around a pencil. Pull out pencil; place rolled wafer, seam side down, on rack to cool. Proceed with remaining batter, reusing cookie sheets, cooled slightly. Store cookies loosely covered in dry place. Makes about 30.

Circle of Lizzies with Rolled Wafers in center

ROLLED COOKIES

SUGAR COOKIES
(shown above)

  2 cups flour
 ¼ teaspoon salt
 ½ cup butter or margarine,
     softened
 ½ cup granulated sugar
  1 egg
 ½ teaspoon vanilla
1½ tablespoons lemon juice
  1 egg white slightly beaten with
     1 tablespoon water
     Colored sugar (optional)

Preheat oven to 350°F. Stir together flour and salt; set aside. In large bowl, cream butter and granulated sugar until light and fluffy. Beat in egg, then vanilla and lemon juice. Stir in flour mixture until blended. Divide cookie dough in half. Wrap each half airtight; chill for several hours.

Roll out ⅛" thick on lightly floured surface. Cut in desired shapes with 2½" cookie cutters. Reroll and cut scraps. Place cookies ½" apart on lightly greased cookie sheets. Brush with egg-white mixture. Sprinkle with colored sugar if desired. Bake 8 to 10 minutes, or until very lightly browned around edges. Remove to wire racks to cool. Store loosely covered in cool place. Makes about 60.

Note: Sugar cookies can be cut in desired Christmas shapes as described for Gingersnaps, and a hole cut near an edge to take a hanging cord. If you prefer the wreath shape in the photograph, this can be made with a doughnut cutter or with round cutters in 2 sizes (the first to cut the round; a smaller second one to cut out the center). With a wreath-shaped ornament, a hanging cord can simply be tied around the edge.

GINGERSNAPS
(shown above)

 ½ cup butter or margarine,
     softened
 ¾ cup sugar
 ⅓ cup water
  1 tablespoon dark corn syrup
1½ teaspoons each cinnamon,
     cloves and ginger
  1 teaspoon ground cardamom
     (optional)
2½ cups flour mixed with
     ¾ teaspoon baking soda
     Decorator Icing (recipe below)
     Colored sugar, silver dragees,
     almonds for decoration
     (optional)

Preheat oven to 375°F. Place butter and sugar in bowl. In small saucepan, bring water, corn syrup and spices to boil. Pour over butter and sugar; beat well. Gradually stir in flour mixture until well blended and smooth. Wrap airtight; chill overnight.

On lightly floured surface, roll out half the dough ⅛″ thick. (Pastry cloth and stockinette-covered rolling pin are helpful.) Cut in desired shapes. Place ¼″ apart on ungreased cookie sheets. Reroll and cut scraps; repeat with remaining dough. For Christmas-tree ornaments, make small hole with wooden pick about ½″ from edge of cookies. Bake 8 to 10 minutes, or until well browned. Let cool on sheets. Decorate as desired with Decorator Icing spooned into small cone made of parchment or double layers of waxed paper. While frosting is still soft, sprinkle with colored sugar and/or press in almonds if desired. Dry on racks or cookie sheets until frosting is firm. Store loosely covered in cool, dry place. Makes about 96 small (2½″) or 36 large (4″) cookies.

DECORATOR ICING

Beat together 2 cups confectioners' sugar, 1 egg white and 1 teaspoon lemon juice until well blended.

WALNUT SHORTBREAD

- **1 cup butter or margarine, softened**
- **1 cup confectioners' sugar**
- **1 teaspoon vanilla**
- **2¼ cups flour**
- **24 walnut halves (about)**

Preheat oven to 350°F. In large bowl, cream butter; gradually add sugar; beat until fluffy. Stir in vanilla and flour until well blended. Cover dough and chill 30 minutes, or until firm enough to handle. Roll out on lightly floured surface to ½″ thickness. Cut with floured 2″ round or other cookie cutter or, with knife, cut in diamonds. Reroll and cut scraps. Place cookies 2″ apart on greased cookie sheets. Press walnut half on each. Bake 20 to 25 minutes, or until very lightly browned around edges. Cool completely on rack. Store loosely covered in cool place. Makes about 24.

ROLLED COOKIES are the usual choice for tree trims because of their firmness and shape-holding ability. Shown here are Gingersnaps and Sugar Cookies (recipes below); for two others, Lemon-molasses and Ornament Cookies, see pages 162-163. (Note that comparative thinness has a bearing, too; directions for these four specify rolling to ⅛″ thickness.) An exception is a pressed cookie, Cream Cheese Spritz Cookies (page 168); made in a wreath shape, it works very well as an ornament.

LEMON-MOLASSES COOKIES
(shown at left)

- 3 cups flour
- 1 teaspoon ground ginger
- ¾ teaspoon baking soda
- ½ teaspoon salt
- ½ cup each shortening and sugar
- ½ cup dark molasses
- 1 egg
- 1 teaspoon lemon extract
  Ornamental Icing (recipe below)
  Colored sugar (optional)

Preheat oven to 375°F. Stir together flour, ginger, baking soda and salt; set aside. In large bowl, cream shortening and sugar until fluffy. Add molasses, egg and lemon extract; beat well. Stir in flour mixture until well blended. Wrap airtight. Chill overnight or at least 2 hours (must be firm enough to roll). Cut dough in thirds; roll out each third (keep remainder in refrigerator) on lightly floured pastry cloth or other surface to about ⅛" thickness. Cut shapes, using small holiday cookie cutters. With broad spatula, transfer to lightly greased baking sheet, keeping cookies ¼" apart. Repeat with remaining dough and scraps. For tree ornaments, make small hole near top of each cookie with wooden pick. Bake 6 to 7 minutes, or until light brown. Remove to racks to cool. Spread or pipe Ornamental Icing (see Note) on top and sprinkle with colored sugar if desired. Let dry in single layer. Store airtight in cool place. Makes about 108 small cookies. **Note:** To pipe icing, make 7" deep cone of parchment, waxed paper or other heavy paper. Seal with tape, then snip off tip to make small opening. Half fill with icing; fold over top; squeeze out frosting in desired pattern.

ORNAMENTAL ICING

In small bowl, beat 2 egg whites with ¼ teaspoon each salt and cream of tartar until stiff. Gradually add 2 cups confectioners' sugar; beat until shiny and stiff. Makes about 1½ cups or enough to frost approximately 108 small cookies.

SPICE RUSKS

- 1½ cups flour
- 1½ teaspoons baking powder
- ½ teaspoon salt
- ½ cup butter or margarine, softened
- ⅓ cup sugar
- 1 teaspoon cardamom or nutmeg
- ⅓ cup milk

Preheat oven to 450°F. Stir together flour, baking powder and salt; set aside. In large bowl, cream butter, sugar and cardamom until fluffy. Stir in flour mixture alternately with milk just until blended. Turn dough out on lightly floured surface and pat or roll out ½" thick. Cut out 1" rounds and place ½" apart on cookie sheet. Bake in 450° oven 10 minutes, or until puffed and light golden. Remove from oven. Reduce heat to 350°. Leave on cookie sheet to cool slightly, then, using fork tines, split each cookie horizontally. Place split side up on cookie sheet; return to lowered oven and bake 10 minutes, or until golden. Turn off heat; leave cookies in oven with door ajar about 30 minutes, or until dry. Remove to racks to cool. Store loosely covered in cool, dry place. Makes about 72.

ORNAMENT COOKIES
(shown above and below)

½ cup butter or margarine

¾ cup sugar

1 egg

¾ teaspoon peppermint extract

1 tablespoon milk

1½ cups unsifted all-purpose flour

⅓ cup cocoa

½ teaspoon baking powder

⅛ teaspoon salt

    Red cinnamon candies

    Colored sprinkles, gumdrops (optional)

    Peppermint Frosting (recipe below)

Preheat oven to 325°F. Cream butter, sugar, egg, peppermint extract and milk in large mixer bowl until light and fluffy. Stir together flour, cocoa, baking powder and salt; add to creamed mixture. Mix until well blended. Divide dough into quarters; wrap tightly. Chill 2 to 3 hours. Roll out dough, one quarter at a time, to ⅛" thickness on a lightly floured surface. Cut the dough with a gingerbread boy or girl cookie cutter, or use star, bell, reindeer, Santa Claus or other Christmas shapes. Or cut half of dough into those shapes and cut remaining dough into 3" x 2½" rectangles to resemble gift tags. With wooden pick, make hole about ½" from edge of cookies to be hung on tree. Place cookies 1" apart on ungreased baking sheet. Make buttons on gingerbread cookies and holly berries on gift tags with cinnamon candies. Bake 8 to 10 minutes, or until firm. Cool on wire racks. Decorate cookies using Peppermint Frosting and, if desired, colored sprinkles and gumdrops. (On gift tags, tuck bits of green gumdrops near holly berries to simulate leaves.) Makes about 24 cookies.

PEPPERMINT FROSTING

With mixer on low, combine 2½ to 3 cups confectioners' sugar, 2 egg whites and ¼ teaspoon peppermint extract in small mixer bowl. Increase speed to high and beat until the mixture is very stiff.

REFRIGERATED AND SLICED COOKIES

LEMON-CARAWAY REFRIGERATOR COOKIES

2⅓ cups flour
½ teaspoon baking soda
½ cup butter or margarine, softened
1 cup sugar
1 egg
2 tablespoons lemon juice
1 teaspoon grated lemon peel
1¼ teaspoons caraway seed
Colored sugar (optional)

Stir together flour and baking soda; set aside. In medium bowl, cream butter and sugar. Beat in egg until light and fluffy. Beat in lemon juice, peel and caraway seed until blended. Stir in flour mixture just until well blended. Shape in roll about 2″ thick. Wrap; chill 1 hour. If roll is flat on bottom, roll on counter so cookies will be round when cut. Chill several hours more or overnight.

To bake, preheat oven to 375°F. With very sharp knife, cut roll in ¼″ slices. Place on greased cookie sheets; sprinkle with colored sugar, if using. Bake 10 minutes, or until cookies are lightly browned around the edges. Remove immediately to racks to cool. Store loosely covered in cool, dry place. Makes about 36.

CHECKERBOARD COOKIES
(shown on page 152)

1 cup butter or margarine, softened
½ cup sugar
2 teaspoons vanilla
⅛ teaspoon salt
2¼ cups flour
¼ cup cocoa, preferably Dutch process

In large bowl, cream butter, sugar, vanilla and salt until fluffy. Gradually stir in flour until blended. Gather into ball. Divide ball in half. With hands or sturdy spoon, work cocoa into one of the halves until well blended. Divide each half in quarters. Shape each quarter into a ½″-thick rope, lightly flouring hands if necessary. Place a chocolate and a white rope parallel to each other, then a white rope on top of the chocolate and a chocolate rope on the white. Press lightly to form a compact roll. Repeat with remaining dough. Wrap rolls airtight; chill several hours or overnight.

To bake, preheat oven to 350°F. Cut rolls in 3⁄16″ slices. Place ½″ apart on lightly greased cookie sheet. Bake 12 minutes, or until white dough turns golden. Remove to rack to cool. Store loosely covered in cool place. Makes about 72.

BARS AND SQUARES

CHOCOLATE-GLAZED OATMEAL BARS

½ cup flour
½ teaspoon each salt and baking soda
½ cup butter or margarine, softened
¾ cup packed brown sugar
1 egg
1 teaspoon vanilla
1½ cups quick-cooking oatmeal
¾ cup finely chopped walnuts, divided
¾ cup semisweet-chocolate pieces

Preheat oven to 375°F. Stir together flour, salt and baking soda; set aside. In large bowl, cream butter, sugar, egg and vanilla until fluffy. Stir in flour mixture, then oatmeal and ½ cup walnuts. Spread mixture evenly in well-greased 13″ x 9″ x 2″ baking pan. With lightly floured palm of hand, flatten surface. Bake 12 minutes, or until golden brown and firm to touch. Remove pan to rack; sprinkle evenly with chocolate pieces. Let stand until chocolate melts. Spread melted chocolate evenly. Sprinkle with remaining ¼ cup walnuts. Cool until chocolate hardens. With small sharp knife, cut in bars about 2″ x 1½″. Store loosely covered in cool, dry place. Ships well. Makes 36. **Note:** For a tender drop cookie, fold chocolate pieces into batter. Drop batter by slightly heaping teaspoonfuls 1½″ apart on lightly greased cookie sheets. Bake in preheated 375° oven 8 to 10 minutes, or until golden brown. Cool 1 minute, then remove with flexible spatula to rack to cool completely. Store loosely covered in cool place with waxed paper between layers. Makes about 65.

CHEWY COCONUT BARS

- ½ cup butter or margarine, softened
- 1½ cups packed brown sugar, divided
- 1¼ cups flour, divided
- 2 eggs
- 1 teaspoon vanilla
- 1 cup each flaked coconut and chopped nuts

Preheat oven to 375°F. In medium bowl, beat butter with ½ cup sugar until light and fluffy. Beat in 1 cup flour until blended. Pat mixture into greased 13" x 9" x 2" pan (see Note). Bake 12 minutes, or until lightly browned; remove from oven. In medium bowl, beat eggs slightly; stir in vanilla, coconut, nuts and remaining 1 cup sugar and ¼ cup flour until well blended. Spread on mixture in pan. Bake 20 minutes longer, or until golden brown. Remove to wire rack and cool slightly. Cut in bars about 2" x 1½". Cool completely in pan. Store in pan, tightly covered, in cool place. Makes 36. **Note:** Recipe can be halved and baked in an 8"-square pan.

MATRIMONIAL BARS

- 1¾ cups flour
- ½ teaspoon baking soda
- ¾ cup butter or margarine, softened
- 1 cup packed brown sugar
- 1½ cups quick oats
- 1 jar (12 ounces) strawberry or raspberry jam (1 cup)

Preheat oven to 400°F. Stir together flour and baking soda; set aside. In medium bowl, cream butter and sugar until light and fluffy. Stir in flour mixture until well blended. Blend in oats (with fingers or wooden spoon). Dough will be crumbly. Press half the dough into greased 13" x 9" x 2" pan. Spread with jam. Crumble remaining dough over top; pat lightly to cover. Bake 20 to 25 minutes, or until lightly browned. While warm, cut in bars about 2" x 1½" and remove from pan. Serve warm or cooled. Store airtight in cool place. Makes 36.

CRISP CHOCOLATE-BROWNIE SQUARES

- ¼ cup butter or margarine
- 1 square (1 ounce) unsweetened chocolate
- ½ cup sugar
- 1 egg
- 1 teaspoon vanilla
- ⅛ teaspoon salt
- ¼ cup flour
- ⅓ cup finely chopped filberts or walnuts

Preheat oven to 400°F. In small heavy saucepan, over low heat, melt butter and chocolate. Remove from heat; stir in sugar, egg, vanilla, salt and flour until well blended. Spread scant ½ cup batter in each of 2 well-greased 8"-square pans (pan size is important; layers will be thin). Sprinkle with nuts. Bake 12 minutes, or until top is firm to touch. Cool in pans on rack 2 minutes. Cut brownies in each into 16 squares. Cool completely in pans. With small flexible spatula, remove squares to racks. (Start in center of pan to prevent cookies from breaking.) Store loosely covered in a dry place. Makes 32.

IF YOU FANCY cookies that are extra easy to make, turn the page for an impressive array. From it, these Pecan-pie Bars and Chocolate Cheesecake Squares (recipes, pages 171 and 168). Other types, too, are well represented.

Ever-so-easy Cookies

On the train, from left: Nutty Chocolate Bars, page 171; Molasses Crinkles, page 168; Peanut Butter-and-preserves Crumb Bars, page 169.

Foreground, from left: Double-chocolate Cherry-bourbon Balls, page 170; No-bake Orange Cookies, page 169; Easy Almond Fingers, page 170; Cream-cheese Spritz Cookies (also on tree), page 168; Coconut-almond Cookies, page 171; Pecan-pie Bars, page 171; Chocolate Cheesecake Squares, page 168.

CREAM-CHEESE SPRITZ COOKIES
(shown above)

   1 package (8 ounces) cream cheese, softened
   1 cup butter or margarine, softened
   1 cup sugar
1½ teaspoons vanilla
   2 cups flour
     Sliced unblanched almonds, sliced red or green candied cherries to garnish wreath shapes
     Jam or preserves for centers of plain rounds

Preheat oven to 350°F. In medium bowl or in food processor, beat or process cheese, butter, sugar and vanilla until fluffy. Add flour gradually, beating or processing until thoroughly blended. Working with 1 cup at a time, press dough through cookie press or pastry bag, fitted with a large star-tip tube, onto ungreased cookie sheets to form 1½" wreath-shaped or plain round cookies. Following photograph above, garnish wreaths with almonds and cherries pressed gently into dough to secure. Make depression in middle of plain cookies with fingertip. Bake 12 to 15 minutes, or until lightly browned on edges and bottom. Remove to racks to cool. Fill depressions in plain rounds with jam. Loop cord or ribbon through wreaths to use them as tree ornaments (see photograph). Makes about 54.

MOLASSES CRINKLES
(shown on pages 166-167)

   2 cups flour
   1 teaspoon each baking soda, cinnamon and ginger
  ½ teaspoon salt
  ½ cup shortening
  ½ cup sugar
   1 egg
  ½ cup molasses

Preheat oven to 375°F. In medium bowl or on waxed paper, mix flour, baking soda, cinnamon, ginger and salt; set aside. In large bowl, cream shortening and sugar until fluffy. Beat in egg and molasses. Stir in flour mixture just until well blended. Drop by teaspoonfuls ½" apart on greased cookie sheets. Bake 12 to 15 minutes, or until lightly browned. Remove to racks to cool. Makes about 48.

CHOCOLATE CHEESECAKE SQUARES
(shown on page 167)

  ½ cup butter or margarine
1½ cups chocolate-wafer crumbs (about 30 wafers)
  ¾ cup finely chopped nuts, divided
   2 packages (3 ounces each) cream cheese, softened
  ½ cup sugar
  ⅓ cup cocoa
   1 egg
   1 teaspoon vanilla

Melt butter in 9"-square baking pan while oven is preheating to 350°F. Stir crumbs and ½ cup nuts into melted butter in pan until well blended. Pat evenly to cover pan bottom. In small bowl, beat cream cheese, sugar, cocoa, egg and vanilla until smooth and well blended. Pour mixture over crust in pan. Sprinkle with remaining ¼ cup nuts. Bake 20 minutes. Cool in pan on rack. Cut into 1½" squares. Keep chilled. Makes 36.

PEANUT BUTTER-AND-PRESERVES CRUMB BARS
(shown on page 167)

1 package (14 ounces) peanut butter-cookie mix

1 egg

¾ cup strawberry or raspberry preserves

Preheat oven to 350°F. In small bowl, combine cookie mix and egg; stir lightly with fork until coarse crumbs form; set aside ½ cup mixture. Press remaining mixture onto bottom of greased 8"-square baking pan. Spread preserves evenly over crumb mixture in pan. Sprinkle reserved ½ cup crumb mixture over preserves. Bake 30 to 35 minutes, or until golden brown. Cool in pan on rack. Cut in 2" x 1" bars. Makes 32.

PEANUT BUTTEROONS

½ cup confectioners' sugar

1 cup each smooth peanut butter and marshmallow-cream topping

Cinnamon (optional)

Preheat oven to 375°F. In small bowl, beat sugar and peanut butter until smooth; fold in marshmallow until blended. Shape in 1" balls; place 2" apart on foil-lined baking sheets. Bake 8 to 10 minutes, or until lightly browned on bottom. Cool on sheet 1 minute. Remove to racks to cool completely. Sprinkle with cinnamon, if desired. Makes about 32.

MINCEMEAT-SUGAR GEMS

1 roll (17 ounces) refrigerated slice-and-bake sugar-cookie dough

¾ cup mincemeat with brandy and rum

Orange Glaze (recipe below)

Chopped candied orange peel for garnish (optional)

Preheat oven to 350°F. Slice dough ¼" thick; roll slices into balls. Place 2" apart on ungreased cookie sheets. Make depression in middle of each ball with fingertip; fill with 1 teaspoon mincemeat. Bake 9 to 12 minutes, or until lightly browned. Cool 1 minute on sheet; remove to rack set over waxed paper. Drizzle 1 teaspoon Orange Glaze over each cookie. Cool completely. Decorate top with orange peel, if desired. Makes about 36.

ORANGE GLAZE

In medium bowl, mix 2 cups confectioners' sugar with 3 tablespoons orange juice until smooth.

NO-BAKE BANANA-PEANUT NUGGETS

2 cups vanilla-wafer crumbs (about 56 wafers)

½ cup each wheat germ, mashed banana and chunky peanut butter

Confectioners' sugar

In medium bowl, mix crumbs and wheat germ with banana and peanut butter until well moistened. Shape in 1" balls; roll in sugar. Makes about 36.

NO-BAKE ORANGE COOKIES
(shown on page 166)

4 cups graham-cracker crumbs (see Note)

1 cup confectioners' sugar

⅓ cup thawed frozen orange-juice concentrate

¼ cup each light corn syrup and butter or margarine, melted

1 cup finely chopped nuts

In large bowl, mix all ingredients until well blended. Shape in 1" balls. Store at room temperature. Makes about 60. **Note:** Gingersnap crumbs can be substituted if desired.

EASY ALMOND FINGERS
(shown on page 166)

- 2 cups flour
- ½ teaspoon salt
- 1 can (8 ounces) almond paste, cut in small pieces
- ½ cup plus 1 tablespoon butter or margarine
- ½ cup packed brown sugar
- 1 egg
- ½ cup semisweet-chocolate pieces

Preheat oven to 325°F. In small bowl or on waxed paper, mix flour with salt; set aside. In medium bowl, cream almond paste with ½ cup butter until fluffy. Gradually beat in sugar and egg until blended. Gradually add flour mixture: blend thoroughly. Shape level tablespoonfuls dough into 2″-long fingers. Place 1″ apart on ungreased baking sheets. Bake 20 to 25 minutes, or until just very lightly browned. Remove to racks to cool. In small heavy saucepan, over low heat, stir chocolate and remaining tablespoon butter until melted and smooth. Dip fork into melted chocolate; moving fork back and forth over cookies, let chocolate drop off tines to make thin lines. Makes about 48.

DOUBLE-CHOCOLATE CHERRY-BOURBON BALLS
(shown above)

- 1 package (6 ounces) semisweet-chocolate pieces
- 3 tablespoons corn syrup
- ½ cup bourbon (see Note)
- 1 package (8½ ounces) chocolate wafers, crushed (2¼ cups)
- 1 cup finely chopped nuts
- ½ cup confectioners' sugar
- ¼ cup finely chopped candied red cherries
- Granulated sugar

In top of double boiler or bowl set over hot (not boiling) water, melt chocolate. Remove from heat; stir in corn syrup and bourbon. In large bowl, mix well wafer crumbs, nuts, confectioners' sugar and cherries. Add chocolate mixture; stir until blended. Let stand 30 minutes. Shape in 1″ balls; roll in granulated sugar. Makes about 54. **Note:** Ginger ale can be substituted for bourbon.

SAUCEPAN CANDIED FRUIT BARS

- 3 cups flour
- ½ teaspoon each baking soda and salt
- 1 cup butter or margarine
- 1½ cups sugar
- 2 eggs
- 2 teaspoons vanilla
- ¼ cup orange juice
- 2 cups chopped mixed candied fruit
- Orange Glaze (recipe below)

Preheat oven to 350°F. In medium bowl or on waxed paper, mix well flour, baking soda and salt, set aside. In medium saucepan, over low heat, melt butter. Add sugar, eggs and vanilla; mix well. Add flour mixture and orange juice; mix well. Stir in candied fruit. Spread in greased 15″ x 10″ x 1″ jellyroll pan. Bake 25 minutes, or until golden brown. While still warm, brush with Orange Glaze. Cool completely in pan on rack. Cut in 2″ x 1″ bars. Makes 75.

ORANGE GLAZE

In small bowl, blend 1 cup confectioners' sugar with 4 teaspoons orange juice until smooth.

COCONUT-ALMOND COOKIES
(shown below)

1¼ cups flour

¼ teaspoon salt

½ cup butter or margarine

⅓ cup sugar

1 egg, separated

1 teaspoon almond extract

1 cup flaked or shredded coconut

¼ cup apricot preserves

Preheat oven to 300°F. In small bowl or on waxed paper, stir together flour and salt; set aside. In medium bowl or food processor, cream butter and sugar until light and fluffy. Add egg yolk and almond extract; beat or process until blended. Gradually add flour mixture; beat or process until blended. Chill dough 2 hours, or until firm enough to shape. Roll in 1" balls. Dip in slightly beaten egg white; roll lightly in coconut. Place 2" apart on greased baking sheets; make depression in middle of cookies with fingertip. Bake 20 to 25 minutes, or until just firm to touch and coconut is lightly browned. Cool 30 seconds on sheets; remove to racks to cool completely. Fill depressions with preserves. Makes about 24.

CHOCOLATE-CHIP PASTRY DROPS

1 package (11 ounces) pie-crust mix, crumbled

1 cup sour cream

½ cup packed brown sugar

2 tablespoons butter or margarine, softened

1½ teaspoons vanilla

1 cup small-size semisweet-chocolate pieces

Preheat oven to 375°F. In medium bowl, beat all ingredients but chocolate until a well-blended, soft dough forms; fold in chocolate pieces. Drop by rounded teaspoonfuls 2" apart onto greased baking sheets. Bake 12 minutes, or until lightly browned. Remove cookies to racks to cool. Makes about 48.

PECAN-PIE BARS
(shown on page 167)

1⅓ cups flour

½ cup plus 2 tablespoons packed brown sugar

½ cup butter or margarine

2 eggs

½ cup light corn syrup

¾ cup finely chopped pecans

2 tablespoons butter or margarine, melted

1 teaspoon vanilla

⅛ teaspoon salt

Preheat oven to 350°F. In small bowl, mix well the flour and the 2 tablespoons brown sugar. With fingers, work in ½ cup butter until dough begins to hold together. Press onto bottom of greased 9"-square baking pan. Bake 12 to 15 minutes, or until just firm. In medium bowl, lightly beat the ½ cup brown sugar and the eggs; add corn syrup, pecans, melted butter, vanilla and salt; mix well. Pour over crust. Bake 25 minutes, or just until edges are lightly browned. Cool in pan on rack. Cut into 3" x 1" bars. Makes 27.

NUTTY CHOCOLATE BARS
(shown on page 166)

1⅔ cups biscuit mix

¾ cup granulated sugar

1 package (6 ounces) semisweet-chocolate pieces

½ cup coarsely chopped walnuts

⅓ cup cocoa

⅓ cup butter or margarine, melted

1 egg, slightly beaten
Confectioners' sugar (optional)

Preheat oven to 350°F. Stir together biscuit mix, granulated sugar, chocolate, walnuts and cocoa. Add butter and egg; stir just enough to moisten dry ingredients. Spread in greased 9"-square baking pan. Bake 30 minutes, or until wooden pick inserted in center comes out clean. Cool in pan on rack. Cut in 3" x 1" bars. Sprinkle with confectioners' sugar, if desired. Makes 27.

CHOCOLATE-CORNFLAKE CONFECTIONS

1 package (6 ounces) semisweet-chocolate pieces

1 can (14 ounces) sweetened condensed milk

1 teaspoon almond extract

2 cups each cornflakes cereal and flaked or shredded coconut

12 candied red cherries, cut in quarters

Preheat oven to 350°F. In top of double boiler or bowl set over simmering water, melt chocolate. Remove from heat; stir in milk and almond extract until smooth and blended. Stir in cornflakes and coconut until well combined. Drop by heaping teaspoonfuls onto baking sheets lined with foil, then greased. Gently press cherry piece in middle of each. Bake 8 to 10 minutes, or until just firm to touch. Remove immediately to racks to cool. Makes about 48.

Cookies that Take to Travel

CREAM CHEESE-COCONUT BROWNIES
(shown at right)

- 1 package (4 ounces) sweet cooking chocolate
- 5 tablespoons butter or margarine, divided
- 1 package (3 ounces) cream cheese, softened
- 1 cup sugar, divided
- 3 eggs, divided
- ½ cup plus 1 tablespoon all-purpose flour
- 1½ teaspoons vanilla, divided
- 1⅓ cups flaked coconut (about)
- ½ teaspoon double-acting baking powder
- ¼ teaspoon salt

Preheat oven to 350°F. Melt chocolate and 3 tablespoons of the butter in small saucepan over low heat, stirring constantly. Cool. Blend remaining butter with cream cheese until softened. Gradually add ¼ cup of the sugar, beating well. Blend in 1 egg, 1 tablespoon flour, ½ teaspoon vanilla and the coconut. Set aside. Beat 2 remaining eggs until thick and light-colored. Gradually add remaining ¾ cup sugar, beating until thickened. Add baking powder, salt and remaining ½ cup flour. Blend in cooled chocolate mixture and remaining 1 teaspoon vanilla. Spread about half the chocolate batter in greased 8"- or 9"-square pan. Alternately spoon remaining chocolate batter and cream cheese batter on top. Zigzag a spatula through batters to marble. Bake 35 to 40 minutes, or until top springs back when lightly pressed in center. Cool. Cut into bars or squares. Makes about 16 to 20.

COCONUT CHERRY BARS
(shown at right)

- 1¼ cups unsifted all-purpose flour, divided
- ½ cup butter or margarine, softened
- 3 tablespoons sugar
- ½ teaspoon double-acting baking powder
- ¼ teaspoon salt
- ¾ cup sugar
- 2 eggs, slightly beaten
- 1 teaspoon vanilla
- 1⅓ cups flaked coconut (about)
- ½ cup chopped maraschino cherries
- ¼ cup chopped walnuts

Preheat oven to 350°F. Combine 1 cup of the flour, butter and sugar; blend well. Press firmly in bottom of 9"-square pan. Bake 25 minutes.

Meanwhile, mix together remaining ¼ cup flour, baking powder and salt. Add sugar to eggs, beating well. Blend in flour mixture and vanilla. Stir in coconut, cherries and nuts. Spread over baked crust; bake 35 minutes longer. Cut into bars while still warm. Makes about 2 dozen.

FINE COOKIE TRAVELERS are great stay at homes, too. In the square box, Coconut Sugar Cookies; in the rectangular box, Coconut Cherry Bars; in the jar, Brownie Drops; on the tray, Vanilla-nut Icebox Cookies and Cream Cheese-coconut Brownies. Recipes complete here and on page 174.

VANILLA-NUT ICEBOX COOKIES
(shown on page 173)

1¾ cups all-purpose flour

1½ teaspoons double-acting baking powder

⅛ teaspoon salt

6 tablespoons butter or other shortening

1 cup granulated sugar

¼ cup firmly packed brown sugar

1 egg, well beaten

1 cup flaked coconut

½ cup chopped nuts

1½ teaspoons vanilla

Two-tone Butter Cream Frosting (recipe below)

Mix flour with baking powder and salt. Cream shortening. Gradually beat in sugars and continue beating until light and fluffy. Add egg, coconut, nuts and vanilla; mix well. Add flour mixture gradually, mixing well after each addition. Shape into rolls 1½" in diameter, and roll in waxed paper. Chill overnight or until firm.

To bake, preheat oven to 425°F. Cut in ⅛" slices; place on ungreased baking sheets. Bake 5 minutes, or until lightly browned around edges. Decorate with red- and green-tinted frosting, if desired. Makes about 8 dozen.

TWO-TONE BUTTER CREAM FROSTING

Combine 2½ cups sifted confectioners' sugar and a dash of salt. Cream 6 tablespoons butter or margarine; add part of sugar gradually, blending after each addition until mixture is light and fluffy. Add remaining sugar alternately with 3 tablespoons hot milk, beating after each addition until smooth. Add ¼ teaspoon vanilla. Divide frosting in half, putting each half in a separate bowl. Tint half the frosting with a few drops of green food coloring and the other half with red.

BROWNIE DROPS
(shown on page 173)

2 packages (4 ounces each) sweet cooking chocolate

1 tablespoon butter or margarine

2 eggs

¾ cup sugar

¼ cup all-purpose flour

¼ teaspoon double-acting baking powder

⅛ teaspoon salt

¼ teaspoon cinnamon

¾ cup finely chopped pecans

½ teaspoon vanilla

Pecan halves (optional)

Preheat oven to 350°F. Melt chocolate and butter in saucepan over very low heat, stirring constantly. Remove from heat; set aside. Beat eggs until foamy. Gradually beat in sugar and continue beating until very thick, about 5 minutes. Blend in chocolate mixture. Add flour, baking powder, salt and cinnamon; blend well. Stir in nuts and vanilla. Drop by teaspoonfuls onto greased baking sheets. Place a pecan half on each cookie, if desired. Bake 10 to 12 minutes, or until firm when lightly touched. Store in tightly covered container. Makes about 3 dozen.

COCONUT SUGAR COOKIES
(shown on page 173)

1¾ cups unsifted all-purpose flour

1½ teaspoons double-acting baking powder

½ teaspoon salt

⅔ cup butter or margarine

⅔ cup sugar

2 eggs, well beaten

1 teaspoon vanilla

1 cup finely chopped flaked coconut

Colored sugar or silver dragees (optional)

Preheat oven to 375°F. Mix flour with baking powder and salt. Cream the butter; gradually add sugar and beat until light and fluffy. Add eggs and beat thoroughly; then add flour mixture gradually, mixing well. Stir in vanilla and coconut. Chill until firm. Roll dough ⅛" thick on lightly floured board. Cut with floured 3" cutter and sprinkle with colored sugar or decorate with silver dragees, if desired. Bake on ungreased baking sheets 12 minutes, or until lightly browned. Makes about 2 dozen.

HOW TO BE SURE YOUR COOKIES TRAVEL WELL

What types travel best? That's the first consideration in making sure that cookies arrive at their destination in good, uncrumbly shape. The cookies in this section are, of course, far from the only "traveling" possibilities, but together they do represent the characteristics to look for. You will note that they are predominantly of the bar, square or drop varieties; such soft and chewy cookies can "take it" far better than crisp ones, especially over long distances. For similar reasons, no-bake cookies are good choices. If crisp cookies are your preference, select either a rolled or refrigerated-and-sliced cookie; pressed cookies tend to be too fragile, unless you are carrying them by hand and not very far. See the discussion below for ways to protect cookies in packing.

Look, as you scan recipe titles, for words like mounds, clusters, balls, chews; in ingredients, for such things as nuts, coconut, fruits, mincemeat and cereals. Avoid cookies with decorations that are likely to break, fall off, drip (jams, for example) or shed (confectioners' sugar).

Packing cookies to go: Whether cookies will be traveling by hand or by mail, you will want their containers to be attractive; you will need them to be firm and strong.

If you are a saver, keep your eyes open for commercial packaging that is in itself good-looking, or can easily be made so. Coffee cans or well-made boxes can be covered with self-stick vinyl, for example. Plastic containers, particularly those with tight-fitting lids, are ideal for packing cookies; a ribbon and bow, with a pretty gift tag, may be all you need to dress them up. Plastic containers, boxes and tins can all be bought inexpensively in variety stores; collect these at holiday times, when they are most plentiful.

In packing, strive for a happy medium: Cookies should not rattle around—this can cause breakage. But don't pack them too tightly either; cookies can damage each other. Fill a container adequately, and take up the slack with crushed tissue or waxed paper.

Arrange cookies in rows, a layer at a time, with heavier ones at the bottom and waxed paper between layers. Wrap fragile cookies individually in plastic wrap (flat ones back to back in pairs). For added elegance (and good protection), consider tucking wrapped cookies in paper or foil baking cups, as commercial cookie packagers do.

COOKIE GIFTS in containers you'd be proud to present. **Far left and right:** decorative tins of No-bake Orange Cookies, page 169, and Double-chocolate Cherry-bourbon Balls, page 170. **In the center:** Cream-cheese Spritz Cookies and Molasses Crinkles in pretty ceramic holders (both recipes on page 168).

Those precautions are sufficient for cookies delivered by hand, but much more must be done if they are to travel by mail.

• Use packing boxes that are sturdy; line them with waxed paper; cushion the bottom with crumpled waxed paper or paper towels.

• For overseas mailing, pack in metal or wooden containers.

• Wrap flat cookies in back-to-back pairs in plastic wrap; wrap others individually.

• Pack wrapped cookies in layered rows, with waxed paper between.

• Top the packed cookies with a cushion of crushed waxed paper or paper toweling, leaving a bit of headspace (about ¼") between cushion and lid.

Beyond that, proceed as you would with any package to be mailed: Tape the box shut; print mailing and return addresses on it; wrap in heavy brown paper and tie securely. Label the front of the package with both addresses; cover with transparent tape; add Handle with Care stickers (or print these words yourself, big and bold, with a felt-tip marker).

EASY-DOES-IT PARTY FOODS

With holidays so social, it can be hard to face giving a party yourself. Yet you must reciprocate, and you want to—entertaining close friends is half the joy of Christmas. To make partygiving a pleasure all around, try an array of appetizer-type foods. They are easy on you and "light" on your guests—a blessing in this overindulgent season. And fantastically varied—just see for yourself!

PATÉS, DIPS AND SPREADS

COUNTRY PATÉ

- 1 **pound beef liver**
- 1 **cup minced onion (1 large)**
- ½ **cup sherry (see Note)**
- ¾ **pound pork sausage meat**
- ½ **pound ground beef**
- 2 **eggs**
- 1 **to 2 cloves garlic, crushed**
- 1 **teaspoon salt**
- ½ **teaspoon ginger**
- 7 **slices bacon**

Preheat oven to 375°F. Chop liver fine in food processor or blender or mince by hand; set aside. In small saucepan, cook onion and sherry, stirring occasionally to prevent burning, until liquid evaporates and onion is tender. In bowl, combine sherry-onion mixture, liver, sausage meat, beef, eggs, garlic, salt and ginger (mixture will be loose). Line 9" x 5" x 3" loaf pan with bacon strips, placing them halfway across bottom and up sides so that a 1½" to 2" end extends over pan edges. Spoon in meat mixture; fold bacon over top. Place pan of meat mixture in large pan containing enough boiling water to come halfway up sides of loaf pan. Bake 1½ hours, or until juices run clear when loaf is pierced with knife. Remove from oven. Cool in water bath with a small pan or foil over top weighted down with cans or other heavy object, then chill. Will keep refrigerated up to 1½ weeks. Makes about 10 slices. **Note:** Beef broth may be substituted for sherry.

MUSHROOM PATÉ

- 1 **pound fresh mushrooms**
- 1 **bunch green onions (about 12 small), trimmed to 5" length**
- 1 **package (3 ounces) cream cheese, softened**
- 2 **eggs**
- ¾ **cup fine dry bread crumbs**
- 2 **tablespoons dry sherry**
- 1 **teaspoon salt**
- ⅛ **teaspoon hot-pepper sauce**

Preheat oven to 375°F. Grease 8" x 4" x 2" loaf pan; line with waxed paper; grease again; set aside. Brush mushrooms clean (rinse only if necessary; pat dry with paper towels). Cut mushrooms in quarters and green onions in 1" pieces. Chop fine with food processor or large knife. Add remaining ingredients; process or mix well until smooth.

If using blender, reverse procedure: Whirl eggs, cream cheese, sherry and seasonings until well blended. Alternately add mushrooms and green onions; whirl until smooth. Add bread crumbs; whirl until blended.

Spoon mixture into prepared pan. Set in pan with 1" of hot water. Bake 50 minutes, or until knife inserted in center comes out clean. Remove from water; cool on rack 10 minutes. Loosen edges; unmold on serving dish; discard paper. Keeps refrigerated about 5 days. Makes about 12 slices.

EAT, DRINK AND BE MERRY as they do in Denmark! **Top,** Danish Glögg, page 187; **center,** hors d'oeuvres platter of Radish-cheese Canapés, Stuffed Mushrooms and Stuffed Cucumber Slices, page 185; **foreground,** Cheese and Olive Bowl and Blue Cheese-pecan Appetizers, page 185.

CARROT PATÉ
(shown on page 134)

1½ pounds carrots, cut in 2" pieces (15 medium)

    Salt

3 eggs

½ cup mayonnaise

2 teaspoons Worcestershire sauce

1 teaspoon white vinegar

½ teaspoon each salt and thyme

⅛ teaspoon hot-pepper sauce

1 teaspoon dried parsley flakes

Preheat oven to 375°F. Grease 7½" x 4" x 2" loaf pan; line with waxed paper; grease again; set aside. Cook carrots covered in lightly salted boiling water about 10 minutes, or until crisp-tender (do not overcook). Drain well and allow to cool.

If using food processor, process carrots until ground coarse; add eggs, mayonnaise, Worcestershire sauce, vinegar, salt, thyme and pepper sauce; process until well blended. If using blender, reverse procedure: Whirl eggs, mayonnaise and seasonings until well blended, then add carrots and whirl until carrots are ground coarse.

Spoon mixture into prepared pan (pan will be quite full). Place in pan with 1" hot water. Bake 35 to 40 minutes, or until knife inserted in center comes out clean. Remove from water; cool on rack 10 minutes. Loosen around edges and unmold on serving dish. Sprinkle with parsley. Slice and serve warm, or chill before serving. Keeps about 3 days. Makes 15 slices.

SPICED MEAT SPREAD

2 cans (5½ ounces each) potted meat (meat spread)

¼ cup drained bottled horseradish

1 tablespoon Worcestershire sauce, or to taste

2 tablespoons minced parsley

In bowl, mix well potted meat, horseradish and Worcestershire sauce. Turn into serving bowl and sprinkle with parsley. Makes about 1⅔ cups.

GUACAMOLE

1 medium-size avocado, peeled, pitted and mashed

½ large tomato, chopped fine

1 small onion, minced (¼ cup)

2 tablespoons lemon or lime juice

½ teaspoon salt

3 to 4 drops hot-pepper sauce (optional)

    Corn chips or tortillas

Mix all ingredients well. Adjust seasonings. Serve with corn chips or toasted tortilla strips as dippers. Makes 1¾ cups.

CHILI-BEAN DIP

1 can (15½ ounces) kidney beans, drained and rinsed (reserve liquid)

3 tablespoons canned hot jalapeño relish

½ teaspoon ground cumin

¼ teaspoon salt

    Corn chips

Mash drained beans until smooth. Stir in relish, 2 tablespoons bean liquid, cumin and salt. Dilute with more bean liquid if desired. Serve with corn chips. Makes 1½ cups.

PEANUT BUTTER DIP

1¼ cups peanut butter

¾ cup chicken broth

¼ cup lemon juice

3 tablespoons soy sauce

2 medium cloves garlic, crushed

½ teaspoon sugar

¼ teaspoon salt

¼ teaspoon hot-pepper sauce

Combine all ingredients in small saucepan. Stir over low heat until well blended and smooth. Serve hot with pork or warm as raw-vegetable dip. (May thicken on standing; if so, reheat over simmering water before serving.) Makes 2 cups.

BEER CHEESE
(shown on page 141)

1¾ pounds Cheddar, shredded fine (about 7 packed cups; see Note)

12 ounces beer

2 tablespoons caraway seed (optional)

In large bowl, combine cheese and beer; cover; refrigerate several hours or overnight. Add seeds if desired; stir until blended and smooth. Spoon into gift or serving container; cover. Refrigerate up to 3 weeks. Makes about 6 cups. **Note:** For "foamy beer," make and layer 2 batches, one with yellow Cheddar, one with white.

BRANDIED CHEDDAR SPREAD

2 cups shredded Cheddar cheese (8 ounces)

1 package (3 ounces) cream cheese

¼ cup crumbled blue cheese

3 tablespoons brandy

2 tablespoons butter or margarine

1 to 2 teaspoons Worcestershire sauce

    Dash of salt

In small bowl or food processor, blend all ingredients until smooth and fluffy. Spoon into crock or other preferred container; cover. Store in refrigerator up to 2 weeks. Makes 1¾ cups.

LOW-CALORIE CHEESE SPREAD
(shown on page 131)

1 clove garlic, halved

1 package (8 ounces) Neufchatel cheese, softened

1 tablespoon chopped parsley

½ teaspoon freeze-dried chives

⅛ teaspoon ground thyme

Rub sides and bottom of small bowl with cut sides of garlic; discard garlic. Add cheese and, with wooden spoon or rubber spatula, cream until smooth. Add remaining ingredients; mix thoroughly. Cover and chill 24 hours to allow flavor to develop. Makes 1 cup.

CHEESE "APPLES"
(shown in photograph on pages 138-139)

- 2 tablespoons sesame seed
- 2 tablespoons brandy
- 1 pound sharp Cheddar cheese, shredded (about 4 cups)
- 1 package (3 ounces) cream cheese, softened
- 1 tablespoon prepared mustard, preferably spicy brown
- 1/8 teaspoon hot-pepper sauce
  Paprika
- 1 cinnamon stick, broken in half
- 4 bay leaves

Combine sesame seed and brandy; let stand 1 hour. With electric mixer, plastic blade of food processor or hands, blend cheeses, mustard, pepper sauce and sesame seed mixture until well mixed. Divide in half. Form each into apple shape. Sprinkle generously with paprika. Press piece of cinnamon stick into apple for stem; press bay leaves at base of stem for leaves. Wrap and chill until ready to serve.

SHERRIED CHEESE SPREAD
(shown on page 181)

- 1 package (8 ounces) cream cheese, softened
- 1/3 cup dry sherry
- 1 teaspoon dry mustard
- 1 teaspoon hot water
- 2 cups shredded Cheddar cheese (8 ounces)
  Chopped parsley (optional)

In small bowl, beat cream cheese with sherry until blended. Mix mustard with hot water; let stand 2 minutes to develop flavor. Stir into cream-cheese mixture with Cheddar. Turn into small crock or bowl. Cover and chill until ready to serve. Garnish with parsley if desired. Makes about 2 cups.

SAVORY LIVER SPREAD

- 8 ounces braunschweiger (smoked-liver sausage), at room temperature
- 1 package (3 ounces) cream cheese, at room temperature
- 1/4 cup finely chopped dill pickle
- 1 tablespoon each grated onion and Dijon-type mustard
- 2/3 cup chopped parsley

Mix well braunschweiger, cream cheese, pickle, onion and mustard. Chill until firm enough to handle easily. With lightly oiled hands, shape into two 6" logs. Roll in parsley to coat evenly. Wrap tightly. Refrigerate overnight to firm and to blend flavors. Makes two 6" logs.

HAM-CHICKEN SPREAD
(shown in photograph on pages 138-139)

- 1/2 cup each chopped cooked chicken and ham (home-cooked or canned)
- 2 tablespoons mayonnaise
- 2 tablespoons brandy
- 1 teaspoon prepared mustard
- 1/8 teaspoon crumbled dried tarragon (optional)
  Salt and fresh-ground pepper to taste
- 2 small bay leaves

In food processor or blender, whirl chicken, ham, mayonnaise, brandy and mustard until smooth. Add tarragon, salt and pepper; whirl until blended. Divide evenly between 2 small ramekins; top each with a bay leaf. Cover with plastic wrap. Will keep refrigerated about 1 week. Makes 1 cup.

SALMON SPREAD

- 1 package (8 ounces) cream cheese, at room temperature
- 1 can (7¾ ounces) salmon, well drained
- 2 teaspoons lemon juice
- 1 teaspoon prepared mustard
- 1/2 teaspoon seasoned salt, or to taste
  Dash of hot-pepper sauce
  Paprika and minced green onions for garnish (optional)

In medium bowl, combine all ingredients except paprika and green onions. Beat until smooth and well blended. Pack in small ramekins; smooth tops. Sprinkle with paprika and garnish with onions if desired. Cover and chill. Will keep refrigerated up to 1 week. Makes 1½ cups.

CURRIED TURKEY SPREAD

- 3¼ cups coarsely chopped cooked turkey (1 pound)
- 2 teaspoons curry powder
- 1 tablespoon hot water
- 1 cup mayonnaise
- 1/2 cup finely chopped celery
- 1/2 cup sliced green onions
- 3/4 teaspoon salt
- 1/4 teaspoon pepper
  Sliced green onions for garnish (optional)

Mince turkey very fine with sharp knife or grind in food grinder or processor. In medium bowl, mix curry powder with hot water; let stand 2 minutes to develop flavor. Stir in remaining ingredients, except garnish, and turkey. Turn into crock or bowl, cover and chill until ready to serve. Garnish, if desired, with sliced green onions. Makes about 3 cups.

MARINATED VEGETABLES, COLD TIDBITS

PICKLED HERRING, SWEDISH-STYLE
(shown on page 131)

½ cup white vinegar

¼ cup sugar

3 tablespoons water

2 small bay leaves

½ teaspoon each mustard seed and whole allspice

1 jar (16 ounces) pickled herring, drained (discard liquid and onions)

1 large red onion, sliced

1 small carrot, sliced

In small saucepan, bring vinegar, sugar, water, bay leaves, mustard seed and allspice to boil. Cool. Cut herring in ½"-wide pieces; layer tightly with onion and carrot slices in wide-mouth 3-cup glass jar. Add cooled pickling brine (should cover contents in jar). Cover and chill at least 2 days before serving. Serve directly from jar. Keeps refrigerated up to 2 weeks. Makes 3 cups (6 appetizer servings).

STUFFED EGGS

6 hard-cooked eggs, shelled

¼ cup mayonnaise

1½ teaspoons lemon juice

⅛ teaspoon each nutmeg and pepper

2 tablespoons chopped toasted walnuts

Halve eggs lengthwise. Remove yolks to small bowl; mash well. Stir in mayonnaise, lemon juice, nutmeg and pepper until blended. Spoon or pipe into whites. Garnish with walnuts. Makes 12. **Variation:** Stir walnuts into yolk mixture; spoon into whites. Garnish with pimiento and parsley.

FISH CUBES WITH MUSTARD-DILL DIP

1 package (16 ounces) frozen fish fillets

1 tablespoon lemon juice
Salt and pepper to taste

2 tablespoons butter or margarine
Mustard-dill Dip (recipe below)

Preheat oven to 450°F. Thaw fish at room temperature 15 minutes. Cut in 36 pieces. With broad spatula, transfer to 12" square of foil, keeping cubes intact. Sprinkle with lemon juice, salt and pepper. Dot with butter. Wrap tightly; place in shallow pan. Bake 40 minutes, or until fish flakes easily. Chill well. Unwrap; discard liquid and solidified butter. Arrange on platter with toothpick in each piece. Serve with Mustard-dill Dip. Makes 36.

MUSTARD-DILL DIP

Mix well ½ cup mayonnaise, 1 tablespoon prepared mustard and ¾ teaspoon dillweed. Chill at least 1 hour to blend flavors. Makes about ½ cup.

HERBED FETA-CHEESE CUBES
(shown in photograph on pages 138-139)

1 cup oil, preferably olive

¼ cup lemon juice

2 tablespoons minced green onion, including tender green tops

1 medium clove garlic, minced

1 teaspoon dried chervil or basil, crumbled

½ teaspoon salt
Dash of hot-pepper sauce

12 ounces feta cheese, cut in ¾" cubes (2½ cups)

In 3-cup plastic or glass container or jar, combine all ingredients except feta. Cover; shake to blend. Add feta; cover tightly and marinate at room temperature at least 1 week. Drain cubes, reserving liquid. Makes 2½ cups cheese cubes and 1¼ cups marinade (makes fine salad dressing).

QUICK PATÉ-STUFFED FRENCH BREAD

2 packages (8 ounces each) cream cheese, softened

1 can (4½ ounces) deviled ham

½ cup chopped green onions

¼ cup chopped parsley

1 jar (2 ounces) sliced pimientos, drained and diced (¼ cup)

1 tablespoon sweet pickle relish

1 loaf French bread (about 7 ounces)

In large bowl, beat cheese with ham until blended. Stir in onions, parsley, pimiento and relish. Cut 1" from each end of bread. With long serrated knife, carefully hollow out bread, leaving about ¼" shell all around. (Reserve insides for bread crumbs.) Stuff cheese mixture into bread. Wrap in foil; refrigerate overnight. Serve cut in 1"-thick slices. Makes 12.

ITALIAN ANTIPASTO
(shown on page 134)

1 cup white vinegar

1½ cups water

2 cloves garlic, crushed

1 package (0.6 ounces) Italian salad-dressing mix

¼ teaspoon crushed red pepper

1½ cups cauliflorets, cut in ½" slices (8 ounces)

2 medium carrots, in crinkle-cut slices ¼" thick

2 large ribs celery, cut in ¾" pieces

18 small stuffed green olives

1 tablespoon capers

½ teaspoon oregano

In large saucepan, mix vinegar, water, garlic, dressing mix and pepper. Bring to boil; add cauliflorets, carrots and celery. Simmer, stirring, 8 to 10 minutes. Add olives, capers and oregano. Cool, then refrigerate in jar or other covered container. Makes 6 cups.

SPICY CAULIFLOWER
(shown below)

- ½ cup each oil and white vinegar
- 2 teaspoons salt
- 1 teaspoon sugar
- ¼ teaspoon hot-pepper sauce, or to taste
- 1 small head cauliflower (about 1 pound), separated into florets
- 1 jar (2 ounces) sliced pimientos, undrained (¼ cup)

In large bowl, mix oil, vinegar, salt, sugar and pepper sauce. Cut cauliflorets in half lengthwise. Add with pimientos and their liquid to oil mixture. Stir gently to coat. Cover and refrigerate, stirring occasionally, several hours or overnight. Drain; serve on picks as an appetizer or on lettuce as a salad. Makes 3 cups.

MARINATED MUSHROOMS

- ⅓ cup white vinegar
- 2 tablespoons water
- 1½ teaspoons Italian herb seasoning or fines herbes
- 1 teaspoon each sugar and salt
- ½ teaspoon pepper
- ½ cup oil
- ⅔ cup dry vermouth
- 12 ounces small fresh mushrooms (about 24)

In small saucepan, heat vinegar, water, herb seasoning, sugar, salt and pepper to boiling; reduce heat; simmer 5 minutes. Stir in oil and vermouth, then mushrooms. Cover and refrigerate several hours or overnight, stirring occasionally. Serve mushrooms on picks. Makes 24 mushrooms and 1½ cups marinade. **Note:** Marinade makes a fine salad dressing.

CHEESE-STUFFED PEPPERS

- 1 package (3 ounces) cream cheese, softened
- 2 tablespoons butter or margarine, softened
- ½ cup shredded Cheddar cheese
- ¼ cup diced celery
- ¼ cup shredded carrot
- 1 medium green pepper
- 4 large slices rye bread, halved

In small bowl, beat cream cheese with butter until blended. Stir in Cheddar, celery and carrot; mix well. Cut stem end from pepper; remove seeds. Pack with cheese mixture. Chill overnight. Slice thin and arrange pepper-cheese slices on bread halves, cutting each half in two. Makes 16 pieces.

OLIVE-NUT STUFFED CELERY
(shown below)

- 1 package (3 ounces) cream cheese, softened
- ¼ cup finely chopped salted peanuts
- ¼ cup finely chopped stuffed olives (12 medium)
- 6 large ribs celery (about 9" long)
- Thinly sliced stuffed olives for garnish

In bowl, mix well cheese, peanuts and olives. Spread in hollow of celery ribs. Cut ribs in 1" pieces. Garnish each with an olive slice. Makes about 54.

GINGER-RAISIN STUFFED CELERY

- 1 package (3 ounces) cream cheese, softened
- ½ cup raisins, chopped
- ¼ teaspoon ginger
- 6 large ribs celery (about 9" long)

In bowl, mix well cheese, raisins and ginger. Spread mixture in hollow of celery ribs. Cut ribs in 1" pieces. Makes about 54.

Counterclockwise from left: Spicy Cauliflower and Olive-nut Stuffed Celery, recipes above; and Sherried Cheese Spread, page 179.

PARTY BREADS, CRACKERS AND CRISP SNACKS

PARTY PUMPERNICKEL BRAIDS
(shown on page 145)

1 package (13¾ ounces) hot-roll mix

¾ cup warm water (105° to 115°)

1 egg

1 egg, separated

¼ cup dark molasses

2 teaspoons aniseed or caraway, cumin or fennel seed, divided

¾ cup medium rye flour

In large bowl, dissolve yeast from roll-mix package in the warm water as directed on package. Stir in whole egg, egg yolk, molasses and 1 teaspoon lightly crushed seed. With wooden spoon, stir in rye flour and roll-mix dry ingredients until well blended. Turn dough out on lightly floured surface and knead briefly until smooth and elastic. Place in greased bowl; turn to grease top. Cover with plastic wrap and let rise in warm, draft-free place until dough has almost doubled, about 1 hour.

Preheat oven to 375°F. Turn out dough and knead briefly until smooth. Cut in 9 equal pieces. With hands, roll each into a 15″ rope. Using 3 ropes for each, braid into three 9″ loaves. Place crosswise on greased baking sheet. Cover with clean towel and let rise 45 minutes, or until light to touch. Brush loaves with slightly beaten egg white. Sprinkle braids with remaining 1 teaspoon seed. Bake 18 to 20 minutes, or until light brown. Remove to rack; cover with towel; cool. Serve in ¼″ slices. Best served fresh, but can be frozen. Makes 3 loaves, 35 slices each.

PULL-APART PARMESAN-GARLIC BUBBLE LOAF
(shown in photograph on pages 138-139)

1 loaf (1 pound) frozen bread dough, thawed

3 tablespoons grated Parmesan cheese

½ teaspoon garlic powder

¼ cup butter or margarine, melted

Cut dough in 16 equal pieces; shape in balls. Place on floured surface; cover; let rest 10 minutes. Stir Parmesan and garlic powder into melted butter. Using spoon, roll balls in butter mixture. In greased 8″ layer-cake pan or 9″ x 5″ loaf pan, arrange balls loosely in two layers. Let rise in warm, draft-free place until doubled. Preheat oven to 375°F. Bake loaf 20 minutes, or until golden brown. Remove from pan. Makes 8 servings. **Note:** Bread freezes well. Thaw at room temperature; reheat in 350° oven.

SOFT CARAWAY PRETZELS
(shown on page 145)

1 package active dry yeast

1½ cups warm water (105° to 115°)

1 tablespoon packed brown sugar

1 teaspoon salt

2 tablespoons caraway seed

2 cups whole-wheat flour

2 to 2½ cups rye flour

Coarse salt

Preheat oven to 425°F. In large bowl, dissolve yeast in water. Stir in sugar, salt, caraway seed, whole-wheat flour and 2 cups rye flour, or enough to make a soft dough. Turn out onto lightly floured surface and knead about 5 minutes, or until smooth. Cut in 12 pieces. Roll each into a 15″ rope. Shape in pretzels; place on greased cookie sheets. Brush with water; sprinkle with coarse salt. *Do not let pretzels rise.* Bake 15 to 20 minutes, or until lightly browned. Pretzels are best warm. Reheat in 325° oven 5 minutes before serving. Makes 12.

FENNEL LOOPS
(shown on page 131)

1 cup warm water (105° to 115°)

1 tablespoon fennel seed

1 package active dry yeast

3 to 3½ cups all-purpose flour, divided

1 teaspoon salt

2 tablespoons oil

1 egg beaten with 2 tablespoons water

In large bowl, combine water and fennel. Stir in yeast until dissolved. Add 1 cup of the flour, the salt and the oil. Beat 3 minutes with electric mixer at medium speed. Stir in 2 more cups flour, or enough to make a stiff dough. Turn out onto floured surface; knead 10 minutes, or until smooth and elastic. (Fennel seed may pop out of dough; just push back in.) Place in greased bowl; turn to grease top. Cover; let rise in warm, draft-free place about 1 hour, or until doubled.

Preheat oven to 400°F. Punch dough down; divide in fourths. On lightly floured surface, roll each piece to a 12″ x 4″ rectangle. Cut 12 lengthwise strips. Shape strips into ovals, loosely overlapping ends by about 1″. Place on greased cookie sheets. Brush with egg mixture. Bake 15 minutes. Cool on rack. Store in airtight container. Makes 48. **Variation (Salted Loops):** Sprinkle egg-brushed loops lightly with coarse salt. Bake as above.

CRISP RYE CRACKERS
(shown in photograph on pages 138-139)

1 cup medium rye flour
1 cup all-purpose flour
1 teaspoon each salt and sugar
¼ cup butter or margarine, slightly softened
½ cup plus 2 tablespoons milk

In medium bowl, stir together flours, salt and sugar. Cut in butter until particles resemble small peas. With fork, stir in milk until dough forms. Knead until smooth. Wrap airtight; refrigerate 30 minutes.

Preheat oven to 400°F. Divide dough in half. On lightly floured pastry cloth or other surface, using stockinette-covered or lightly floured rolling pin, roll each half ⅛" thick. Prick whole surface with fork. Cut out rounds with 3¼" doughnut cutter. Reroll and cut scraps. Place rounds ½" apart on ungreased cookie sheets. Bake on middle rack in preheated oven 12 to 14 minutes, or until golden brown and crisp. Remove to rack to cool. Store airtight in dry place. Crackers keep well. Makes 32.

GOURMET POPCORN

1 tablespoon oil
½ cup popcorn
¼ cup butter or margarine
2 cloves garlic, crushed
¼ teaspoon salt

Heat oil in large heavy saucepan or skillet with dome lid. Add popcorn and, shaking pan, cook over moderate heat until all corn has popped; turn into large bowl. In small saucepan, melt butter; add garlic and cook over moderate heat about 3 minutes. Pour over popcorn with salt; toss well. Makes about 4 cups. **Variation:** Toss prepared popcorn with 2 tablespoons grated Parmesan.

WHOLE-WHEAT-AND-OATMEAL CRACKERS
(shown on page 131)

3 cups whole-wheat flour
2 cups rolled oats
1½ teaspoons salt
½ cup shortening
¼ cup butter or margarine, softened
½ cup sugar
1½ cups milk

Stir together flour, oats and salt; set aside. In large bowl, cream shortening, butter and sugar until fluffy. Stir in flour mixture alternately with milk. Dough will be soft and sticky. Turn out onto well-floured surface and knead lightly. Divide in fourths; wrap and refrigerate several hours.

Preheat oven to 350°F. On floured surface with floured rolling pin, roll out each piece ⅛" thick. Cut in 3" rounds, using scalloped-edge cookie cutter. Prick surfaces all over with a fork; place on ungreased cookie sheets. Bake 20 to 25 minutes, or until golden brown. Remove to racks to cool. Makes about 60.

HICKORY-SMOKED ALMONDS

1 tablespoon butter or margarine
2 cups (12 ounces) whole blanched almonds
1 teaspoon hickory-smoked salt, divided (see Note)

Melt butter in large shallow pan in oven while preheating oven to 325°F. Add almonds to melted butter in pan and stir to coat. Sprinkle with ¾ teaspoon smoked salt. Bake, stirring twice, 15 to 20 minutes, or until well toasted. Spread on absorbent paper; sprinkle with remaining ¼ teaspoon salt; cool. Pack airtight; store in cool, dry place. Makes 2 cups. **Note:** If desired, substitute seasoning blend of salt, pepper, and garlic and onion salts for hickory-smoked salt.

PARMESAN ROUNDS
(shown in photograph on pages 138-139)

¾ cup grated Parmesan cheese
½ cup flour
⅛ teaspoon cayenne pepper
¼ cup butter or margarine,
2 tablespoons cold water
2 tablespoons finely chopped walnuts
1 tablespoon parsley flakes, crumbled

Preheat oven to 375°F. In small bowl, stir together cheese, flour and cayenne. Cut in butter until particles resemble small peas. Sprinkle with water; work with hands until dough holds together. Shape in 1½"-wide roll. Roll firmly in mixture of walnuts and parsley. With serrated knife, cut in ¼" slices. Place ½" apart on ungreased cookie sheet. Bake 12 to 15 minutes, or until bottoms are light golden. Remove to rack to cool. Makes 24.

TRAIL SNACK MIX
(shown on page 131)

2 cups puffed-rice cereal
1½ cups bite-size crispy corn-square cereal
1 cup bite-size shredded-wheat cereal
1 jar (4¾ ounces) soy nuts
2 cans (1½ ounces each) potato sticks
6 tablespoons butter or margarine
1 small clove garlic, crushed
1 tablespoon chili powder
½ teaspoon each onion and celery salts
⅛ teaspoon cayenne

Preheat oven to 350°F. In large bowl, combine cereals, soy nuts and potato sticks; set aside. Melt butter in small saucepan over low heat. Stir in remaining ingredients. Stir into cereal mixture. Place in 15" x 10" x 1" pan. Bake 15 minutes, stirring twice. Cool on paper towels. Makes 8 cups.

PARTY PICKUPS

Open-faced Sandwiches

Based, canapé-style, on sliced pumpernickel or rye bread, sliced thin and quartered. Toppings are tasty and colorful bits and pieces, maybe elegant holiday leftovers. References are to photograph at left.

Upper left: Danish Fontina or Tybo creamy Havarti with green pepper ring and radish slices; blue cheese with pecan piece and grape half; Camembert with mandarin orange segment.

Upper right: Thinly sliced roast beef topped with tartar sauce, chives or onion, and chopped tomato; roast beef with cranberry sauce and mandarin orange segment; roast beef with sautéed onion, beet twist and grapes.

Lower left: To a ham base, add cranberries and an orange twist; double cucumber twist; carrots and peas mixed with mayonnaise.

Lower right: Top turkey, pork or ham with a spiced crabapple, piece of pickle, a cucumber-tomato "flower," pairing of prune and orange.

Cold Hors d'oeuvres Medley
(shown on page 177)

Radish-cheese Canapés: Referring to photograph, carve radish roses; chill in cold water until opened; drain. Cut cubes of Danish Fontina cheese. Insert wooden pick through each radish into a cube of cheese.

Stuffed Mushrooms: Bring cream cheese with herbs and spices (can be bought already combined, or mix it yourself) to room temperature. Clean mushrooms; carefully remove stems. Put cream cheese into pastry tube and press into mushroom cavity to form a rosette.

Stuffed Cucumber Slices: Wash cucumbers, scraping lightly to remove wax; trim off stem ends. With apple corer, hollow out center. Pack firmly with softened cream cheese (same kind used for mushrooms). Chill until firm. Cut into ¼" slices.

Blue Cheese-pecan Appetizers: Sandwich 1" cubes of blue cheese between pairs of pecan halves, pressing to stick.

Cheese and Olive Bowl: Arrange a bowl of mixed cheeses, cut in bite-size wedges and cubes, along with pimiento-stuffed olives. Have a supply of picks nearby.

Hot Hors d'oeuvres

OVEN-FRIED CHICKEN DRUMLETS
(shown below)

3 pounds broiler-fryer wings (about 24)

⅓ cup butter or margarine, melted

5 cups cornflakes cereal, crushed

½ teaspoon salt

Sweet-sour Sauce (optional; recipe below)

Preheat oven to 400°F. Cut drumlet (meaty section) from rest of wing at joint (use wing tip and center piece for soup). Dip drumlet in butter, then into mixture of cornflake crumbs and salt. Line shallow baking pan with foil; lightly grease foil; arrange chicken in single layer in pan. Bake 45 minutes, or until chicken is cooked through and coating browned. Serve hot or cold, with Sweet-sour Sauce if desired. Makes 8 appetizer servings.

SWEET-SOUR SAUCE

1 jar (12 ounces) apricot preserves

1 jar (6 ounces) bottled horseradish, drained

Mix ingredients well. Serve with Soy Pork Balls or Oven-fried Chicken Drumlets. Makes about 1⅔ cups.

SOY PORK BALLS
(shown below)

1 pound pork sausage meat

1½ cups fresh bread crumbs (about 3 slices bread)

¼ cup packed brown sugar

½ teaspoon dry mustard

¼ cup each soy sauce and water

Mix sausage and bread crumbs well. Using heaping teaspoonfuls, shape mixture into 1" balls. In hot heavy skillet, brown half at a time. Remove from skillet; set aside. Wipe skillet clean. In skillet, mix sugar and mustard well. Stir in soy sauce and water. Add meatballs. Bring to boil, reduce heat, cover and simmer 5 minutes, or until meatballs are cooked through. Serve warm on picks, or on skewers, alternating with pineapple and green-pepper chunks. Strain liquid to use as dipping sauce or serve with Sweet-sour Sauce (left). Makes 56.

Soy Pork Balls (on skewers) and Oven-fried Chicken Drumlets. Recipes above.

MINI CHINESE ROLLS

½ pound ground beef

1 cup canned bean sprouts, drained

½ cup chopped canned water chestnuts, drained

1 envelope (2 ounces) onion-mushroom soup mix

2 tubes (8 ounces each) refrigerated crescent rolls

Preheat oven to 375°F. In skillet, sauté beef, stirring to break up, until brown. Drain off fat. Stir in sprouts, water chestnuts and soup mix; set aside. Carefully unroll dough from one crescent tube; separate into two rectangles of four triangles each. On lightly floured surface, roll each rectangle into a 7" square. Cut into four 3½" squares. Place 1 tablespoon meat mixture in center of each square. Fold one side over filling, turn sides in and roll (like egg roll). Place seam side down on large baking sheet. Repeat with remaining dough and filling. Bake 10 to 13 minutes, or until golden brown. May be baked, then frozen; thaw, then reheat before serving. Makes 32.

CHEESE-SOUFFLE CANAPÉS

1½ cups shredded Cheddar cheese (6 ounces)

¼ cup butter or margarine, softened

1 egg, beaten

1 teaspoon dry mustard

Dash of hot-pepper sauce

26 slices party rye bread, toasted on one side

In small bowl, stir together Cheddar, butter, egg, mustard and pepper sauce until well mixed. Spread a heaping teaspoonful of mixture on untoasted side of each bread slice. Place on ungreased cookie sheet. Broil 6 inches from heat source 2 to 3 minutes, or until puffed and golden. Serve immediately. Makes 26.

CHINESE-STYLE CHICKEN LIVERS

1½ pounds chicken livers

½ teaspoon aniseed

1 tablespoon sugar

1 teaspoon ginger

¼ teaspoon crushed red pepper

3 green onions, cut in 1" pieces

⅓ cup each soy sauce and dry sherry

¼ cup cornstarch

½ cup oil

Mustard Catsup (optional; recipe below)

Cut livers in half; set aside. Crush aniseed with sugar. Place in shallow dish with ginger, pepper, green onions, soy sauce and sherry. Stir in livers; marinate 30 minutes. Remove livers from marinade with slotted spoon; dry very well on paper towels. In small saucepan, bring marinade to boil; strain; set aside. Dredge livers in cornstarch. Heat oil in skillet and fry about a fourth of the livers at a time until well browned on all sides. Drain on paper towels. Serve warm or cold on wooden picks, with marinade for dipping or Mustard Catsup. Makes 12 appetizer servings.

MUSTARD CATSUP

Place ¼ cup catsup in small shallow dish; set aside. Make waxed-paper cone; seal sides with tape. Cut small opening at tip. Place 1 teaspoon prepared mustard in cone and pipe in spiral on catsup. Makes about ¼ cup.

OLIVE-CHEESE PASTRY WHEELS
(shown in photograph on pages 138-139)

½ cup minced onion

1 tablespoon butter or margarine

1 cup shredded Cheddar cheese (4 ounces)

1 can (6 ounces drained weight) pitted ripe olives, drained and chopped fine

2 teaspoons chili powder

Cream-cheese Pastry (recipe below)

Prepare Cream-cheese Pastry; chill while preparing olive-cheese mixture.

In small skillet, sauté onion in butter until golden. Place in bowl; add cheese, olives and chili powder; mix well. On floured surface, roll out pastry to 15" x 10" rectangle. Spread cheese mixture evenly over surface. Roll up tight from long side as for jelly roll. Wrap in waxed paper; refrigerate until very firm, several hours or overnight.

To bake, preheat oven to 400°F. With sharp knife, cut in ⅜" slices. Place cut sides up ½" apart on greased baking sheet. Bake 12 minutes, or until lightly browned. Remove from baking sheet; cool on racks or serve warm. Store tightly wrapped in refrigerator; reheat in 350° oven 10 minutes to serve. Makes about 36.

CREAM-CHEESE PASTRY

4 ounces cream cheese, softened

½ cup butter or margarine, softened

1½ cups flour

½ teaspoon baking powder

2 tablespoons ice water

In medium bowl, with fork, combine all ingredients. With generously floured hands, work mixture 3 minutes, or until smooth dough forms. Chill until time to use.

CHEESE-CLOUD CASSEROLE
(shown on page 177)

- 1 cup mayonnaise
- 1 cup sour cream
- 1 tablespoon lemon juice
- 1 tablespoon finely chopped onion
- ½ teaspoon curry powder
- ⅛ teaspoon cayenne pepper
- 1 cup thawed frozen peas
- 6 cups cooked, cubed chicken, turkey or ham
- 5 cups shredded Danish Fontina cheese, divided
- 6 egg whites
- ½ teaspoon cream of tartar

  Parsley or watercress sprigs

Preheat oven to 300°F. In large bowl, blend mayonnaise, sour cream, lemon juice, onion, curry powder and cayenne pepper. Fold in peas, cubed meat and a little less than half the cheese. Spoon into buttered, shallow, oven-to-table dish; cover and bake about 20 minutes, or until warm.

While casserole is baking, beat egg whites with cream of tartar until stiff peaks form. Gradually fold in remaining cheese. Remove dish from oven and spoon meringue onto warm mixture, forming 6 to 8 mounds. Increase oven temperature to 400°, return dish to oven and bake 8 to 10 minutes, or until meringue is golden brown. Garnish with parsley or watercress. Serve at once. Makes 6 to 8 supper servings, about twice as many appetizers.

SPINACH QUICHE

- **Pastry for 9″ pie shell**
- 4 eggs, beaten
- 1 cup milk
- ¾ teaspoon salt
- ¼ teaspoon each pepper and nutmeg
- 1 package (10 ounces) frozen chopped spinach, thawed and drained well
- 1 cup (4 ounces) shredded Swiss cheese, divided

Preheat oven to 425°F. Roll out pastry to fit 9″ pie plate. Flute edges; prick bottom. Bake in preheated oven 8 minutes. In medium bowl, mix well eggs, milk, salt, pepper and nutmeg. Layer spinach and ½ cup cheese in pie shell. Sprinkle with remaining ½ cup cheese. Bake in preheated oven 10 minutes. Reduce temperature to 325°; bake 25 minutes longer, or until knife inserted in center comes out clean. Let stand 5 minutes before serving. Makes 12 appetizer servings.

SPIRITED SEASONAL BEVERAGES

DANISH GLÖGG
(shown below)

- 3 cinnamon sticks, 2″ to 3″ long
- 20 whole cloves
- 1 cup water
- 1 cup raisins
- ⅔ cup slivered almonds
- ¼ cup sugar
- 1 half-gallon red burgundy
- 1 bottle (⅘ quart) port wine
- 1 cup light rum
- 1 cup aquavit or brandy

  Very thin orange slices

In small saucepan, combine cinnamon sticks, cloves and water. Cover and bring to boil. Reduce heat and simmer about 30 minutes. Strain and discard spices. In 4-quart pan, combine spiced water with all remaining ingredients. Heat over medium-low heat, but do not boil. Serve garnished with orange slices in warmed punch bowl. Makes 8 to 10 servings.

Punch bowl on warmer filled with Danish Glögg.

MULLED CIDER

1½ quarts apple cider (6 cups)
2 tablespoons sugar
4 cinnamon sticks, 3" long
10 cloves
   Cinnamon sticks for stirrers (optional)

In saucepan, bring all ingredients to boil, stirring to dissolve sugar. Reduce heat to low and barely simmer 30 minutes. Strain and discard spices. Serve warm in mugs with cinnamon stick, if desired. Makes 6 cups. **Note:** May be kept warm on electric hot tray or in a slow cooker.

DOUBLE CRANBERRY PUNCH

3 cups cranberry-juice cocktail
2 cups vodka (see Note)
1 cup orange juice
2 tablespoons lemon juice
½ cup sugar
   Cranberry Ice Cubes (recipe below)

In large pitcher, stir all ingredients except ice cubes until sugar dissolves. Chill; serve over Cranberry Ice Cubes. Makes 6 cups. **Note:** If desired, substitute club soda for vodka. Add just before serving.

CRANBERRY ICE CUBES

Half fill ice cube tray with water; freeze. Add several cranberries and another ⅛" water to each cube; freeze. Fill tray completely with water; freeze until needed.

BLUEBERRY LIQUEUR
   (shown in photograph on pages 138-139)

1 cup Blueberry Syrup (page 140)
1 cup vodka

Pour syrup and vodka into sterilized bottle or jar. Close and shake to blend. Let age in cool, dark place, shaking occasionally, 1 month. Makes 2 cups.

SPICED WINE

   Cinnamon stick, 3" long
1 teaspoon whole cloves
1 small piece (½" square) dried ginger root (optional)
½ cup each sugar and raisins
1 cup water
1 cup aquavit, gin or vodka, or to taste
3 cups dry red wine
½ cup blanched whole almonds (optional)

Tie spices in 5"-square double-thick cheesecloth. Place in heavy saucepan with sugar, raisins and water. Cover; cook over low heat about 10 minutes. Add aquavit and wine; heat uncovered over low heat (do not boil) about 30 minutes, or until mixture has good spicy flavor. Remove spice bag (can be used again). Add almonds, if using. Serve hot in punch cups with demitasse spoons for eating raisins and almonds. Makes 4 cups.

SPICED CRANBERRY GLÖGG
   (shown in photograph on pages 138-139)

1 orange
1 teaspoon whole cloves
   One 3" cinnamon stick, broken in half
½ cup raisins, divided
1 can (6 ounces) each frozen cranberry- and apple-juice concentrates, thawed
6 juice cans water

With small knife, cut peel (include some white part) of orange in 1"-wide long strips (they will form spirals). (Save orange for another use.) Stud peel with cloves; divide between two wide-mouth 1-quart clear-glass bottles. Add ½ cinnamon stick and ¼ cup raisins to each bottle. Mix juices with water; pour half into each bottle. Refrigerate. Before serving, heat in saucepan over medium heat. Makes 8 servings. **Note:** If desired, add vodka to taste before heating the glögg.

HOT-BEVERAGE GIFT MIXES

Spice mixes to tie on gift bottle of wine or cider (one is for hot tea).

SPICED CIDER
   (shown in photograph on pages 138-139)

In sandwich-size plastic food bag, combine ½ cup sugar, peel from 1 orange cut in long strips, 2 teaspoons whole cloves, 1 teaspoon whole allspice and two 3" cinnamon sticks, broken in pieces. Tie securely.

To serve: In saucepan, bring contents of bag and 4 cups unsweetened apple cider to boil. Reduce heat; cover and simmer 30 minutes; strain. Makes 1 quart.

TEAHOUSE PUNCH

In sandwich-size plastic food bag, combine ½ cup sugar, 1 tablespoon each grated orange and lemon peel, ½ teaspoon each ground allspice and nutmeg and one 3" cinnamon stick, broken in half. Tie securely.

To serve: In saucepan, bring contents of bag and 4 cups water to boil. Strain over 3 tea bags in serving pot; steep 5 minutes. Makes 1 quart.

MULLED WINE
   (shown in photograph on pages 138-139)

In sandwich-size plastic food bag, combine 1 cup sugar, 1 tablespoon each whole allspice and cloves, peel from 1 lemon cut in long strips and two 3" cinnamon sticks, broken in half. Tie securely.

To serve: In saucepan, stir contents of bag and 1 cup water over medium heat until sugar dissolves. Simmer 5 minutes; strain; return to saucepan. Add 1 liter burgundy or claret. Heat slowly to just under boiling point. Makes 5 cups.

HOW TO ENLARGE PATTERNS

You will need brown wrapping paper (pieced if necessary to make a sheet large enough for pattern), a felt-tipped marker, pencil and ruler. (If pattern you are enlarging has a grid around it, you must first connect lines across pattern, preferably with colored pencil, to form a grid over the picture.) Mark paper with grid as follows: First cut paper into a true square or rectangle. Then mark dots around edges, 1" or 2" apart or whatever is specified, making same number of spaces as there are squares around edge of diagram. Form a grid by joining dots across opposite sides of paper. Check to make sure you have the same number of squares as diagram. With marker, draw in each square the same pattern lines you see in corresponding squares on diagram.

MAKING POMPONS Cut 2 circles of cardboard the desired diameter of pompon. Cut hole in center of each from ¼" to ½" in diameter. Cut slit from outer edge to center. Place circles together, matching slits. Wrap yarn around and around cardboard rims, sliding it through slit for each wrap. When hole is filled and rim almost covered, slip scissor point between circles, clip yarn around edges, separate circles slightly and tie piece of yarn tightly around center of strands. Remove circles and strands will puff out to form pompon. Trim if necessary to even the ends.

For a tiny pompon, such as a nose on toy, cut a number of 1" yarn strands, tie together tightly at center and trim to desired size.

MAKING FRINGE AND TASSELS To make either, cut strands as specified. **To make fringe tassel:** Hold strands together and fold in half. With crochet hook, draw fold through stitch or space, draw ends through loop and pull to tighten. **To make simple tassel:** Hold strands and fold as above. Tie at center with a strand of yarn; wind several times around the top near the fold. Tassel may be finished off by threading yarn end, passing needle *up* through tassel, and securing yarn at top. Or needle can be taken *down* through tassel so that winding yarn becomes one of the ends.

INDEX

CHRISTMAS CRAFTS

CHRISTMAS FOODS